Presumed Intimacy

One of the most striking characteristics of the new mass media – radio, television, and the movies – is that they give the illusion of face-to-face relationship with the performer ... We propose to call this seeming face-to-face relationship between spectator and performer a para-social relationship.

Donald Horton and R. Richard Wohl

When I first got out in the yard I heard groups of men talking about how Sarah was going to marry Jim or how Frank had betrayed Susan, I thought, 'Damn, these cats all know each other and their families. That's odd.' But after a few minutes I realized they were talking about soap operas. Television in prison is the great pacifier. They love *Basketball Wives* because it is 'T and A' with women of colour. They know how many cars Jay-Z has. But they don't know their own history. They don't understand how they got here. They don't understand what is being done to them. I tell them to read and they say, 'Man, I don't do books.' And that is just how the empire wants it. You can't fight power if you don't understand it.

Mumia Abu-Jamal (political prisoner in the USA,
serving life without parole)

As the term accountability implies, people want to know how to trust one another, to make their trust visible, while (knowing that) the very desire to do so points to the absence of trust.

Marilyn Strathern

Presumed Intimacy

Para-Social Relationships in Media, Society and Celebrity Culture

Chris Rojek

polity

First published in 2016 by Polity Press

Polity Press
65 Bridge Street
Cambridge CB2 1UR, UK

Polity Press
350 Main Street
Malden, MA 02148, USA

ISBN-13: 978-0-7456-7110-9 (hardback)
ISBN-13: 978-0-7456-7111-6 (paperback)

A catalogue record for this book is available from the British Library.

Library of Congress Cataloging-in-Publication Data

Rojek, Chris.
    Presumed intimacy : parasocial interaction in media, society and celebrity culture / Chris Rojek.
       pages cm
    Includes bibliographical references and index.
    ISBN 978-0-7456-7110-9 (hardcover : alk. paper) – ISBN 0-7456-7110-1 (hardcover : alk. paper)
– ISBN 978-0-7456-7111-6 (pbk. : alk. paper) – ISBN 0-7456-7111-X (pbk. : alk. paper)   1. Social
interaction.   2. Intimacy (Psychology)–Social aspects.   3. Celebrities.   4. Mass media–Social
aspects.   I. Title.
    HM1111.R65 2015
    302–dc23
                                        2015012744

Typeset in 10.5 on 12 pt Sabon
by Toppan Best-set Premedia Limited
Printed and bound in the UK by Clays Ltd, St Ives PLC

Epigraphs:

Donald Horton & R. Richard Wohl (1956) 'Mass Communication and Para-Social Interaction' *Psychiatry* 19 (3): 215–29. Reprinted by kind permission of The Washington School of Psychiatry. (http://www.wspdc.org)

Marilyn Strathern (2000) 'The Tyranny of Transparency' *British Educational Research Journal* 26 (3): 309–21. Reprinted by permission of John Wiley & Sons, Inc.

For further information on Polity, visit our website: politybooks.com

Contents

Contents

1

Living with Statistical Men and Women

Modern democracy is speared with a sharp paradox. Formally, it is a body of life and blood equals, primarily consisting, at the level of experience, of empty apparitions. For the greater part we are oblivious to the details of the real circumstances and destines of the human species of which we are a part. Yet we glimpse fractured aspects of them through media transmissions of various sorts. It is certainly not out of the question that we may be moved by the apparent circumstances, conveyed via the media, relating to multitudes of people, who we have never met, do not know and, in all probability, will *never* know. For a variety of reasons, relating chiefly to the force of the media in organizing moral density, we may have the temerity to feel that we *belong* to their story and vice versa. Notwithstanding this, for the most part we confine ourselves to issues surrounding our families and friends. Of course, some of us are passionately devoted to justice and matters of human dignity involving the lives of others. Nearly everyone respects a person of this stamp, even if they disagree with their specific political views. However, despite paying lip service to venerated Enlightenment ideals of individual responsibility and civic action, we are wary, highly provisional, travellers in the art of global human fellowship. The global media provide an outline of the conditions of the lives of the aggregate. As watchers we are party to the shallow surface of what we see. Because the TV eye and the world wide web seems to be empowering in exposing data for us, we may even affect to grasp a little bit more than the ordinary person might know about what is going on, out there in the world of people who are separated from us by the magnitude of distance. [1] Some of us care enough to dig deeper. There are cases of individuals in the afflu-ent societies of the West forsaking all, to engage in struggles that are situated way beyond their doorstep. A case in point is the activism and horrific death of the 23-year-old American protester, Rachel Corrie, killed in 2003 by an Israeli armoured bulldozer, while protest-ing against the policies of Palestinian land clearance. [2] The Rachel Corries of this world are brave, idealistic, worthy of our respect. [3] Still, they are very much exceptions to the rule. We may register global emergencies, injustice and suffering but for the most part we let them pass us by as distant, glancing relations having no direct, durable bearing on our personal responsibilities or sense of self. This is not necessarily a cause for self-reproach. How can knowledge of the global aggregate be anything other than shallow? The numbers in the world are so huge and diverse that their details exceed the capacity of the individual brain to capture them. We identify with the lives of others, but only with strings attached. Our lives, and the lives of those immediate relations who depend upon us, impose obli-gations and duties that are too relentless and unyielding. Their clamour for our attention, even while we register and feel for the pain and mortality of others, is insistent. So we devote the greater part of our lives to pursuing our narrow, private ends and those of the kith and kin networks to which we are attached.

However, global media society insistently imposes a counter-life upon us. We are constant, often furtive, watchers of the lives of others. Usually, we become activated only when the media seize upon an event, episode, incident or emergency deemed worthy of public attention. Even then, our emotional connection is tenuous and capri-cious. We live in a world of statistical men and women. Typically, our leaders speak of abstract numbers, rather than flesh and blood people, and champion or condemn them through briefings via press attachés and researchers rather than direct experience. There is a real sense in which relations in democracy are stamped with the mark of being once removed. Much of the mandate for official action is sheer word magic. The political challenge in the art of political rhetoric is to utter passable empathy with others. The combination of democ-racy and the global media impose presumed intimacies of the counter-life upon us. Not to care about the lives of others, or the condition of the planet, is to risk being stigmatized as selfish, irresponsible and heartless. Fiormanti (2014) shows convincingly that credit ratings, growth figures and other 'hard data' have a powerful influence in public debate. But he also raises the point that these numbers are often misleading and are typically *selectively* constructed and applied in order to suit the needs of vested interests. Presumed intimacy can be a political tool. It gains votes. In public life its assembly and presentation often follow hidden agendas. Global statistical men and women constitute a multi-dimensional category. Yet they are generally politically represented too us in no more than one or two dimensions. Can we really know the lives of those who live in politically troubled areas such as Sudan, Syria, the Gaza or North Korea? Can we truly grasp the actual context in which they find themselves or the indivertible forces which they confront (with only a slender chance for inserting their own agency to make a difference)? Yet governments and activists reduce complexity by making schematic statements about the lives of others in these geo-political hot spots. This should not be a cause for surprise. Social statistics are not independent of social relationships. Rather, the correct way to analyse and understand them is to see them as products of social relationships (Best 2001). If we incubate and exhibit presumed intimacy for the lives of others, it is partly because our propensities in these respects are framed by political leaders and media pundits. It would be rash to proclaim that the fundamentals here are new. Humans have always passed their lives with others who are obscurely acknowledged, but never encountered. They are impenetrable features of our social landscape. Their co-existence is recognized as a fact of life, but it hardly prohibits us from going about our own lives. It has been ever thus. At the same time, possessing awareness about the lives of others is a more prominent aspect of what might be called, *favoured identity*, that is, the positive status differentiation which represents a relevant, decent, caring person. The sheer volume of data about the lives of others that we are privy to, is unprecedented. Everyday cable, satellite and other forms of digital communication carry fact-finding bulletins and op-ed pieces on conditions in distant places, the geography, culture, religion and history of which are fuzzy to us, but about which we feel obscurely connected. Numerical force is frequently the basis for moral force.

News about the lives of others is often troubling or downright bad. The media tend to concentrate upon dramatic episodes that correlate with high human interest potential because this is what wins ratings wars. In communicating troubling data to us, they have developed codes of propriety and conventions of disclosure to convey and register emotions in an approved, acceptable manner. These instruments of exchange marry up with emotional management technologies developed in professions and occupations where handling and communicating bad news is a significant element in case-load performance (Furedi 2003). In this study, the term *presumed intimacy* will be used to refer to the skills required to provide concrete feedback to an individual who has done something wrong, to deliver bad news to those who may be dismayed or troubled by it, and to assert authority over those with whom one disagrees at work or in other public settings. It is a tool to smooth-out awkward situations and avoid negative or destructive behaviour. Typically, it works through the disclosure of empathy and offers an action plan to overcome blockages, disruptions or difficulties of one sort or another. In a wired-up world, where more people are in one way or another in touch with each other than ever before, it is ubiquitous. Agents of persuasion use statistics about the relationships of opportunity, risk and threat with statistical men and women as the pretext for moral and economic action. The role of the media in delineating these issues for the public is decisive. However, framing only has purchase because we spend a large part of our life alone or with others, not acting, as such, but secretly watching.

That old technological determinist, Marshall McLuhan (2001) knew this only too well. He famously speculated that 'cool' technologies of audio-visual communication would galvanize human sympathy, break down social, political and cultural divisions and create 'the global village'. For McLuhan, it was inevitable that watchers of the world would unite. History has not turned out like that. On the contrary, cool technologies have proved fully compatible with thin readings of social reality. Greater data about the lives of others does not necessarily assist sound moral judgements or moral action. Our lives are passed in a condition of data overload. Under its sway, we find it difficult to work out what data to believe and what to question and reject. The more informed we are, the more we hedge our bets, since we are conscious that the information upon which our perspective is founded is necessarily partial. For every point of view, there is a counter-point of view. Modern men and women are mostly sharply conscious that they lack the knowledge and time to decide on global issues by themselves. Democracy is a proxy form of government which empowers elected representatives to take these decisions for us, and to subject themselves to accountability via the due electoral process. This has ramifications for the emotional density of the counter-life they share with others.

Amid a sense of obscurity about the lives of statistical men and women, naked fear is an element that it would be unwise to underrate. Since 9/11 the West has learnt to view globalization more widely than questions of deregulation and outsourcing. [4] The terrorist threat, itself mostly obscure, is acutely stressed by the authorities, especially in metropolitan cultures. Vigilance and awareness are promoted as public necessities. It is short sighted to soldier on without even a dim awareness of the world out there and the hidden risks that it conceals. But it is a peculiar feature of modern life that this awareness, which can be like lighting blue touchpaper when it comes to emotional transference, is actually a darkling place where it is difficult to see the wood for the trees. 9/11 has been instrumental in standing the logic of vulnerability upon its head. We are inured to thinking of men and women in the developing world as worthy recipients of aid. The unbearable, patronizing backdraft of this outwardly benign Western outlook has been rightly deplored by critics (Moyo 2009). Now the statistical men and women who share our world may take our jobs, claim welfare benefits that we have paid for and may plot and take steps to kill us. *Removed intimacy* is the opposite side of the coin of presumed intimacy. That is, the social condition in which presumed intimacy based in care and respect for the lives of statistical men and women is withdrawn and inverted by redefining them as a threat or risk.

This darkling sensibility in the public mind is exploited and developed by political leaders of all stripes. Presumed intimacy can turn into aggression in the wink of an eye. It also points to something sociologically important, and little considered, in the ways that we go about relating to others in the world. What does it mean to live with statistical apparitions? And how is this category used by leaders for the ends of power and influence? And what does it mean to be a furtive watcher?

Familiar Strangers

Goffman (1963) put 'the nod count' (the number of people with whom we are on 'nodding terms'), at a hundred. The core consists of primary relationships with family and friends. Nonetheless, a considerable proportion fall into the fascinating and little understood category of 'familiar strangers' (Milgram 1992: 67–9). That is, persons who populate our known social landscape, yet with whom we never interact beyond a glancing recognition. Like the famous 'lost letter experiment', the subject reveals Milgram's lifelong interest in the nature of modern altruism. [5] The springboard for this research question was the anonymous people Milgram saw regularly on the station platform where he caught his subway train into Manhattan. The familiar stranger relationship is not the absence of a relationship, but a 'special kind of frozen relationship' (Milgram 1971: 71). Basic to it is a history of principled non-communication and the acceptance of this as the normal state of affairs. This supports a system of non-negotiated, restraining conventions which is mutually accepted, but turns out to be rather odd on closer inspection. For example, you are more likely to ask a total stranger for the time than a person that you have seen for years but never spoken to. Why? What is the inhibition that stops us from asking someone who we have watched as a familiar stranger for months or years, and what is behind the preference for asking a *bona fide* stranger? Doubtless, it is a matter of not wishing to be emotionally beholden to familiar strangers. The glance or the nod are enough.

Still, Milgram held that in exceptional circumstances familiar strangers may become 'real people'. As an example, he (1992: 68) refers to a woman who slipped and hurt herself on a Brooklyn street, close by her apartment. She had been known as a familiar stranger by another resident for years. The resident immediately came to the assistance of the woman. Not only that, she organized an ambulance and accompanied her to the hospital to ensure that she received proper care. This suggests that triggering real interaction seems to be associated with out-of-routine encounters. Yet typically, the chief identifying characteristic of familiar strangers is that they remain recognized but unknown to us. By extension, we do not want to know more about them.

The analytical import of Milgram's discussion is that there are latent 'background expectancies' in social relationships with persons who are manifest to us as strangers in everyday life. [6] There are unwritten rules that govern the extent of our moral involvement with men and women that we do not directly know. Familiar strangers seem to switch to direct encounters only when a crisis or emergency occurs. Milgram (1971: 74) is very much a man of his time in posing the question: 'Is there any way to promote solidarity without having to rely on emergencies and crises?' However, this over-dramatizes the occasions in which familiar strangers become 'real people' for us. For example, should you bump into the man who has sold your bottle of mineral water to you for years, some form of greeting, more elaborate than a nod, is highly likely. The decisive factor in unfreezing the relationship is not the presence of an emergency or crisis, but a de-routinized encounter. Yet in our day the question of using this as a basis for constructing solidarity seldom arises. Routine and semi-detachment are ascendant. When they do break down can we really be certain that it leads to emotionally satisfying, durable relationships? As we shall see in the last chapter of the book, the de-routinization that accompanied the *Occupy* demonstrations in the autumn and winter of 2011 to 2012 established the broad notions of the 99 per cent and the one per cent. But at the society-wide level there is little evidence that the notion of the 99 per cent has endured. It has not moved from a rhetorical interjection to revitalize civic life into an actual, meaningful force capable of marshalling and directing transformative collective behaviour.

The research front that Milgram does not expand very much, is the question: What role do the media play in humanizing familiar strangers by introducing new categories of screen amity and fluid sub-communities organized around celebrity culture and the counter life of recognition with the lives of others? To be clear, our immediate environment remains peopled with familiar strangers with whom a nod count still means something. At the same time, the field of screen apparitions in life has multiplied and vastly grown. With *Facebook*, *Twitter*, *Instagram*, *Snapchat* and other social networking sites and digital chat rooms, we live under the illusion of 'being connected'. Celebrity culture *is* the global village of the present day (McLuhan 2001). Most of us may have nothing but a vague knowledge of rural life conditions on the Ivory coast or political relations in the Ukraine, but we know about the Kim (Kardashian) sex tapes and how Kim is handling the challenges of motherhood with West, her baby daughter; and we are aware of what Chris (Martin) and Gwynneth (Paltrow) went through in their 'conscious decoupling' and the tough road they face in bringing up their children on different sides of the Atlantic. Celebrity culture insistently imposes onto our radar private, emotional data relating to public figures who are socially and geographically remote. We feel close to them, or at least, well informed about key aspects of their private lives. You may be totally unaware of the personal traumas being faced by the person who works in the office with you, but you know what Mel Gibson and Oscar Pistorius went through in their respective, very different trials with the media. The cases of celebrity culture and statistical men and women require a rethink of both Goffman's notion of 'nod count' and Milgram's concept of 'familiar strangers'. Unprecedented media expansion constitutes a technological re-casting of relationships with others, which is partially based in a history of principled *non-communication*. One interesting aspect of this is social networking. This has contributed much to our general sense of being connected. We receive postings from people we may know slightly, or who post because they share the same surname, or went to the same school or university. Even if we make no direct response we are conscious of these wraith-like presences in the background. Yet, while we record communication with others in this format, we do not necessarily reciprocate. We are conscious of relationships, but we deal with them by principled non-communication.

An embarrassing irony for the philosophy of modern liberalism is that the concept of individual autonomy to which it cleaves is articulated at a moment in which consciousness of co-presence is greater than ever before. Even the most diehard neo-liberal is conscious of being *alone, together*. Consecutive to the autonomy to act however I please, so long as it does not damage the interests and wellbeing of others, is now a freedom to record the intention of others to communicate with me without my taking any action whatsoever to reciprocate. Certainly, social networking makes Goffman's nod count of a hundred seem hopelessly outdated. The disconnected awareness we have of familiar strangers has proliferated and become more hierarchical, with layers of celebrity culture and ranks of statistical men and women crowding in for our attention. It is part of the social landscape and contributes to our sense of modern personal and social order. Yet, save for exceptional circumstances, we go through our whole lives without making contact, and with no more than superficial, fleeting knowledge of the apparitions and the actual conditions of life in which they are situated. Even in the closer world of celebrity culture, we scarcely have the means of discovering what is really going on in the lives of public figures. Which, of course, is not to say that, as with statistical men and women, they are not without weight in the cultural, political and economic conduct of our everyday lives.

Conversely, it must be granted that social networking partly unfreezes the essence of not knowing, which Milgram (1971) attributed to the concept of familiar strangers. Social networking is not only about recording, snooping, the absence of communication or the political positioning of a measureless entity to support vested interests. It is a relatively new form of communication and social association. Its format encourages exchanges that reward displays of personal disclosure and *screen amity*. As with the pen-friend culture of old snail-mail days, screen amity is perfectly capable of building ties with people separated from each other by great spatial and cultural magnitude. But why bother with a pen friend when you have instant contact available to Skype at your fingertips? Through these means we may acquire a deeper sense of the lives of others. Yet the exchange is not natural. It does not unfold in the way that a direct, physically co-present relationship develops. It is a semi-detached, removed relationship, which often complies, in obvious ways, with the logic of commercial media culture. For many of us, screen friends are becoming more numerous. It is too early to reach conclusions about how they influence moral density, that is, our awareness of the mutual rights and obligations that obtain between people. Yet unquestionably, their presence constitutes a new relational hub in 'society'.

During the course of this, old notions of co-presence are being recast. An interesting new insight into this may be gleaned from work on new digital technologies of communication. Researchers into the psychological and social consequences of webcam have devised the concept of the technology being 'always on'. (Miller and Sinanan 2014: 54–60). That is, webcam is left in the background while we get on with cleaning the house, cooking or writing an essay, without paying attention or having a direct conversation with the pixillated other. Webcam is therefore compatible with two types of intimacy. The first is face-to-face, often intense, conversation. The second is 'the intimacy of taking for granted the co-presence of the other' (Miller and Sinanan 2014: 55). A few words of explanation are necessary. When we are 'always on' we are digitally co-present, but physically absent from our nominated interlocutor. But what does it mean to be 'co-present' in these circumstances? We allow a webcam interlocutor or a webcam familiar stranger into our dwelling space, just as we bring our boss in our work appraisals 'into confidence' about the reasons for not reaching our work targets having to do with personal relationship problems. A new gestural economy has emerged in which a high degree of personal disclosure is accepted as a quality of good civility. But it is by no means clear if disclosure is clarifying reality or a personal technique to manipulate outcomes.

So, to summarize, since Goffman's day, the nod count of familiar strangers has grown massively and proliferated new relations of presumed intimacy. New media have augmented the social presence of statistical men and women, and celebrities. These 'familiar strangers' are people with whom there is no history, and little obvious prospect, of communication in the social landscape. Not all forms of social networking avoid principled non-communication. The type of communication that occurs, its intensity and social meaning, is the subject for another study. In this book my focus is upon emotional relations in which the history of communication takes the form of principled non-communication. Despite permeating into our lives mostly as screen presences, the subjects with whom we do not communicate and have no history of communication are not blank slates. To be sure, a characteristic of modern life is that we often know a good deal about the private lives of others, *before* we meet them. The data about statistical men and women are certainly uneven, but can be accessed without too much trouble. A visit to *Wikipedia* now provides a window on a good deal of the world. Of course, much is left out of *Wikipedia* accounts. But that is precisely the point about the social category of statistical men and women; that is, in our counter-life as secret watchers we do not need or, generally, seek to access, anything more than superficial data about them. Flanking this category, is the qualitatively distinct category of celebrity culture. This is also defined by a history of non-communication. But, unlike the category of statistical men and women, interaction with celebrity culture is with famous personalities, about whom much private data percolates into, and is retained by, the public domain. Celebrity blogging sites and web chat rooms affect to offer a backstage pass to the real lives of the famous. They provide the patina of emotional closeness that affords status differentiation for participants. In the case of celebrities and statistical men and women, social interaction around presumed intimacy is commonplace. The emotional intensity of this interaction varies according to setting and content. If a celebrity is involved in a scandal, or statistical men and women are caught up in an 'incident' or 'emergency', our emotional interest magnifies. In both cases our response is aided, abetted and some might say, orchestrated by the media. The remarkable thing to note, which is the real subject of this book, is that personal, emotional involvement occurs without a history of communication or any real prospect of direct communication. We live our lives with familiar strangers. The relationships that we have with them are second order, that is they are not based in bloodline or direct kinship. Nevertheless, at the level of meaning, they often give our lives direction and a rewarding sense of place and purpose. Yet familiar strangers are also apparitions whom we never encounter and never really get to know.

Moral Density and Human Sympathy

Since they obviously influence the emotional composition of populations, statistical men and women and celebrities have bearing upon moral density. That is, the background expectancies of obligations and responsibilities that we recognize with each other. In the history of non-communication a palpable moral dimension exists. In its original formulation, Durkheim (2013: 202) insisted that moral density is inextricably tied to physical density. As the division of labour concentrates populations into urban settings, with well-defined national boundaries, 'the mutual acting and reacting with one another', which is the basis of moral density, increases. 'This act of drawing together morally', writes Durkheim (2013: 202) 'can only bear fruit if the real distance between individuals has itself diminished'. The awareness of moral density is enshrined in human rights legislation and debates. However, the dynamics that compel us to exercise these moral provisions in the form of concrete action are fuzzy. Nearly everyone would say that they feel some sort of responsibility to help those who are in urgent need. But this is again, closely bound up with issues of setting, content and hidden motivation. Our responses are structured by presenting need as a temporary emergency, incident or episode. The questionable rider to this is that action will produce lasting solutions. In an earlier work, I coined the term 'event consciousness' to refer to an orientation to the world that presents social reality as a succession of disconnected incidents, emergencies and events (Rojek 2013). [7] Event consciousness privileges the episodic over the structural and rooted processes. Need in the third world is a grinding, perpetual sorrow that requires a major transfer of resources from affluent societies and well-off strata (Bourdieu 1999; Easterly 2007). By framing it through the lens of event consciousness, supplied via television and other branches of the media, the causes of sorrow are often mis-attributed and the solutions prepared in its name misfire. Incidents, episodes and emergencies are not adventitious. They are the result of traceable structures and identifiable processes. But this level of interpretation is confined to the lecture hall or the 'serious' media. The main currents of popular media are events or episode based.

Our lives play out amid a vast aggregate of statistical men and women. When we speak of 'aggregate' we are referring to the seven billion with whom we presently co-exist. When an emergency or incident occurs which puts some of them in danger, through, for example famine, earthquake, industrial catastrophe, most of us immediately empathize with them. We have a relationship of presumed intimacy with them, which proceeds on the basis that we 'know' their pain, we 'care' and we are prepared to 'act'. The same species of presumed intimacy prevails for many of us in our relationships with celebrities. Because we know so much more about their private lives, it is apt to be more intense and enduring. Some of us follow the private lives of stars like Rhiannon, Lana Del Ray, Justin Bieber, Oscar Pistorius, Kanye West or Kim Kardashian, so that they become virtual members of our kith and kin networks to whom, in some cases, we maintain life-long attachments. How are we to explain the contagion of emotions that pass with the utmost ease and facility from one person to another when physically and socially remote statistical men and women or superstars are portrayed as being at risk?

One answer emerged over two and a half centuries ago. It was provided by the philosopher David Hume (1742). In common with other Enlightenment figures, he sought to develop the concept of society as a community of moral and material interests in conditions in which, through rapid industrialization, competing individual interests and prejudices run amok. He found the seat of community in the passions, especially the capacity for sympathy. For Hume (1742) sympathy is a natural passion without which human society cannot abide or prosper. Sympathy extends beyond the affect of limited company to describe all social relations. It runs through human confederacy like blood through a vein.

On this account then, there is no real surprise at the transfer of emotions. For Hume, human sympathy is innate. When one of us ships water, natural sympathy produces a 'correspondent feeling' in 'all human breasts' (Hume 1742). Adam Smith (1790: 10, 12) too defined human sympathy as 'our fellow feeling with any passion whatsoever . . . (which) derives from . . . the situation which excites it'. So there you have it. In the classical Enlightenment tradition, the transfer of emotions is a reflection of the innate quality of human sympathy that enables everyone to recognize vulnerability and suffering when the circumstances arise. Routinely, we may think of ourselves as separate, self-absorbed individuals. But when a crisis and emergency occurs we come through in our true colours and assume the mantle of 'team world'. This account possesses a high feel-good factor, because it points to a common thread of human decency running through life. By the same token it is obviously unsatisfactory. For decency is not always applied when others are obviously in pain and distress. We may profess to feel their pain, to care and to act when statistical men and women or celebrities are in *extremis*. But on a society-wide basis, action is very uneven, and for most, may run no deeper than a glib statement of sympathy.

Hume (1751) himself later moderated his position. He found himself wondering if sympathy in mankind is not in fact unequally distributed by the same social divisions that divide people into what he referred to as 'clubs and companies' (Mullan 1988). In other words, he came to believe that the intensity of human sympathy is not universal. Rather, it is rationed via social attachments and choices. We care for others, but we do not do so equally or indiscriminately. Smith (1790) added a further reservation by proposing that the intensity of sympathy is an inverse of physical and social distance. The capacity to imaginatively 'change places with the sufferer' (Smith 1790: 10), diminishes with physical and social magnitude. That is, generally speaking, human sympathy for our kith and kin and fellow countrymen and countrywomen is greater than for people who are not connected to us by bloodline or who are foreign nationals. In fine, Hume and Smith recognized equilibrium between physical *proximity* and human sympathy. Where physical proximity is absent, both took the view that emotional disequilibrium must follow. This is also, by the way, the essence of Durkheim's (2013) position in *The Division of Labour*. While we can recognize the validity of the argument to relations of sympathy in our own time, the hub of screen-friend relations and the collateral expansion of the category of statistical men and women in social consciousness through the media-sphere mean that Smith's formula of an inverse relationship between the strength of sympathy and physical distance can no longer be taken for granted. Human sympathy has moved from merely being tied to physical proximity to co-presence. To put it in a nutshell, the instant, electronic representation of emotional need has the power to overcome the magnitude of physical distance. Particularly when exceptional circumstances obtain, statistical men and women may become symbolic *causes célèbres*, marshalled into emotionally meaningful relationships with us by a numinous *esprit de corps*. Attention has shifted from viewing sympathy as an innate characteristic of the human species to the relations of power that make emotional identification with others, with whom we have no history or prospect of communication, possible.

Para-Social Interaction

Although massively under-developed since Milgram's untimely death, the concept of familiar strangers resonates with most readers. From the 1950s, Horton and Wohl (1956) were working with the parallel idea of para-social interaction. This is a concept with more powerful emotional implications for the conventional senses of social responsibility and reciprocity than Milgram's concept of familiar strangers. It refers to relationships of presumed intimacy between media figures and network spectators. Robert Merton (1946) strayed into this ground in his account of the astonishing achievement of the singer and radio star Kate Smith who, during the Second World War, raised $39 million war bonds in a marathon of one day of broadcasting. His (1946: 83. 142) analysis noted the relationship between feigning personal concern and manipulation. He argued that in the newly emerging arena of television media figures consciously call upon audiences to become emotionally involved not only with the content of the broadcast, but to identify with them as personalities. The

...pparent authenticity of media figurers were com-
...y emerging performative economy in which rela-
...nunication over the airwaves produced emotional
...ween audiences and performers. Merton's (1946)
...ates on the new potential of media celebrities to
...strangers in preferred trajectories. He called this
'mass persuasion'. He did not advance further to explore the undergrowth of social psychology of emotional identification with media
figures.

It was left to Horton and Wohl (1956), writing at the dawn of
national network television in North America, to forge a path into
this area through their investigation of para-social relationships. They
maintained that audiences were forming close emotional relationships with media figures (news readers, anchor men, chat show hosts,
weather men, etc.) that went far beyond interludes of air-time broadcasting. Emotional identification with media figures is the heart of
the para-social relationship. For Horton and Wohl (1956) it perme-
ates spectators' cognition of the social components of everyday life
and spills irresistibly into ordinary behaviour. [8] In a word, para-
social relationships alter the balance of emotional attachment we
have with others. Horton and Wohl (1956) surmise that these secondary relations were competing with primary (kith/kin) relations in the
organization of social life. What is more, TV producers and directors
were exploiting this new emotional economy by encouraging TV
figures to become, not merely presenters, but personalities by adopting forms of behaviour and engineering organized settings of exchange
that refer to domestic conditions. Bespoke forms of presentation were
introduced and exchanged using stylized linguistic cues (wisecracks,
catch-phrases, deadpan jokes, off-the-cuff remarks, self-deprecation,
sharing apparently private thoughts) and, in some cases, making
on-screen revelations or engaging in emotional disclosure. This was
reinforced by set design that strategically employed domestic furni-
ture, potted plants, framed family photographs, coffee tables, sofas,
cushions, rugs and so on in order to convey the impression that the
studio is an extension of the home. All of this contributed to a televisual ethos of emotional disclosure. In this vein, Barry King (2008)
later introduced the notion of the *para-confession*. That is, the institutionalized revelation of celebrity secrets, which often involves ritualized celebrity repentance, designed to increase bonding with audiences. He argues that this has become an accepted part of talkshow
culture. Its objective is to draw the audience *into confidence*. The
ethos of the para-confession is to magically transform a star in
trouble into a friend in need. The underlying aim is to boost audience

ratings and the persuasive authority of the star. An atmosphere of *staged authenticity* is perpetuated (MacCannell 2011: 22–8). That is, an artificial environment, based upon the obliteration of spatial divisions and emotional barriers to elicit the veneer of co-presence and open exchange between familiars. The fundamental goal of these settings is to achieve *accelerated intimacy* between spectators and media figures. [9] The para-social confession is the institutionalized expression of relations of para-social interaction which soak much deeper in popular culture.

Nowadays, it is too limiting to confine para-social interaction to the relationships between media personalities and spectators. The electronic eye of the media has turned statistical men and women into screen presences with whom emotional relationships are built and developed in spite of the absence of physical co-presence. The media are adept at personalizing these conditions of life and presenting dilemmas as objects with which spectators can rapidly transfer emotional investment. In the process, there has been an explosion in social consciousness of the throng of statistical men and women and celebrities, that we recognize as having 'relations' with, and about whom we seek to be informed. Parallel to the bonds that we have with family, friends, fellow students and co-workers, we conduct relationships, often of appreciable emotional intensity, with familiar strangers with whom we pass through life, but never directly encounter.

It comes as a jolt to observe that we pass our lives conversant with what might be termed *second order relationships* with people with whom we never communicate. It might be said that the novel and poetry played this role in traditional culture. But today's celebrities and statistical men and women are not experienced or interpreted as fictional characters. They are real flesh and blood people whose existence is understood to be independent and consecutive with our own. The mental apparatus that handles this information is heavily influenced by the media. One consequence of the enlargement of the media is to populate ordinary life with 'uninvited guests' (Mullan and Taylor 1986). We pass our time with a batch of TV news readers, characters in soap operas, musical icons, sports stars, famous actors, actresses and swathes of nameless statistical men and women, who furnish our lives with vital aspects of fragmented meaning. This is indeed one dimension of what Horton and Wohl (1956) mean by para-social interaction, but the scale of their concept needs to be much enlarged to take account of the scope of modern mass communications. Because of media saturation, it is perverse to submit that our knowledge and ontological identification with the lives of others is confined to celebrity culture. The same channels of communication that supply us with data about the lives of the famous and the glamorous, provide information about ordinary people from whom we are separated by the distance of physical space and the banal necessities of culture. The human sympathies that we develop with them may not be built upon the sculpted, granular knowledge that allows some of us to identify closely with celebrities. All the same, it admits the presumption of intimacy. Consecutively, questions of content and context relating to, *inter alia*, the extremity of their plight, our knowledge that they are on the edge of the abyss, is perfectly capable of eliciting the rapid transfer of deep emotions. The media switchpoint that permits cathexis with people who are nameless, unmet and unknown to us is a major influence in our contemporary personal sense of personal identity and civic membership. Yet the psychological forces and depth of commitment involved are strangely under-examined. When we pledge £10 or $20 to a global media event like *Live Aid* (1985) and *Live Earth* (2007) we may bask in the light that we have made a concrete difference to our starving brothers and sisters, or to the fate of the planet itself. Yet the impulse that underwrites charity is also connected to fiscal prudence. The same emotional intensity behind a charitable donation may be switched to resisting an increase in the attempts of the state to increase personal taxation to combat poverty in the developing world or correct climate change (Easterly 2007, 2014). The worry that afflicted Hume in later life, namely that human sympathy is not a universal constant, but is disproportionately allocated through self-interest with 'clubs and companies', has lost none of its force. Further, we should recognize the possibility that a pledge to donate money is merely an example of votive behaviour. That is, it is a statement of intentionality which may never be realized. The purpose of making a pledge to ease suffering in others that will never be delivered is to garner social approval. *Votive behaviour* carries the appearance of presumed intimacy, but what is often driving it is the demand for recognition, approval and acceptance.

The moral density of our relationships with strangers with whom we communicate on the basis of para-social relationships is not indiscriminate or constant. Dramatic events, incidents and emergencies, such as a terrorist attack or an epidemic, inject the outward conditions and emotional circumstances of strangers more insistently into our moral universe. We presume to have meaningful knowledge and, in some cases, develop strong opinions, about others who mostly exist for us as screen apparitions. The ubiquity of the media, and the obligations of individuals to fulfil the mundane requirements of the division of labour, mean that ordinary knowledge about the lives of others is both plentiful and superficial at the same time.

The Cult of the Individual

This is a far cry from 'the cult of the individual' that Durkheim (2013) envisaged as emerging in moral density as mechanical solidarity gives way to organic solidarity. Before coming to the question of this social category it is necessary to prepare the ground by briefly setting down the main differences between the two types of solidarity. In making the distinction, Durkheim (2013) was stressing the more complex social differentiation, diversity of roles, beliefs, sentiments and values in the organic form, as opposed to what he took to be the relatively undifferentiated conditions in the mechanical form. Under mechanical solidarity, individual conscience corresponds closely to collective conscience (collective authority, belief and values). This correspondence is usually expressed in a tribal or religious vernacular. Rituals, in which personal deviation from collective beliefs are subject to censure. Under organic solidarity, where the division of labour is appreciably more complex, personal roles, beliefs, sentiments and values have, relatively speaking, greater autonomy. Under organic solidarity the content of collective conscience is more secular, humanistic and rational. In these conditions, respect for the individual becomes a type of humanistic civic belief system. Respect for personal dignity and material wellbeing are shared throughout society. These collective beliefs are not abstract, but focused and realized in ordinary inter-personal relations. Thus, respect is not merely a theoretical matter, but a practical undertaking. It is buttressed by the state working in conjunction with a variety of associations that Durkheim envisaged establishing in the workplace and the community. The purpose of this partnership is to conceive, operationalize and monitor individual rights and check abnormality to ensure healthy social equilibrium. This is what Durkheim means by the term, 'the cult of the individual'.

What distinguishes moral density under organic solidarity is that it is more cognisant of human needs (and rational) than under the mechanical precedent. Individuals are not compelled to prostrate themselves before the mysterious ways of a supreme being, nor are they understood to be the blind servants of nature. Where the cult of the individual takes root and flourishes, it is enough to exhibit and practise respect and justice for the dignity of all, without distinction (Lukes 1973: 147–67; Fournier 2013). While Durkheim regards these qualities to be aspects of ordinary social encounters, the ultimate repository is what he calls 'restitutive law'. That is, a legitimate, universal legal framework that recognizes the ultimate social value of individual rights.

In the course of a subsequent contribution to understanding the social glue of modern civil society, Jürgen Habermas (1996, 1998), makes an analogous case in proposing 'constitutional patriotism' as, among other things, the guarantor of individual rights in contemporary multi-cultural, multi-ethnic conditions. Constitutional patriotism may be regarded as the cognate of moral density. It sets out and defends the rights of the individual and, as such, presupposes mutualities and reciprocities. These are ultimately enshrined in law, but Habermas also understands them to be ordinary qualities of civil culture. Under constitutional patriotism then, respect for the individual is pronounced. It consists of the aggregate of recognized legal and supererogatory responsibilities and duties beyond kith and kin networks, that citizens acknowledge and apply in relations with each other. Durkheim's notion of moral density applies to civil relations contained by national boundaries. For Habermas, the spatial application of the idea is broader. He mainly uses it to refer to relations in the partner states of the European Union. Other writers have taken over the basic idea and applied it more freely to refer to borderless groupings in which global strangers recognize mutuality and reciprocity and the level of background expectancies relating to rights and obligations. For example, 'care for the other' is a primary obligation in the philosophy of Emmanuel Levinas (2005). In this case, the other is not confined to strangers in national or federated civil society. It refers to an extra-territorial, cosmopolitan outlook to strangers in the world who are *in extremis*.

To return to the question of fluctuation, a moment's reflection establishes that moral density is not constant in social affairs. It undergoes cycles of amplification and recession through circumstances and representation (via media communication). In his own day, Durkheim was aware of the role that the media played in representing the Dreyfus scandal, in which an innocent French artillery officer of Alsatian Jewish descent, was convicted and imprisoned on trumped-up charges of treason (Fournier 2013: 285–308). The Dreyfus scandal, and the subsequent campaign to pardon him, shamed the French establishment and received high levels of media coverage. While he did not comment upon it in detail, Durkheim would surely have been aware of an intensification in the moral density of ordinary public life in relation to indignation and unease with respect to the Dreyfus question. To be precise, media communication (and amplification) of the episode multiplied the volume of moral density surrounding Dreyfus as a familiar (celebrity) stranger. In the *Division of Labour* Durkheim (2013: 202–4) hypothesized that the prime levers determining the concentration of moral density are (a) the growth and urban concentration of populations; and (b) the number and speed of the means of communication. His only comment on the latter lever is terse to the point of being consecutively vague and suggestive. 'By abolishing or lessening the empty spaces separating social segments', writes Durkheim (2013: 203), 'these means (communication) increase the density of society.' It is unclear whether he regarded the mutuality and reciprocity in moral density produced by population growth and concentration as equivalent to that which stems from communication. Not the least of the difficulties in unravelling this question is the comparatively primitive nature of the communications of his own day. Print, telegraph, rail and the radio deliver a very different circuit for building reciprocity and mutuality than digital society, tablet culture and air travel. To prejudge here is to err. Screen amity is not necessarily the bedfellow of depth, nor is the telegraph inevitably the companion of superficial communication. Once again, content and context are important variables here. With these caveats, Durkheim clearly identifies a connection between communication and moral density. That is, moral life with others is not confined to direct physical interaction. It also embraces representation of others through the means of communication. Crucially, Durkheim cites communication as an element in the concentration of moral density. We will return to the relationship between the quality of moral life and its equation with physical nearness and remoteness later in the study. Durkheim believed that group associations, based in work and community, would emerge under organic solidarity to translate moral constitutional issues into everyday life. While today, these association do exist (in the form of trade unions and voluntary associations), the central players of moral force are the state, corporations, interest groups and the media. This implies that neither organic solidarity nor constitutional patriotism function as Durkheim and Habermas would wish. In their accounts, the citizen is a knowledgeable, active participant in democratic processes. Above all, Durkheim saw moral density as the free reciprocal relation to impartial civic principles classified by the state, but subject to civic revision by the action of the people. Nowadays, the execution of these rights and responsibilities is not exactly freely vibrating with the state or corporations in the way that Durkheim envisaged. Contemporary conditions involve the inflection of these rights and responsibilities through the media and the vested interests that manage and control them. Vital civic membership is heavily influenced by the gatekeepers behind the distribution of information. The scope of mutuality and reciprocity is not confined by legal distinction and classificatory schemas laid down by the state, but mediations of these qualities through the lobbying of vested interests and the Public relations/ Media hub (PR/Media hub).

The question of mediation raises the issue of how powerful elements see others. Turning the metaphor upon its head, to the powerful, *we Western* statistical men and women need to have our minds furnished with the right information and our hearts won over to desirable causes (Wolin 2008). The statistical men and women of the nation are so numerous that when one speaks of them in aggregate their individual characteristics and differences blur; which is one reason why powerful interests in society are so agitated by the city and what to do about it.

Cities are full of statistical men and women with differentiated, variable forms of moral density. But it is a more visible, tangible aggregate than national or world populations. The street or the neighbourhood come closer to achieving the relations of moral density envisaged by Durkheim. The presumed intimacies that develop in cities as people go about their business with each other are potentially threatening to authority. This is because they constantly raise questions of power, inequality and control. It is difficult to speak of them deeply in aggregate terms, because difference and diversity are such obvious and ineradicable features of their composition. But as people go about defending public space, protecting access and helping each other, they cannot avoid politicization. Occupational groupings and trade unions are perceived as sectional nowadays, for the casualization of work mean that many careers in paid labour are episodic, and temporary. The insecure, spatially diffuse character of workplace settings (in which many workers now work at home), undermine the moral force of occupational settings as a conduit for moral density. In contrast, the city provides opportunities for building close relations of moral density that transcend sectarian interest and are experienced as continuous, adhesive forms of relation. [11] The powerful may outwardly celebrate urban space as exciting and vigorous, but they also harbour deep fears that it is a potential axis for intrigue and disturbance. Stephen Graham (2010), a major voice among critical commentators on the new ways of policing urban space in the West, maintains that, since the declaration of 'the war against terror' after 9/11, the diverse, variable moral densities that characterize cities have been subject to transparent authoritarian pressures designed to achieve consent and containment. Urban space has been subject to a massive upgrade in securitization and militarization. Its hallmarks include the multiplication of CCTV cameras, police checkpoints, biometric testing, helicopter surveillance, satellite monitoring, phone-tapping, the construction of gated communities and the encasement of the metropolitan perimeter with 'rings of steel'. Domestic policing in the West borrows from police marshalling tactics devised to control the demonized, 'risky' Palestinian population in Jerusalem, dissidents in Damascus, seditionaries in Islamabad and other 'unstable' metropolitan hot spots. It adapts military technologies and communication surveillance networks pioneered and refined by the armed forces in the bloody wars in Afghanistan and Iraq.

Our biggest, most ceremonial displays of brotherhood and liberty are in fact tightly regimented and externally controlled. The Beijing Olympics (2008) involved a security force of police officers, professional security staff and volunteers numbering 80,000. It was part of a trend toward escalating armed security for mass sporting and festive events (Perelman 2012: 6). The constellation of high-tech missiles, drones and military personnel deployed during the London Olympics (2012) was unprecedented in the postwar era (Rojek 2013).

Most people are divorced from real power by virtue of the scale of modern urban-industrial populations and isolation from the PR/Media hub that frames the public agenda (Castells 2009; Keane 2009). This hub conditions the semantic field of cognitive responses to issues, incidents and emergencies (Castells 2009: 142–3, 155–65). It is set up to follow a defensive, pro-capitalist agenda, rather than a programme of system change committed to egalitarianism and freedom. These predatory developments in Western civil society are legitimated on the pretext that urban space is the breeding ground for 'feral' moral densities that put the silent majority at risk. It has become a profound obligation of moral density today to keep a watchful eye on what might be called 'risk incubation'. That is, maintaining vigilance and effective policing against sections of the population or gatherings that are perceived to carry risk to the majority. Since 9/11 the idea of 'homeland security' has entered the political lexicon. The statistical men and women with whom we share politically territorialized space are assumed to be no less 'at risk' than leaders and figureheads. The PR/Media hub places all of us in the firing line. The common, mostly unparticularized, threat is the pretext for the goal of blanket protection, which has escalated securitization and the militarization of everyday life. Tellingly, the nature of risk incubation also revolves around statistical men and women, labelled as belonging to, or carrying the genes of the 'feral' type. No elected leader, whether they be a President or military/police commander in chief, knows how many people are intent on harbouring or have the capacity to mount terrorist attacks on the silent majority and its property. If risk is nowhere and everywhere at the same time, it makes vigilance and risk incubation at one and the same time supreme and inconsequential. These are the perfect conditions for the harmonious expansion of control and authoritarian populism. [12]

2

Chimerical Risk Management

The term 'chimerical risk' may be introduced at this point to refer to the putative, *represented* threat posed to life and property by antagonistic agents. It is different from real risk, which involves confirmed knowledge of perpetrators and informed knowledge of would-be perpetrators. It is worth noting that it is also based upon principled non-communication. Surveillance of risk incubation certainly generates data about so-called 'risky populations', but it is sieved through complex power struggles in the corporate-state axis to financial strategies to achieve lucrative, no-bid contracts (Johnson 2010: 103). Chimerical risk is a matter of educated guesses and it may be inflated by politicking, scare-mongering and financial skullduggery. It is proportionate to the volume of media in a territorially bounded space. To be sure, given the financial and political stakes involved in securitization, it is inconceivable that some element of risk distortion is not at play. By inflating the clear and present danger posed by perpetrators theoretically antagonistic to Western interests, politicians gain votes and the power of police/military commanders increases and security companies gain orders. Chimerical risk orchestrates particular kinds of presumed intimacy. As a general principle, chimerical risk management prospers most when the information about the real level of risk is imprecise and ambivalent but the emotional reaction to an episode, incident or emergency apparently produced by terrorist agency is bourgeoning. A moral climate in which danger lurks around every corner makes it easier for authorities to achieve compliance and fight the war against risk incubation (Wolin 2008). Correspondingly, the incentive for bold, courageous chimerical risk

management expands. Imprecise and ambivalent risk consciousness
has a strong tendency to be self-perpetuating. Chimerical risk management involves a version of Pascal's wager. [1] When a terrorist
incident occurs, the belief in omnipotent and omnipresent risk is
vindicated; when nothing happens, the requirement to be vigilant
does not abate, since apparent inactivity is often interpreted as potentially concealing the gradual unfolding of carefully hidden plans and
preparations by 'evil men and women'. It follows that chimerical risk
is properly seen as an asset for three sets of vested interests: corporations involved in the security sector, for authority legislators and
executives (hawkish politicians/acquisitive military chiefs/police commanders), and owners and managers of some sections of the media.
The intensification of homeland security is funded by powerful political and economic elements and is packaged to the public that 'eternal
vigilance' is the price paid to protect the people from terrorist insur-
gents. What Chalmers Johnson (2010), Graham (2010) and others
make abundantly clear, is that these authoritarian measures can also
be switched from an external foe to domestic settings. In other words,
securitization and militarization are advanced to cover reciprocal
relations in the moral density of the population defined and segregated by the prognosis or diagnosis of being labelled as 'dysfunctional', 'destabilizing', 'threatening' and, in other ways, 'risky'. The
mature and sophisticated mutual social relationships identified by
Durkheim in the discussion of 'organic solidarity', and Habermas in
his account of 'constitutional patriotism', are supplanted by crude,
emotional boundaries of social inclusion and exclusion. Emotional
management here works through the politics of fear. Typically, inclusion and exclusion are mapped around totems of nationalism and
religion. The object is to create and buttress the impression that those
who are not with us must be against us.

Some critics, notably Sheldon Wolin (2008: 284–7) go further and
maintain that politics and culture in democracy is an 'enclosed',
'elite managed' process that *excludes* the citizenry. Of course, this is
not done by banishing individuals from democratic participation.
Rather, it takes the form of boosting notional aggregate security
measures over individual interests and lording the 'dynamism' of
private property over public ownership. [2] The protection of the
majority requires subjecting all to the 'managed democracy 'of tele-
photo surveillance, hacking and a clandestine system of informers.
What Wolin (2008) is driving at is that the citizenry are excluded
from direct involvement in this by the authorities because *inclusion*
is defined as a security risk. The citizenry are systematically disem-
powered *for their own good*. A sort of undisclosed higher ('we know

best') democracy is invoked to justify this; that is, those with the power over national security are in the best position to decide what is in our best interests. This is the opposite of Durkheim's cult of the individual. It implies that individual freedom is often a curse that imperils the common good.

Chimerical risk management involves powerful elements in society creating familiar foes, about whom public knowledge is rationed or repressed for the security of all. Therefore capacity to render authoritarianism accountable is impeded. Elected authorities are represented as acting in the best interests of all to protect us from mortal danger. The efficacy of this action is portrayed as being predicated in the need for secrecy. Again, this runs counter to what Durkheim expected in organic solidarity, and Habermas proposes in constitutional patriotism. They assume the full *transparency* of representative power. Such a state of affairs presupposes not only openness on the part of the authorities, but an educated, informed public with real powers to challenge elected leaders. This state of affairs exists in theory in Western democracy, but its practice is not so cut and dried.

Fugitive Democracy

For Wolin (2008: 287), modern democracy has a 'fugitive' quality, since it operates on the principle that the democratic process can only work through remote chains of delegation, data release and representation. The people are segregated from open and full participation in regulatory mechanisms notionally designed and applied to protect them. This happens for two reasons. Firstly, because they are too far removed from the seat of power to make a difference. [3] Secondly, because the powers that be decide that there are some things that are better handled discreetly. The reasons to feel uncomfortable about this extend further than the realization that an enclave of 'representative' interests refuse the public the right to know, and therefore preside over the disenfranchisement of the electorate. They centre on the objection that property qualifications and the rank of officialdom are preconditions for meaningful (rather than ceremonial) engagement with democratic process (Keane 2009). That is, on *a priori* grounds, some strata are excluded from informed involvement in the democratic process. Defenders of the system have every reason to insist that the machinery to realize popular aspirations is in place. To which critics respond that what is absent is the general distribution of the effective (especially economic and specialized knowledge) means of allowing general participation to drive the machine. Wolin's

(2008) case, in brief, is that current democracy offers a first class service to the minority who possess the economic and political means to participate, and confines the overwhelming majority to cabin class. Once again, it must be observed that this is very different from how Durkheim believed organic solidarity, and Habermas submits constitutional patriotism, should work. For them, meaningful democracy requires resources of time, education and sound data to be awarded to the *polis*.

At this point, commentators are entitled to object that there is all the difference in the world between democracy as an ideal and democracy as a reality. Since the dawn of the Ancient Athenian experiment, it has been ever thus. In response Keane (2009), argues reasonably that we pay too much attention to the ingredient of the *demos* ('people') in democracy, and too little to the *kratos* ('rule'). If democratic leaders turned the searchlight on rule they would see that the people *en masse* are being comprehensively deprived of precisely what they need most. Namely, meaningful engagement with democratic process. The hiatus is filled by what Keane (2009) terms *monitory democracy*. That is, the over-loaded, inefficient form of democracy today in which the question of public accountability is subject to a multitude of competing and overlapping interests composed of watchdog committees, ombudsmen, audit trails, quality assurance programmes and internet blogging sites, which end up leaving the public with the message that nobody is fit to rule. The sheer scale of administrative support systems designed to deliver egalitarianism and due process means, *a priori*, that all leaders are viewed as flawed and potentially, corrupt. This militates against the effective application of democratic process. On this account, democracy is dysfunctional not on the grounds that it *excludes* citizens. The real problem is that it encourages all citizens to have a say, to make their case, to 'meaningfully' challenge authority. Rather like Foucault's (1981) famous argument in the history of sexuality, society does not so much repress freedom as turn it into a perpetual debating point. This complicates direct action and progressive change. The din cancels out how democracy should work by producing a stalemate between competing voices, each intent on presenting their own view of affairs as privileged. Free speech and self-determination are cardinal features of democracy. Unlike autocrats and plutocrats, the principal representative forces democratically elect leaders to be accountable. Yet in the monitory form, these principles have assumed an inverted value in which democratic leadership is automatically associated with double dealing and broken promises. Politicians are forced to assume the mantle of hypocrisy in affecting presumed intimacy with the people

(Runciman 2008: 202–26). This forms a toxic environment in which the electorate often feels helpless and powerless. An electorate that feels helpless and powerless is also psychologically susceptible to authority figures that claim to feel its pain, understand its perplexity and share its frustration. In party politics, presumed intimacy has developed as a mechanism to boost media attention and accumulate votes. The emotional identification played out in front of the TV cameras or on the hustings bears no necessary relation to what is being thought or done behind the scenes. When democracy is paralysed by the hubbub of competing voices and the bugaboo of fatal threats, the political acts of reaching out and displaying empathy buys space for covert decision making to seize the initiative. Presumed intimacy of this type chokes off criticism and allows managed democracy to prosper.

Self-styled 'friends of democracy' have long insisted that leadership requires flattery and rationing information because the public is culturally illiterate (Lippman 2007, originally 1922). This is a lofty proposition that rests more on group prejudice than solid evidence. It is more difficult to maintain today when the level of monitory democracy is much higher than a century ago. Monitory democracy depends upon effective networks of information gathering and distribution (especially the media) and cultivated public discernment (principally through the discipline of education). Western citizens live in an age of media saturation and unprecedented levels of participation in higher education. Yet the data and the capacity of the public to read events and processes in the world in different ways negates the democratic imperatives to understand clearly and to act purposefully. Democracies are at their best when crises dramatize issues and demand decisive action. Even then decisiveness may be impeded by the requirement to please the electorate. All democratic leaders must subject themselves periodically to the electoral process. This tariff of selection complicates clear decision making, which is in the public interest. It is a price that must be paid for the democratic process *per se*. David Runciman (2012) is right to maintain that democracy mostly involves muddling through. This reinforces the 'fugitive' quality of modern democracy, to which Wolin (2008) alludes, since it logically suggests a separation between the theory and practice of the cult of the individual. It introduces the idea of what might be called, controlled elasticity, in moral density. Wolin's analysis makes no bones about relating moral density to vested interests. It proposes that density is subject to elite piloting and the manipulation of the PR/Media hub. So the modern Western citizen is confronted with more data on statistical men and women with whom some sort of emotional relationship can be formed than at any time in human history. Emotional relationships take place in an imperfect market of knowledge and information. We are supplied, and supply for ourselves, bundles of aggregate knowledge about the lives of others. This makes it easy for us to provide positive emotional responses when the curtain is pulled back and one or more of the nameless and unknown strides out of the shadows to become an embodied personality in the media. This only goes to reinforce the point that monitory democracy sees veils and shadows everywhere. We are aware that data that come our way are subject to rationing and may, in any case, be designed by leaders to encourage 'preferred readings'. The articulation of this is now a constant feature of democratic process. When statistical men and women step out of the shadows we cannot trust our positive emotional responses to the representation of their circumstances because we have the background consciousness that hidden veils may be holding something back. As we shall see more clearly in Chapter 6 of the book, the concept of personality should not be taken at face value. To be sure, face value is often the only value that it has. Its content is a matter of context and setting. Where the media are involved in disclosing personality to the army of watchers, it is entirely right to ask if we are being given the real thing or a package tailored to suit media schedules and the vested interests that inform them. Unlike totalitarian regimes which impose monolithic rule, in monitory democracy everything is being questioned all the time, with complex and costly administrative systems to support interrogation and auditing. These systems develop an independent momentum which fetishizes due process so that the ends of proper democratic process are thwarted. This reinforces the general sense of muddling through (Runciman 2012). Nihilism and opposition may accompany totalitarian regimes. Under monitory democracy, doubt and scepticism are much more probable responses. Every question is exposed, every proposed solution is parried, to the point where social reaction is subject to constant interrogation and deconstruction, i.e. the postmodern mind set. This is a negative politics because the type of engagement that it summons forth cannot transcend the treadmill of querulous criticism and build hope for a genuine progressive platform. Despite the attachments and positions that are stirred up, monitory democracy proliferates deep level emotional and political paralysis. Again, this raises the ante for leaders to reach out and display intimacy with the muddled, the bewildered and the perplexed. Among the culturally literate this contributes to a deeper sense of bad faith that the system is rigged to manipulate emotions and cultivate compliance.

Bystander Mentality

Stan Cohen's (2001) investigation into the difficult problem of social denial may be referred to here in order to expand the argument. The Watergate and Iran-Contra cases in the USA and the findings of the Scott 'Arms to Iraq' Inquiry in the UK, clearly reveal deep tensions between the real, free expression of moral density and social orchestration of public opinion designed to accomplish obedience and compliance (Cohen 2001: 67–8). In these cases, statecraft based in the release of faulty information, was interpreted as a legitimate component of government. [4] Through direct falsification of the truth the government seized the option to act (which consequently turned the majority of the citizenry into 'bystanders', powerless to influence events that were, automatically, portrayed as too big for them to fully appreciate). In the bargain, the corporate-state axis is 'naturally' presented as the only meaningful (and honest) actor capable of responding positively to events, emergencies and incidents. The postmodern version of antagonistic politics rejects this on the grounds that there is no such thing as 'original meaning' and that the assertion to rule is the contamination of power (since it necessarily marginalizes contrary standpoints). It need hardly be laboured here that the querulous criticism encouraged by postmodernism is not the stuff of board-room decision making, cabinet room policy formation or the strategies of military and police command staff. Historically speaking, those who agonize over who they are and where they have come from have difficulty in deciding what to do; while those, for whom these questions are beside the point, are more adept at following through their interests.

Cohen's (2001) discussion sheds much light on the nature of human connectivity today and in doing so clarifies the contemporary character of moral density. 'We Make Us' has become a motif of activists of all stripes, ranging from campaigners against hunger in Africa, torture in Darfur, poverty in Europe and North America, racial injustice and umpteen other *causes célèbres*. [5] The motif is a truism. We are all interrelated, and the needless suffering or death of one, diminishes everyone. Yet the sheer moral weight that comes with this acceptance requires its own type of emotional rationing. Cohen (2001: 10–11) points to an entire category that is a mundane part of social life consisting of *cultural denial* in which knowledge of the suffering and extreme plight of others is developed as a coping strategy. We excuse our personal engagement with a familiar language of denial consisting of phrases such as: 'It's not my problem'; 'What difference can a single individual make?'; 'It's worse elsewhere.' Emotional disengagement of this sort is one aspect of bystander mentality; that is, a frame of mind and personal outlook that acknowledges emergencies, incidents, events and risks involving strangers, but decouples knowledge from action.

One reason for this mentality is compassion fatigue. Figley (1995) defines compassion fatigue as overexposure to the suffering of strangers: human brutality, war, disasters, loss, illness, rape and other catastrophes. We have seen it all before. There is nothing new under the sun. The depth of western charity is unable to extinguish the cauldron of pain, misery and suffering in the world. Technically, this mentality advances by moving along three interrelated fronts. Firstly, social consciousness of inexhaustible global needs expands at a rate beyond the personal means of achieving solutions. Secondly, the responsibility to act is transferred from the private realm to humanitarian aid agencies and the state. Thirdly, the media ceases to cover emergencies, events and incidents after the drama and consequences are judged to have ceased to be newsworthy. To be sure, high profile events receive media amplification which, in turn, boosts charity. Western responses to crises, such as the famine in Ethiopia (1985), the earthquake in Turkey (1999) and the Indian Ocean Tsunami (2004), are often generous. However, even here, the primary response is emotional rather than strictly based in reason. In the wealthy countries of the Northern hemisphere, the request to dig deep into pockets when a disaster occurs disguises the requirement to reform the fiscal systems and globally revitalize the ethic of care for the other. The central defect of this response is, as Taithe (2007: 135) remarks, that 'one is not asked to contribute to a global form of a national insurance scheme – one is called upon using the register of emotion'. The *exhibition* of humanitarianism, the *display* of care and the *drama* of concern overshadow the construction of sound economic arrangements to manage global problems. They are also at the core of votive behaviour, through which statements of action masquerade as genuine contributions of action. [6] In all of this the repertoire of presumed intimacy is refined and expanded. The visual dynamics of reaching out become the focus of social consciousness. The monitoring of aid and charity is secondary. The primary focus is upon doing something, doing anything, *together* to relieve pain and suffering.

It is tempting to discount the emotional exhibitionism and drama of charity as sheer posturing. This would be to do a disservice to the quality of emotions involved. Most people really do care, and they are genuine and steadfast in their belief that 'We Make Us'. The trouble is that, consecutively, they are onerously aware that the problems of the world are part of a perpetual conveyor belt of troubles that is beyond the capacity of any country, let alone a group or leader, to master. Hence, bystander mentality is not merely a result of indifference, but also, acute consciousness of the sheer scale of human problems that is (not irrationally or cynically), judged to be beyond the capacity of human agency to remedy (Clarkson 1996). The fugitive quality that Wolin (2008) detects in the practice of democracy is paralleled in the practical observance of moral density. In terms of caring for strangers who are in need, mostly we do not practise what we preach. Some of this has to do with what the social category of what the familiar stranger means.

The Unity of Nearness and Remoteness

To understand this better, consider, Simmel's (1950: 402) classical designation of social equilibrium as a combination of relations consisting of a 'unity of nearness and remoteness'. Simmel was critical of consciousness and behaviour that fell on the side of either extreme. In the first instance we might be said to live in a bubble, and in the second, we might be scolded for living in a vacuum. If we care too much for strangers we will be regarded as slightly odd, perhaps even unhinged. On the other hand, if we show ourselves to be indifferent to strangers, we run the risk of being denounced for our shameful inhumanity. Evidently, Simmel regards the relationship between strangers and groups to be one of very delicate balance. His understanding operates on the assumption that social boundaries are analogous to spatial boundaries. Relations of nearness are well defined and incomparable, whereas relations of remoteness are vague and general. Thus, with strangers we have general connections in common, whereas with people with whom we are organically connected characteristics are shared that separate them from that which is vague and general. This is similar to the inverse relationship between human sympathy and social/spatial distance identified by Hume (1742) and Smith (1790) alluded to in the previous chapter.

The spatial analogy that forms part of Simmel's account of the place of strangers in social equilibrium, loses explanatory force in the age of digital communication. The remoteness of strangers appears to be dissolved by our personal accessibility to their lives and their conditions through electronic communication and the incentives of para-social interaction that it invites. Accessibility affords the presumption of intimacy, which is massaged and glossed by the media. It turns blank slates into familiar strangers. In a word, para-social relationships stand Simmel's account of social equilibrium and the place of strangers, upon its head. Via terrestrial and satellite transmission (and the print media hub), organic connections with familiar strangers, with whom we have no history or real prospect of communication, are routinely made. Para-social relationships create well-defined, tangible connections with those with whom we have no face-to-face connection. The stranger is no longer precisely vague or general. Through the media network, the stranger enters the private sphere and becomes familiar, in ways that Simmel, or for that matter, Milgram, failed to foresee. This is not confined to victims of incidents, emergencies and events. Social networking sites and chat-rooms create a portable switchboard in our personal space, occupied by, what might be called, pixillated people. Illouz's (2007) work on online dating shows clearly the exaggerated emotional investment that is frequently made in pixillated strangers. In most human relationships we develop emotional attachments as we become more literate with a person's conditions of life and character. With pixillated strangers the reverse applies. Emotional involvement is urged to precede cultural literacy. This does not stop with the practices of online dating agencies. Ehrenreich's (2009) study of medical counselling and human resources shows how approaches to difficult labour issues, such as redundancy or failed attempts at promotion, reveal a well-developed repertoire of standardized emotional responses that precede cultural literacy about what the person is going through and feeling. Counselling and therapy, which have done so much to expose the dangers of partial, prejudiced perspectives, also create a climate in which emotional mutuality and reciprocity are impertinently assumed without being 'won' (Furedi 2003). It is not enough to acknowledge that the walls of the group are arbitrary. In addition we are under strong informal pressures to embrace the conditions of life of the stranger, not merely as relevant, but as constitutive of the group. In the economically advanced countries of the West this is exacerbated by a high dose of historical guilt. We emote with strangers in the developing world because we accept that our colonial ancestors did much to create conditions of global inequality and injustice. We are not to blame, but, regrettably, blame runs in our blood.

The relations of intimacy that we express for spatially remote people are part of a gestural economy of civic culture. That is, they belong to the imperative of being seen to do the right thing and not being bogged down in indefensible colonial prejudices. Presumed intimacy is a major component of this economy, and in Chapter 9 we will see how it works in greater detail. At this point it suffices to note that the economy demands that we visibly empathize with oppressed groups like the Palestinians, the Kurds and the Rohingya (a small, oppressed Muslim group in Northern Myanmar). However, because they are external to our spatial boundaries there is a weak incentive to develop culturally literate knowledge about their lives and conditions. Presumed intimacy relies on an emotional 'nearness', a strong sense of presumed intimacy, supplied by the media. Our switchboards of global knowledge are mainly supplied by media representations and are susceptible to the self-cancelling qualities of monitory democracy. We embrace them on our television screens and hand-held devices, much as Milgram embraced the familiar strangers that he photographed at rush hour on the platform of his local subway station. Our knowledge about the details of their lives and aspirations depends upon an imperfect market. Simultaneously, it lends itself to value distortion and snap judgements.

Para-social familiarity is most highly developed in celebrity culture. This is because here relations involve familiar strangers to whom the media give primary, concentrated and usually glamorous attention. The private lives of stars has developed into a global communication industry. In this case, while most of us do not know celebrities, we often possess high cultural literacy about their private lives, for example, health issues, financial matters, political interests, leisure pursuits. Not coincidentally, cultural literacy also carries over into the world occupied by statistical men and women.

Analytically, we may make a purely quantitative distinction in the concept of familiar strangers, between Category A relationships and Category B relationships. In both there is scant history or real pros-pect of communication. The former refers to high-volume, focused para-social interaction (e.g. mostly with celebrities), whereas the latter refers to low-volume, wide-angled para-social interaction (e.g. with victims of incidents, events and emergencies, or, more prosai-cally, the aggregate in general). The high-volume data typical in Cat-egory A relationships reflects media concentration and transmission. In each case the relationship is based on a density of interconnections from which face-to-face contact is absent. Despite this, Category A relationships yield higher levels of emotional investment, ontological identification and presumed intimacy. With the Category A type we feel that we intimately know the personal lives of the individuals concerned, because many of the private details have been aired, often in dramatic format, through a variety of media channels, from televi-sion interviews, newspaper features and chat-room websites.

Category B relationships are based on weaker data. Knowledge about the private lives of statistical men and women is generally scant and mostly superficial. Yet, here too these details are often dramatically promoted to the public in the wake of an incident, episode or emergency. It is the human response to these dislocations in social order and the suffering that they produce that elicits presumed intimacy. Indeed, events like *Live Aid* (1985), *Live 8* (2005) and *Live Earth* (2007) suggest that Category B relationships have become an important marker of civic virtue. As with Simmel's equation of nearness and remoteness, living in a bubble or living in a vacuum, isolated from the multitudinous pulses of mankind, is regarded to be a social negative. A pre-condition of being recognized as a relevant, virtuous person in modern society today is to be seen to be *connected* with those who we do not know in a world that we acknowledge to be interdependent. A good deal of emotional labour goes into displaying identification. Of course, when we (Westerners) see film reports of starving villagers in Africa or Latin America, the families of victims of chemical warfare in Syria (2013) or survivors of the Fukushima Daiichi nuclear plant disaster (2011), we engage at some emotional level, with their plight. However, caution should be exercised in interpreting the moral density of this emotional identification. The quality of emotional engagement with extreme events is highly variable. For some, it may be life-changing, but for the majority it is just part of the event stream that is perpetually relayed to us through the media. As we have seen, Adam Smith ventured that human sympathy is expressed in inverse relationship to spatial distance. Likewise, in contemporary society the emotional nearness that we feel to statistical men and women who are in need or distress is closely tied to media coverage. [7] The televised plight of others may persuade some who live in comfort to launch a strong personal crusade against specific conditions of want and misery. This outcome is rare indeed. For others the emotional connection carries the moral weight of a goose feather. Intense identification with remote people who are portrayed as being in need of assistance, soon becomes yesterday's news. Category B relationships have a high propensity to be tokenistic. They lend themselves to the exhibition of presumed intimacy. It is a matter of gaining acceptance and approval from the group. Nor, whether it be strong or light, in the moment, is there firm evidence that the emotional connection will prove durable. Even in the matter of direct experience of high-impact traumatic events there is a good deal of obscurity about the persisting character of psycho-social effects.

3

The Shockwaves of Trauma

Research into psycho-social responses to natural disasters and terrorist incidents provides much food for thought on the question of the depth and longevity of emotions transferred to statistical men and women who are represented as being in crisis. This is of moment to the subject of presumed intimacy, since it has a bearing on the question of how deep our emotions with respect to screen apparitions go. Not surprisingly, common responses to natural disasters and social high-impact incidents are anxiety and stress. So much so, that a regular conclusion in research is that mental health workers attending post traumatic populations can expect to devote substantial resources to treating symptoms of Post-Traumatic Stress Syndrome (PTSD) (Norris and Rosen 2009). There are important distinctions to be drawn. PTSD is more likely to occur among primary victims, i.e. those who have significant emotional attachments with the dead or injured, first respondents and support providers (Fullerton and Ursano 2005: 15). Research suggests that on average, 25 per cent of adults initially experience PTSD after a traumatic high-impact event (Hagan 2005). Research into traumatic high-impact events finds that psycho-social reactions are variable. In this respect a comparative study of psycho-social responses to the bombing of the Murrah Federal Building in Oklahoma City (1995) and New Orleans victims of Hurricane Katrina (2005) is instructive (North 2010). [1] The Oklahoma City survey consisted of White, middle-aged males with a minimum of two years' college education, directly exposed to the blast. It was conducted a year after the event. It found that the majority of survivors did not develop a psychiatric disorder. By 'direct exposure' is meant individuals who were in the Murrah Building at the time of the explosion or in unprotected locations outside or in nearby buildings. However, 34 per cent of the sample had symptoms of PTSD and 23 per cent suffered from major depression.

A survey of 421 Hurricane Katrina evacuees from New Orleans, with histories of mental illness, conducted two weeks after the storm, discovered contrasting results. The survey consisted of 55 per cent female, 76 per cent African-American, aged in their forties. The sample was classified as economically disadvantaged, with 32 per cent uninsured, 48 per cent on public insurance schemes and 11 per cent on private schemes. Research found that PTSD was not a major problem. It was diagnosed in only three per cent of the sample. The most prevalent psycho-social problems were depression (25 per cent) and schizophrenia (21 per cent). Over one-quarter of the sample had pre-existing histories of serious and persistent mental illness. Alcohol disorders were identified in 20 per cent of the sample and cocaine disorders in 17 per cent (North et al. 2008).

The two events were very different. The Murrah Building incident was an event of horrific impact lasting only a few seconds, while the Hurricane Katrina evacuees experienced days of extreme weather and extensive property destruction. The Oklahoma City sample consisted of randomly sampled survivors who had business in the Murrah Building, whereas the Hurricane Katrina group consisted of economically disadvantaged respondents with a history of pre-existing chronic physical and mental health problems. The PTSD symptoms among the Oklahoma sample suggest that 34 per cent mark may be reasonably taken as the upper level of the amount of PTSD that can be expected from an extreme traumatic event of this type. Research discovered a much lower rate of PTSD symptoms among the New Orleans sample (three per cent), but a much higher rate of serious or severe mental health effects (40 per cent with a pre-disaster history of mental retardation, autism, attention deficit disorder, delerium and dementia; and 24 per cent who showed post-disaster onset of these conditions). The research suggests that psycho-social reactions to traumatic high-impact events are conditioned by time frame, setting and socio-economic characteristics (North 2010: 46). In particular, pre-trauma conditions of life and the latitude of victims to resume a regular life after the trauma are key factors. It is likely that this extends into social responses to representations of 'common' risks and emotional responses to events, incidents and emergencies.

Clinical research into the psychiatric effects of high-impact incidents posits that six factors influence the strength of reaction. These are, the extent of the incident to risk of life, degree of bereavement, physical suffering, extent of displacement of life changes, proportion of community affected and whether the incident was produced by nature or human action (Gleser, Green and Winget 1983). The variation in social reactions to traumatic events is likely to be paralleled by risk perception *before* traumatic events. One implication of this, is that chimerical risk management cannot operate on the assumption that uniform perceptions and reactions exist. Another is that presumed intimacy is strictly conditional.

On the question of the durability of effects, Galea et al. (2003) studied New Yorkers who had witnessed the 9/11 bombings on TV, at intervals of one, three and six months after the event. They found that PTSD declined from an initial 75 per cent to 0.6 per cent within six months. Long-term effects were more severe among people living directly near the high-impact incident. [2] For example, research into the traumatic effects of 9/11 three years after the event discovered that trauma symptoms were stronger in people who had been living within a radius of 1.5 miles of the World Trade Center on 9/11, relative to those resident more than 200 miles away (Ganzel et al. 2007). The general finding of research is that the majority recover from exposure to traumatic events fairly rapidly unless they, or their family, are directly affected (Pine and Cohen 2002; Barnes et al. 2005). However, a small minority may develop chronic problems (Masten and Chatsworth 1998).

If emotional involvement of people directly involved in high-impact traumatic events appears to fade with time, what are we to make of the declarations of support and identification made by those who have no direct connection with the same events? By the same token, how are we to read the commitments of elected political leaders and other public figures to derailments of social order caused by high-impact events? The first thing to state is that it is dangerous to equate emotional engagement with figures on the screen of a communication device with cultural literacy. No one would deny that we live in a state of co-presence with others in one world. For most people, the primary expression of our relation to the lives of others is through arithmetical currency. We learn that this volume of people applied to be asylum seekers in the last calendar year, or that number of people died in a distant plane crash; we know that the massacres in Santa Monica (2013) and the Navy Yard, Washington DC (2013), claimed so many lives, and we have a shadowy image of the perpetrators that we assemble, courtesy of the media. [3] In general, our contact with these flesh and blood people is purely quantitative, although this may not, of course, prevent us from forming strong qualitative opinions about them. This is not without consequences for social psychology and politics. As we have already noted, statistical men and women have their uses in managing democracy. The numerical relationship is an asset for political leaders who can at whim, mobilize demographic weight to endorse any position that lobbyists and focus groups flag as a source of political worth (Wolin 2008). When political leaders use a collective noun ('the American people', 'the British people') to support their policy and strategy statements, they are playing games with words. There is no psephological basis to validate the proposition that an elected leader speaks on behalf of an entire people. It need hardly be added, there has never been a democratically elected leader of an urban-industrial country that has achieved 100 per cent of the vote! Despite this, in managed democracy, modern leaders often resort to 'the people' as a flag of convenience to mobilize popular support, especially in response to violent incidents, economic challenges, natural disasters and other projections of shared risk. This holds good for the responses of leaders to traumatic events in the nation.

For example, on Patriots' Day (15 April 2013) terrorists launched double bombings near the finishing line of the Boston Marathon. Three people died and over 260 were injured. In short order, President Obama issued a statement which declared, 'the American people will say a prayer for Boston tonight. And Michelle and I send our deepest thoughts and prayers to the families of the victims', adding there is no hiding place for the perpetrators (*Guardian* 16.04.2013). The statement reinforces the President's faith and the emotional backing of his wife and, by implication, their two daughters. Public knowledge that Obama is a family man with a close and loving family apparently united at this moment in grief and national danger, adds to the emotional payload of the broadcast. The personal touch and knowledge of personal issues are fundamental because they tranquilize criticism and dissent. But there is something obviously and profoundly, unsatisfactory about his response. It may be a figure of speech to maintain that 'our deepest thoughts and prayers' are with the bereaved and the dead. But, it is hardly tenable. Surely, like everyone else, the President reserves his deepest thoughts and prayers for genuine, not *presumed*, intimates. The relationships involved here, with family, are of a different order to even close (or 'near') relationships with strangers. His wife, daughters, relatives, close friends and trusted advisers have a claim upon his deep emotions that the dead and bereaved in Boston cannot equal. If the counter-factual obtained, namely, if the President truly invested his deepest thoughts and prayers in people who are strangers to him, his thinking would be widely condemned as cranky. It would be said that his heart is in the right place, but his head is on back to front.

Presumed intimacy then is empathetic behaviour designed to assume a condition of ontological identification, while witholding ultimate commitment. The purpose of the behaviour is to achieve prestige and trust among others. It belongs to a gestural economy that denotes the display of compassion as a signifier of civic virtue. While the ends of trust are various, and are different in commercial and political contexts, they always include the object of attaining and managing compliance. Presumed intimacy uses many of the devices familiar in relationships that are based in the doctrine of ultimate commitment. Namely, emotional solicitude, reaching out, expressions of loyalty, familiarity and reassurances of reliability. Para-social inter-action multiplies the settings and channels through which presumed intimacy operates. It provides opportunities for distanced ontological identification with strangers. The delicate balance, to which Simmel alludes, between relations of remoteness and nearness in the interac-tion between groups and strangers is violated. Para-social interaction means that a high ratio of moral density in contemporary life is made up of relations with famous media figures and statistical apparations. In the case of statistical men and women, the presumption of intimacy is typically based upon very low levels of cultural literacy and very high levels of media exposure. Further, the social importance of pre-sumption may be to enhance the honorific status of the civilian rather than administer meaningful assistance and care to strangers.

The question raises the issues of the depth of moral density and the prevalence of bystander mentality as a coping strategy for the sheer instability of the world. For vested interests, public cynicism is far from being deplored, because it contributes to political demoral-ization and langour (Wolin 2008: 139). Presumed intimacy, which has no real force because it is built on sand, is a desirable and prized asset in governance. It is a form of civic engagement that recognizes a sense of participation without demands or responsibilities.

What About Category A Responses?

So far, the discussion has mostly dwelt on responses in Category B para-social relationships. That is, emotional reactions to statistical men and women based on fairly low levels of cultural literacy with respect to their conditions of life. Most casualties of the Murrah Building bomb did not develop long-term symptoms of PTSD because they did not have primary relations with the victims. There was no 'career' or evolutionary aspect to their relations. Similarly, Obama's public statement after the Boston Marathon attack was not made in respect of acquaintances or relations. It carried the emotional insulation of leadership separated from direct reciprocal bonds and obligations. Category A interaction is quite different. Because it involves emotional propinquity, despite the absence of mutually agreed reciprocal bonds and obligations, it is reasonable to hypothesize that it goes emotionally deeper than Category B interaction. That is, the *elan vital* that spectators have with celebrity figures is typically founded upon high levels of cultural literacy with the subject in question. Fans have appreciable background knowledge about the biography and conditions of life of the celebrity to whom they are attached. Moreover, the balance of evidence shows that attachment has significant effects on the organization and presentation of personality. To expand, if I say I care about everybody in the world, I am immediately (and rightly) dismissed by many as a screwball. On the other hand, if I display ontological identification with George Clooney's humanitarian campaign to halt human rights violation in the Sudan, or Angelina Jolie's work as United Nations High Commissioner for Refugees (UNCHR), my profile of 'responsible citizenship' is enhanced. [4] The ontological identification of Clooney and Jolie with their respective causes has the benefit of field trips and advice from professional advisers. My claim for responsible citizenship is obtained by proxy. That is, it is acquired by my interest and support for the humanitarian response of Jolie and Clooney. This of course conflates two issues: identifying with the humanitarian injustices identified by Jolie and Clooney and having the illusion of being on their 'team'. Superstars of the magnitude of Jolie and Clooney have a halo effect in culture. By supporting the causes that they champion, part of my motivation may be to hope that some of the halo rubs off on me and I am respected by others as a responsible, attractive personality. There are separate issues about the depth and duration of the ontological identification obtained by proxy. The spin-off here may not be confined to acquiring distinction for supporting a good cause. It may also be a way of investing private life with public attention capital. I call this aspect of the complex relations between private life and celebrity culture *skimming*. By skimming I mean goal-driven ontological identification with a celebrity that aims to transfer a level of attention capital from the celebrity to deploy it in self promotion activity. In their classic article, Horton and Wohl (1956: 216) note that spectator imitation of the gesture, voice, conversation and conduct of media personalities is a common feature of para-social relationships. Skimming consists of emulating these aspects and the value set attached to the celebrity, and projecting them in particular settings and relationships for the purpose of self promotion. Needless to say most cases of skimming are unlikely to provoke cases of crises or transformation in depth psychology. They take the form of superficial, trivial expressions of *esprit de corps* with individuals who possess high attention capital. At the same time, research also suggests that in some cases the depth and longevity of emotional identification at play here may be life changing. For example, Elliott (2010: 464) commenting upon changes in body culture, argues that celebrity identification is a factor in the growing phenomenon of cosmetic surgery. Fans do not necessarily seek a full body makeover. Imitations of celebrity body parts have an expanding attraction as lifestyle accessories. Elliott (2010: 469) observes, the most requested imitations in celebrity body parts are the nose (Nicole Kidman, Reese Witherspoon, Ben Affleck, Jude Law), eyes (Halle Berry, J-Lo, Brad Pitt, Ralph Fiennes), lips (Liv Tyler, Uma Thurman/Brad Pitt, Matt Damon) and so on. The proposition that facets of private life are being turned by some individuals into public spectacle intersects with the thesis in social psychology that celebrities are an increasing site of identification, imitation and desire. [5] The direction of cultural literacy and ontological identification takes the form of absorption with the lives of others. Para-social interaction is relevant inasmuch as these types of behaviour may unfold on the basis of having a real, reciprocal relationship with the celebrity in question. There is an evolutionary core in serious para-social interaction by which the relationship between fans and celebrities grows, despite the absence of direct, reciprocal contact (Chia and Poo 2009). This can tip over from viewing the celebrity as a person with whom one can identify, into an object that one seeks to discipline and control, both symbolically and, on some occasions, in direct social encounters. As Jenkins (1992: 13) notes, the root of the term 'fan' is 'fanatic'. The shading between shallow levels of cultural literacy and ontological identification with celebrities and more disturbing affective responses is not separated by bold, hard and fast lines. Studies of fan communities suggest that it is reasonable to conceptualize the movement from low to high affective responses in terms of drift. That is, disordered fan reactions to celebrity do not necessarily refer to separate personality types but, as the term continuum implies, to stages in a single personality that may be reached and passed through when specific psychological, social and political factors apply e.g. isolation, low levels of self esteem, peer-group influence, and so on (Maltby et al. 2006).

The scale of disordered para-social relationships with celebrities is hotly disputed. Phillips (1974) in a study of suicide rates in the USA and UK in the month following the suicide of Marilyn Monroe claims that rates rose by 12.4 per cent in the USA and 9.8 per cent in the UK. Corroborative findings of 'the Werther effect' cite the volume of publicity given to celebrity suicides as a key predisposing variable in cases of imitation suicides (Stack 1987: 409–10). [6] More recent research in South Korea supports the proposition that the suicide of some celebrities results in copycat suicides, although it stops well sort of positing a uniform cause and effect relationship. Again, what comes through most unequivocally is the conditional nature of pre-sumed intimacy. For example, the research cites the age and gender of the celebrity suicide, and the nature of the media reporting of the event, to be crucial variables (Fu and Chan 2013). The findings imply that Category A relationships are widely distributed in society with the proviso that a continuum obtains between entertainment-social and borderline-pathological orientations.

Conversely, although Stever (2011) points to the expansion of ontological identification and compulsive imitation with celebrities in private life, she pours cold water on the inference that entertain-ment-social fan behaviour frequently shades into more disruptive behaviours. She insists that serious fans and celebrity worshippers are categorically different types. Her research confirms that the practice of what is called here, skimming, is well established and widespread in popular culture. But she qualifies the argument by insisting that most people, or the social circles around them, put on the brakes before they risk falling into disruptive addictive behaviour. Interest-ingly, she (2011: 1367) also notes that Twitter, Facebook, MySpace and other social networking sites are increasingly being exploited by celebrities to create 'an intimate, day-to-day connection' with fans. [7] In some cases the mediation between agency and conforming to the expectations of fans threatens the division between the private and public face of celebrity. Stever (2011) raises the interesting notion that the private face of celebrity is, in some cases, colonized by the public face. That is, the celebrity becomes the social construct invented by cultural intermediaries. This is a clever twist on the familiar argu-ment made in discussions about para-social interaction that the private life of fans appropriates aspects of celebrity culture through skimming. The prospect of celebrities engaging in projection and self promotion without end does not seem faulty when one considers the likes of Kim Kardashian, Chantelle Houghton, Jim Davidson, Paris Hilton or Justin Bieber.

The issue that Category A relationships pushes to the forefront is the role of personality to accumulate attention capital. Performative and emotional labour designed to achieve social impact is at the heart of celebrity culture and, by extension, the culture of presumed intimacy. While important ancillary questions on the role of cultural intermediaries and the appetites of the crowd are necessarily posed by this, the crux of the matter is the complex relationships between personality, self-promotion and exposure management. Because achieved celebrity involves occupying new public space, it challenges the social boundaries of stratified society. We need to address the subject of personality and the adjoining concept of character in detail later. At this point in the discussion I want to state in a fairly unqualified way that the rise of presumed intimacy in everyday life is closely related to the triumph of personality over character in the game of achieving attention capital and social impact. Before coming to that point, it behoves us to return again to the topic of moral density. If our connectedness to personalities and entire social categories (statistical men and women) who are physically absent from our life settings and with whom we have no history of communication is often strong and in some cases, life changing, what does it say about the balance of nearness and remoteness that applies in ordinary social life? Morally speaking, how close are we to the lives of others?

4

The Lost Neighbour Proposition and the Collateral Damage Problem

Presumed intimacy is a sub-branch of emotional labour. Despite the fact that she usually refers to it as 'emotional work' (not labour), the basics of the latter concept were set out by Arlie Hochschild (1983, 2003). She famously elaborated the idea in a study of the commercial setting and labour of airline stewardess. Emotional labour refers to the practice of workers 'to induce or suppress feeling in order to sustain the outward countenance that produces the proper state of mind in others' (Hochschild 1983: 7). This is also at the crux of presumed intimacy and, by extension, modern civic culture. The emotional labour of the workers studied by Hochschild differs from para-social interaction in that it is based in direct facework and is conducted on the basis of strictly provisional commitments. An airline stewardess is likely to make you comfortable and feel at home on your flight. 'What can I get you?'; 'Are you comfortable?' 'Relax and enjoy the flight', are familiar entreaties delivered with the sincerity of a salaried service worker trained to put paying customers at their ease. She is unlikely to offer prayers to celebrate your presence in the world or to develop an interest in accumulating detailed knowledge about your history or life course. Hochschild's (1983) account is at pains to insist that the emotional labour of airline stewardesses is a required aspect of social relationships, and not merely a facet of personality (Hochschild 2003: 100). Through facial gesture and somatic presentation, the worker pursues the object of achieving compliance and obedience in others. The airline stewardesses in Hochschild's study went about this by inhibiting negative feelings to passengers by creating an atmosphere of concern and solicitude.

Emotional labour is a *front* of activity since it conceals the determination of the worker to confine concern and solicitude to the strict parameters of a business relationship, and absent themselves from the doctrine of ultimate commitment. To change tack a little by introducing the labour of a different kind of emotional service labour, a redundancy counsellor may state that she feels your pain or a President may appeal to an entire nation to pray with him for healing, as if you are each part of one big family. This form of emotional service labour involves taking others into your confidence and giving the impression that, despite outward differences, you share the same concerns. We are all in the same boat together. It is the technique of appearing to be everyman in a handshake or a soundbite. Workers who labour on the front of presumed intimacy absent themselves from delivering ontological identification to the letter. However, the personal element stresses the limited, conditional display of outward identification with the plight of others.

There are many good and stimulating things about Hochschild's (1983) discussion. However, in stressing that emotional labour is primarily a feature of social relationships, Hochschild (1983) underestimates its centrality in the struggle of personality to build attention capital and achieve social impact. Civic culture now requires gestures of empathy and concern for others whether they be related to us by (media induced) emotional nearness, despite being geographically remote. Physically speaking, presumed intimacy is a matter of facial gesture and somatic presentation. Like emotional service labour it is a front designed to create a climate of concern and solicitude with respect to the celebrity or the abstract social category (with whom direct face-to-face contact is absent, e.g. statistical men and women). However, in this case the spectator operates on the state of mind of others by applying a doctrine that may appear to lead all the way to ultimate commitment. For example, the spectator goes beyond confining concern and solicitude to insinuate *ontological identification* with the other. [1] Presumed intimacy is not just a prelude and condition of giving a good service, it is also about having an imaginary, ultimate, trust relationship with others.

The obverse to presumed intimacy may be called *removed intimacy*. That is, a personal relationship in which individuals negate emotions for others. This again raises the questions of denial and bystander mentality. Now, although denial has already been mentioned, it is necessary to return to the subject because it raises crucial issues about the operation of presumed intimacy in general life. Cohen (2001: 7) submits that there are three types of denial: *literal*, *interpretive* and *implicatory*. Literal denial is based upon the assertion that something did not happen, or is not true. Since I did not malign you, there can be no basis for holding negative emotions against me. Extreme nationalists or congregationists go through the same thought process in refusing to accept that their leaders and armies are guilty of atrocities or war crimes. They stifle anger, regret and guilt because they refuse to accept that the alleged events actually happened. Thus, many think it inconceivable that a national hero and global celebrity like Oscar Pistorius could have killed his girlfriend, Reeva Steenkamp in 2013; or that in 1994, O. J. Simpson could have murdered Nicole Brown Simpson and Ronald Goldman. People who take this view may even see these celebrities as victims of smear campaigns organized by the international media and the 'vested interests' that own and control them.

Interpretive denial means accepting that something happened but revising its meaning. For example, President Clinton smoked marijuana when he was a student, but he didn't inhale; ethnic cleansing was really just population exchange; illegal invasion is not really illegal because the war on terror is just (Cohen 2001:7). Typically the aim is to redraft morally unacceptable behaviour and render it tolerable.

Implicatory denial also accepts that something happened but qualifies it by claiming that the reports and consequences may be exaggerated and, in any case, it is beyond the capacity of any individual to do anything meaningful to solve the issue. The thought process here frequently falls back onto bystander rationalization. 'It's not my problem'; 'It's for the government to act'; 'There are far worse cases elsewhere in the world.'

Cultivating indifference or negating intimacy is a demanding process because we live under strong public pressures to demonstrate civic virtue. This involves opening up our emotions and connecting with those less fortunate than ourselves (Furedi 2003). [2] Denial is a means of excluding issues from our mental horizon so that we do not have to deal with them. It involves *cognition* (refusing to accept the facts); *emotion* (refusing to feel, or identify); *morality* (neutralizing misdemeanours and wrong doing); and *action* (refusing to take steps to help (Cohen 2001: 9). By these means, our intimacy with others is rationed. All of these responses call into question the real moral density of our relations with one another. The rhetoric of civic virtue and constitutional patriotism calls upon us to display compassion and concern for others. The voluntary carer is one of the most noble and admirable of all roles in society. Yet it is also quite rare. Moreover, it is concentrated in kith and kin networks. Thus, one may care for a relative who is house-bound or an elderly resident in the street who cannot cook. The proportion of the world's population that offer consistent meaningful care to strangers is comparatively small. The probability is that the mundane necessities of life make the response of meaningful care mostly tokenistic. How might this proposition be tested?

In the spirit of Stanley Milgram, one thought experiment that could be imagined might be called *the lost neighbour experiment.* [3] Suppose you research an inner-city apartment block in which the residents are mostly on nodding terms with one another. The volume of their social interaction may be more dense than that which obtained between Milgram and the rush-hour passengers at his local train station in New York. It may involve giving regular greetings or passing the time of day as you encounter each other on the corridor or board the lift. Now, suppose a neighbour is paid by researchers to vanish. He or she is paid to take extended leave from the block, but the absence is unexplained to other inhabitants. How do the familiar strangers in the apartment block process the lost neighbour? They may presuppose that absence is down to illness, abduction, abandonment of the partner or some form of institutionalization, such as long-term care or imprisonment. Speculatively, some may take the trouble to make a point of making a direct enquiry to the household. Others may wait to let it come up through circumstantial contact in the corridor or elevator. Still others can be expected to pretend that they are unaware of the lost neighbour and continue with their normal conduct until the loss is again disclosed to them. The experiment would test the social connectivity of residents. It would also reveal the moral density of relations in the apartment block.

The lost neighbour experiment is a methodological, and admittedly provocative response to the problem of the nature and depth of moral density. I am suggesting the experiment as an imagined way of testing the reality of altruism that is embedded in the notion of civic virtue. Postmodernism and the cultural turn of the 1980s and 1990s included the principle of 'care for the other' as a core theme. The work of Emmanuel Levinas (2005) is frequently cited to provide philosophical support for this principle. The principle is widely applied in civil law. As we have already seen, the concept of 'constitutional patriotism', coined by Jürgen Habermas (1996, 1998), refers to the political attachment of persons to the norms, values and procedures of a liberal democratic constitution. Civic virtue is at the heart of constitutional patriotism. That is, respect and active concern for the wellbeing of fellow citizens. This also comes close to what Durkheim (2013) means by moral density under organic solidarity.

But what does it mean to have respect and concern for fellow citizens? How deep and consistent should these undertakings be? For example, a common reaction in war to battle casualties in an enemy country is indifference or even exultation at the injury or death of the foe. But what if the casualties are not enemy soldiers but 'innocent' civilians? Must constitutional patriotism be confined to territorial boundaries? And what if the deaths are defined by combatants as 'collateral damage' in countries that are not formally at war with each other, as is the case in the current American drone attacks in the Yemen and Pakistan borderlands? Do the constitutional values of respect and active concern for citizens resident under the writ of the constitution necessarily imply humanitarian attachments of a related order to foreign citizens?

Collateral Damage

These are not merely abstract questions. Media reports strongly suggest that they were among the primary motivating factors that led to the actions of the two Boston Marathon bombers, Tamerian and Dzhokhar Tsarnaev. They were angry that the American 'war against terror' involved illegal Unmanned Aerial Vehicles (UAVs) and drone attacks on suspected terrorists thought to be resident in nations not at war with the United States. In their eyes, American civil society was in the grip of bystander mentality on this question. President Bush launched the campaign after 9/11. Under Obama, the numbers of attacks escalated, and the geographical radius of drone warfare expanded (Wall and Monahan 2011: 242; Bhatt 2012: 220; Hudson et al. 2012: 142–3; Sauer and Schornig 2012). During the Bush years, missile attacks were concentrated in Pakistan's Federally Administered Tribal Areas (FATAs), and thought to number fifty strikes. In Obama's (2009–10) first two years in office FATA strikes tripled. They declined to seventy in 2011 and twenty-five in the first half of 2012. Since 2004 there have been 365 drone strikes against Pakistan, 313 of them under Obama's period in office (Randle 2013). In terms of death rates, the decline in missile strikes is misleading. Targets have been ramped-up to so-called 'signature strikes'. That is, focused attacks upon 'high-risk' militant groups outside the FATA zone, notably in the Yemen, employing bombs with heavier detonative capacity (capable of many more deaths). This reflects a decision in the White House, following the assassination of Osama bin Laden in May 2011, that the campaign against 'al-Qaeda 1.0' was over. The cadre in control of al-Qaeda was judged to have been rendered impotent by the high trophy Bin Laden kill. The focus transferred to so-called 'al-Qaeda 2.0' attacks in high-risk areas of militant recruitment and agency mainly in the Yemen. Under Obama, targeted killings widened from the category of *known terrorists* to *suspected* terrorists.

These military assaults are very controversial because the USA is not officially at war with Pakistan or the Yemen (Gregory 2011: 190). It is not clear how far the governments of each country are complicit with US military and political strategy or to what extent their assent is tied to pledges of US aid provision. Der Derian (2009: xxi) submits that the military and political command axis behind drone campaigns routinely justifies them as 'virtuous warfare'. By this uncomfortable, term, is meant military action based in 'hygenic' technology that minimizes risks to combatants by focusing attacks in machine-based technologies directed at 'surgically' pinpointed targets. The discomfort and ambivalence here derives from the fact that all 'counterinsurgency' measures hazard so called 'collateral damage', i.e. the death or injury of innocent citizens. It is estimated that between 2004 and 2010 deaths in FATA's range from 1338 to 2144, of which approximately one-third were innocent civilians (Bergen and Tiedemann 2010). These figures have been challenged by other commentators who claim that in Pakistan alone, the numbers killed are as high as 3577, including 197 children (Randle 2013). [4]

Militarily and ethically, the use of the adjective *virtuous* in this regard is legitimated by the principle of *proportionality*. That is, in the ultimate struggle to rid terrorism from the face of the earth *some* collateral damage is judged to be unavoidable and, by implication, *acceptable*. The logic here is questionable and relies on Manichean assumptions. It runs – perhaps *races* would be more accurate – along the lines that in the *a priori* 'noble' struggle against 'men of evil' it is hardly reasonable to expect the enforcers of law to behave like angels. Extrajudicial assassination is somehow vindicated by the contentious objective of eliminating 'the enemy within' from so-called 'ungoverned' or 'lightly governed' independent states exerting nominal territorial jurisdiction. Because these states are militarily and politically defined as being in need of further 'nation state-building', enforcer nations take it upon themselves to administer what might be called *tough justice* (Boat 2012: 822). So-called wiser counsel and action are invoked and implemented over what are implicitly deemed to be less sophisticated power regimes. 'Failed states' are defined as fair game for enforcer nations, namely the USA and its allies, to bring into line. Virtuous warfare thus becomes permitted, since it is portrayed as doubly blessed. Practically, it 'cleanly' eliminates people labelled as terrorists (even though they have not faced legal charges or open trial), while at the same time offering failed, but aspiring, nation states the improving *pedagogy* of, for want of a better phrase, we might call, the *sagacity* of older hands. It is hard to deny the echo here of discredited colonial principles of 'manifest destiny' and 'the White-man's burden'.

The difficulty with this argument is that there are no agreements that justify the use of drones in territories which are not official war-zones. No declaration of war against Pakistan or the Yemen has been made. Instead, aggression is bow-ribboned by the insistence that it virtuously prevents terrorist acts from taking place by eliminating known or suspected perpetrators. Yet this line of reasoning brings difficulties of its own which multiply like bindweed. It dispels the judicial principle that the individual is innocent until proven guilty by an open trial of peers. It replaces this with a position that casts the military-political axis in the roles of prosecutor, jury and executioner. For moral philosophers this is untenable. Technically, it is objectionable on a number of counts. Most seriously, it puts all the cards in the hands of one party, denies transparency to the victim and removes the burden of public accountability from the kill. Morality depends upon principles. If a principle means anything it means a standard and code of conduct that is trusted, objective and universal (Dworkin 2011: 104–5).

On moral grounds therefore, President Obama is right to condemn the killers who planted bombs at the Boston Marathon. His public reticence at the state-sponsored murder of high-value targets collateral damage (i.e. the death and mutilation of untried, alleged terrorists and innocent people) in the border between Afghanistan and Pakistan, the Yemen and elsewhere, is morally wrong. Together with the use of questionable methods of interrogation at Abu Ghraib and CIA 'Black Sites', it continues the policy, initiated after 9/11, at the instigation of the so-called 'War Council', led by Vice President Cheney's Chief Counsel and close associate, David Addington which decoupled the Presidency from the restraints of the Geneva Convention, the UN Convention against torture and the federal laws attached to these treaties (Scharf 2010: 130–1). Under the dubious guise of American exceptionalism, the Obama administration presided over an escalation of the drone campaign on 'high-value' targets and the use of rendition (the enforced seizure of suspects on foreign soil and consignment to American-run facilities for the purpose of interrogation). The moral dilemma is exacerbated because the Obama administration originally campaigned on the promise of providing a new direction to American foreign policy by returning to the traditional values upon which the Republic was founded: liberty, justice and freedom (Boys 2011).

The juxtaposition of Obama's presumed intimacy with the victims of the Boston bombings and his presumed indifference (removed intimacy) to the suffering of the innocent victims of illegal drone attacks in the FATA Zone and the Yemen lifts the lid a little on the wider politics of presumed intimacy in public life. The recognition of loss and injury is partial and coded to curry favour with the media, the electorate and foreign power regimes seeking American financial support. Some political commentators assert that this is a functional requirement of contemporary large-scale, urban-industrial democracies. For example, Sheldon Wolin (2008: 107) has written (critically) of the combination of statecraft and communication power in these terms:

> American rulers prefer to manage the population as would a corporate CEO, manipulatively, alternately soothing and dismissive, relying on the powerful resources of mass communication and the techniques of advertising and public opinion industries.

The same could be said of state undersecretaries and many university vice chancellors!

The notion of 'managed democracy' throws into relief one disturbing aspect of the psychology of living with statistical men and women. It is the dubious expression of genuine sympathy with one set of domestic victims, together with apparent indifference for innocent victims elsewhere, that make vigilante, militant Muslims, like the Tsarnaev brothers, seek publicity and revenge. This illustrates an important point about presumed intimacy which should be stated plainly. Presumed intimacy must not be taken at face value. The emotions that it stirs may draw on heartfelt feelings, affects, moods and sentiments, but they are of a different, more calculating stripe. The social device it uses to pursue the goal of achieving a 'proper state of mind' is the gesture of ontological identification (Hochschild 1983: 7). [5] With respect to the display of this gesture by public leaders, there may be genuine sympathy for the victims of a terrorist incident or a natural disaster. However, the affirmation of intimacy is a requirement of leadership intent upon exploiting and developing conviviality with audiences and creating the impression that something is being done.

In a study of this type the role of the media quickly emerges as fundamental. The media are our gatekeepers, furnishing us with the data that inform our habitual take on the world. What is unusual and artificial (for in ordinary life we have so little occasion to practise it) is the task of really trying to get under the skin of the statistical strangers we encounter on screen or in the press. What does it mean to suffer from malnutrition in Burundi, Eritrea or Chad? How can we really understand the risks and state of mind of African farmers in Darfur who are subject to the programmes of genocide conducted by the Arab Militia *Janaweeds* ('devils on horseback') loyal to General Omar Bashir's governing *National Islamic Front*? The same questions are raised by conditions closer to home, such as the plight of the unemployed, those on minimum wage, the disabled and so on. To proffer ontological identification in these matters is often awkward, not to say downright impertinent.

Therapeutic culture teaches us to reach out and rejects inhibition and witholding as invalid responses (Furedi 2003). But we have left the meat of the business of really understanding the lives of others to specialized professionals, namely psychoanalysts, counsellors, social workers, anthropologists, psychologists and sociologists. In Sociology, ethnography is precisely a set of qualitative principles and techniques designed to achieve cultural disclosure among strangers. A complex code of ethics has been developed to minimize bias and ensure transparency in the data collection process. Civic virtue is built upon the concepts of respect and active concern. However, the practicalities of modern life mean that these functions are often delegated to experts and bracketed out from the experience of ordinary men and women.

Ethnography is usually thought of as a qualitative method aimed at people who are different from us. However, from the early days of the Chicago School it was also applied to reveal the stereotypes, caricatures, fuzzy knowledge and blanking devices that we employ in piloting through the complexities of modern social life (Whyte 1943; Drake and Clayton 1945). In a word, the best ethnography *de-familiarizes* native commonplace preconceptions and working principles of communication. It reveals co-presence to be a curious thing, replete with unexpected ontological assumptions, antithetical conventions for establishing trust and surprising rituals to separate truth statements from bogus communication. Ethnography highlights the lives of others, but it also reveals the multitude of social issues and relations that we 'bracket out' of our lives merely by going single-mindedly and pragmatically about our daily business. Our subjective lives are conducted as if objective social and economic conditions are mere background details. In general, customary public behaviour rations emotional identification with strangers. It is concentrated in the social relations pertaining to kith and kin and media representations of the lives of others. Globalization and social networking have obviously widened social consciousness of episodes, incidents and emergencies in the world. But the real circumstances and interest of the people caught up in these disturbances are as mysterious and impenetrable from us as they have ever been.

The above is less a comment on how callous modern men and women are, than a reflection of the accumulated effects of the scale, distribution and mobility of modern populations and the centrality of the media in imparting the lives of strangers to us. There are now over seven billion of 'us'. This super-prolific multiplicity is hard to grasp. In terms of emotional intelligence this has resulted in a psychological exactitude that is associated with what can be called a *gestural economy of the emotions*. That is, an order of second-class para-social relationships in which emotional expressions are mostly tokenistic and glib. Emotional labour and presumed intimacy are part of the core currency that make this economy go round. The gestural economy involves staged empathy and votive behaviour disguising shallow psychological identification designed to produce reactions that award social merit. The dressing of public emotion is designed to achieve social acceptance and facilitate trouble-free interaction. In a word it is a *front* that does not necessarily correlate with what we really feel inside. The dead, the injured and the assailants in the Boston Marathon massacre (2013) are social statistics with whom, in public, we emotionally identify in either positive or negative ways. At the same time, they are divorced from us by seemingly infinite social and spatial magnitude.

The greater our sense of living in a human world that appears to us mainly in the shape of statistical men and women, combined with the benchmarking of every life around rational-legal, 'objective' standards of constitutional patriotism and civic virtue, the more society invests in professionals and experts dedicated to therapy. The scale of modern populations, especially in urban concentrations, and the massive expansion of global mechanisms of communicating knowledge about their conditions and development, has vastly increased the quantitative dimension in the 'moral density' of life. The only way to handle our emotional connections to the lives of seven billion people is to assign abstract legal-rational principles and rights to them and to recognize this as a condition of a morally acceptable life (Dworkin 2011). People skills and rational-legal technologies of presumed intimacy, and all of the emotional obtuseness and psychological frustrations that go with them are the inevitable by-products of the moral density of modern urban, mobile populations. Combating the sense of powerlessness and vulnerability, by encouraging people to get in touch with their true feelings and develop a 'can do' attitude has become a major activity of industrial proportions (Furedi 2003: 50). We assume that making visible that which is invisible or semi-visible is a boon to the cause of transparency and justice in social relations. Consecutively, this is regarded to be a social good since transparency is a commonly accepted prerequisite for trust. But what does making visible the invisible or semi-visible *conceal* (Strathern 2000)? Presumed intimacy prejudges emotional commitment. It need hardly be added that pre-judgement is a dangerous means of achieving balanced conclusions and rightly informed actions. The mechanisms employed rely upon a standard of presumed intimacy, which is often as questionable as the staged response of elected leaders and salaried experts to social traumas and natural disasters. In a sense, an important function of elected leaders and salaried experts is to exhibit emotion and care on our behalf. They communicate, even if we cannot get beyond the non-communication or votive forms of care in personal responses, because our lives are too full-on, too busy. It is a peculiar state of affairs to live daily in a society that has developed a veritable squad of professional care spokesmen to do the bulk of its public emoting for it. Yet this is the condition of presumed intimacy today.

Panoptical Intimacy

Presumed intimacy is often the accessory of so-called positive thinking. 'Getting over' a terrorist incident or 'pressing on' regardless of economic and social adversity, or being made redundant – 'transitioning' in the troubling argot of human relations-speak – is frequently urged as an invitation to develop a positive response. Barbara Ehrenreich (2009) gets it right, in firing a broadside against 'positive thinking' on the grounds that it is actually based in a programmatic style of intimacy. That is, it obeys the mechanism of being near to us in emotional terms, while at the same time, retaining remote distance on the questions of what is 'right' to restore or attain equilibrium. When diagnosed with breast cancer, Ehreneich was indignant at the presumption of professional strangers claiming to 'feel' her pain, 'know' her suffering and imploring her to 'embrace' the 'opportunity' of cancer. She rightly took this 'positive thinking' to be a controlling device, partly based upon the questionable proposition that 'positivity' boosts the immune system. As she (2009: 45) notes, the use of presumed intimacy by professionals is not confined to the health industry. The same human skills package of positive thinking is applied in the field of work (dealing with redundancy or the reduction of work hours or pay), penology (learning from enforced confinement), marital issues (divorce), gerontology (life enrichment from growing older) and, one might add, reacting to high-impact traumatic events. The entreaties of life coaches, drug companies, prison counsellors, support groups and all the rest to 'battle disease', 'learn' from imprisonment and see old age as a 'gift' are more accurately described as techniques designed to engineer compliance and stifle complaint.

Lorna Rhodes (1998: 285–6) speaks of *panoptical intimacies*. By this term she means the intensive personal management techniques applied in prisons to 'turn someone around' through counselling and monitoring (Rhodes 1998: 291). By promoting intensive self-questioning, and declaring care and concern for wellbeing, prisoners are encouraged to internalize the standards applied by supervised discipline and thus, volunteer for rehabilitation. The concept can be expanded to apply to therapeutic interventions in health, welfare, psychiatry and education. According to Rhodes (1998) , at the heart of panoptical intimacy is a profound conservatism. The task is to re-enter existing paramount conditions, rather than to query the validity of the social order to which the individual is being, notionally, rehabilitated. The support groups that dismayed Ehrenreich (2009) so much do much the same thing. In perpetuating positive thinking they eclipse alternatives. Positive thinking involves a form of emotional bullying in which individuals who venture to criticize are made to feel that there is something rum with them. One of the best sociological accounts of this is set out by Theodor Adorno (2000) in a book that comparatively few have read. *The Psychological Technique of Martin Luther Thomas' Radio Broadcasts* deal with the means of persuasion and affectation of what I call presumed intimacy, used by an evangelical Christian Right demagogue in the USA during the 1930s. The book can also be read as exploring a form of panoptical intimacy organized around technology (radio transmission) in which a moral system is applied to corral behaviour by imprinting responsibilities, inhibitions and prejudices upon listeners. For our purposes the study is noteworthy because it offers a powerful analysis of an early attempt to construct 'personality' over the air-waves for the purpose of engineering consent. The bullying style of positive thinking is here pioneered in the form of 'right thinking', conveniently backed up with biblical authority. Winning consent is not so much a matter of producing the best arguments as creating instant, automatic, uncritical identification with the radio personality.

Adorno's book is divided into four parts: 'The Personal Element'; 'Thomas's Methods'; 'The Religious Medium'; and 'Ideological Bait'. For our purposes what Adorno has to say about 'the personal element' and 'the personal interest' device is especially suggestive. In Part I, he comments on the intensely emotional style used by Thomas in building what I refer to as presumed intimacy. 'The talk is personal', writes Adorno (2000: 1). 'Not only does it refer to the most immediate interests of his listeners, but also it encompasses the sphere of privacy of the speaker himself who seems to take his listeners into his confidence and to bridge the gap between person and person.' Ontological identification is sealed by conveying the impression that talk is 'in touch' with 'our story' and can tell a home truth from a dud. It focuses on promising to do everything possible to alleviate the plight of the individual without engaging for a moment with the social and economic conditions that give rise to personal problems. Emotional release is promised to all who obediently follow the course of action dictated in the broadcasts. Adorno (2000: 19) is quick to note that Thomas repeatedly equates emotional release with making financial donations to his Church. The style of presumed intimacy involved 'wavers between very small, practical, down-to-earth matters, and grandiose statements which are brought together without any intermediary logical stages' (Adorno 2000: 22). The exaltation of determination, courage and grit builds a fiction of personal closeness and intimacy. Thomas presents personal involvement with the world as a matter of constant struggle and assures his receptive audience that they will go the whole nine yards together. The worthy life objectives that are lavishly praised and the wrong turnings in personal life that are scorned are designed to spread lifestyle tips that bind the group more closely together. The place of the leader is to take tough decisions and impart the lessons of life that have been learned the hard way. The logic of Thomas's speeches is that he has been, or purports to have been, in the same emotional pit and economic straits as his audience, and he is a man that has come through. By this means ontological identification is proclaimed and the foundations of panoptical intimacy are dug deeper. The Freudian overtones of Adorno's analysis of Thomas's psychological technique (the righteous paterfamilias device, 'cloaks', 'screens', 'the subconscious of the crowd', the 'personal experience' device) anticipate central themes in today's sociology of the emotions.

Frank Furedi's (2003) essential account of how therapy culture has come to colonize everyday life, and Illouz's (2007) discussion of the sorcery of capitalism in regulating human emotion for the purpose of commodification, both point an accusing finger at the role of psychiatry and psychology in multiplying the presence of personality in everyday life. These disciplines are attacked for promoting positive thinking as the royal road to self-help and equilibrium. Counselling and the talking cure take the form of helping people get in touch with the real causes of their suffering. By expert delving into the tangled branches and twisted roots of personality, individuals are prevailed upon to develop a more positive, robust self-image. Illouz (2007), in particular, shows how the psychological language of personality, emotions and motivations is channeled into a new type of, ultimately exploitative, management in the workplace. That is, the type organized around 'human relations'. Consecutively, the caring emotional cure permeated education, health, welfare and most other areas of daily life. Presumed intimacy becomes the first port of call that a salaried carer applies to a person *in extremis*.

It is perfectly valid to read the Thomas broadcasting type as a veiled tribute to the disclosures of personality achieved by psychology and psychiatry. However, to do so is unsatisfactory because it focuses on the aetiology of subjective behaviour rather than the distinctive aesthetic and social core of Thomas's broadcasting appeal. Without much subtlety, Thomas aims to achieve direct, emotional arousal and a relationship of presumed intimacy in the crowd. The main instrument he uses is not logical argument but sheer force of personality. His broadcasting style is a shotgun wedding between a fairground barker and an old-style revivalist preacher. Frequently, it resorts to violent indignation. It puts it to the crowd that any person standing in his shoes would 'naturally' share the same point of view. A concomitant argument is that anyone faced with the same dilemmas would see the world in the same way. Emotional conviction, based upon ontological identification, is the primary means used to forge emotional intimacy between Thomas and the crowd. This does not rely upon face-to-face contact. Thomas's instrument is verbal, exploits the secret or half-hidden fears, anxieties and prejudices of the audience, and uses the means of radio transmission to cajole, persuade and seal primitive trust relations.

Of course, the revolutions in psychology and psychiatry partly created the conditions for this style of ontological identification. What boosted it was a shift in the means of identification from character to personality. In common speech, character and personality are often blurred. Actually, their content is quite distinct. According to the classic definition, provided by Brown (1926: 126), 'character is the result of the building up of habits of action on the basis of circumstances and heredity, and thus we are thrown back to earlier and earlier years for the source of their responsibility'. Essential to this

idea is the notion of a *career*. Brown clearly recognizes an evolutionary foundation in character. Hence, the reference to heredity. However,
character is not just the 'result' of evolution. It is built upon 'habits
of action' developed through 'circumstances' (and heredity). Reference to the essential social dimension acknowledges that the concept
of career is integral to character. The hammer and anvil of character
is experience in the school of life. Through *habitus*, role models, self-
discipline, responsibility and self-determination the pupa of character
moves into its fully fledged form.

In contrast, while an evolutionary dimension is acknowledged,
most treatments of personality examine the characteristics of
behaviour as *situational*. A distinction is drawn between outer and
inner experience. The person we appear to be in the classroom,
the workplace or the supermarket does not necessarily match the
person we are at home. Unlike the concept of character, which is
founded upon deep-rooted patterns of behaviour and expresses
consistent patterns of conduct, personality is more circumstantial
and calculated. Individuals invest considerable thought and effort
to evaluate the impressions they make in the eyes of others and
conduct their actions to produce favoured responses (Leary and Allen
2011: 1192).

Doubtless, public intimacy has always been a mixture of relations,
having to do with both character and personality. However, the
central thesis of this book is that over the last century there has been
a decisive shift in the balance of social encounters from character to
personality (appearance) based exchange. 'Screen', 'front', 'appearance', 'stage', 'frame', 'cover up', 'image' and 'method' are the key
metaphors that capture public interaction today. Needless to say,
much of this derives from techniques developed in celebrity culture
(Sternheimer 2011). Successful social life now requires adaptation,
nimble improvisation, deft impression management and principled
non-communication. Life coaching is a perpetual undertaking, not
something that one learns with one's mother's milk. Accomplishments
in performance and presentation are at the top of the list of valuable
people skills. Since most of the boundaries in social life are acknowledged to be arbitrary, social vitality depends upon testing frontiers
and going the distance. Moral density in individuals that is built
around strong, inflexible values and habits of behaviour may be
grudgingly applauded because it reveals integrity. However, in the
fast-moving, changing constellation of social encounters it is ultimately a weakness, because it reflects a tanker mentality, unable
to adapt, change course and compromise. Hence, the proliferation,
in public settings and public encounters, of presumed intimacy.

Accelerated intimacy, delivered with appropriate social finesse, puts people at their ease, and gets results.

In order to understand what is at stake here more fully, we must turn to the meaning of character and the challenge thrown down to it by personality (appearance) culture. A useful symbol to investigate this question is the notion of a frontier in human relationships. In most nineteenth-century accounts, pushing back the spatial/property frontier was understood to be character-forming. For example, Thomas Carlyle (2012) portrayed the modern hero as overcoming obstacles and hurdles to gain self-knowledge and status via struggle and property ownership. As we shall see in the next chapter, Frederick Jackson Turner (1893) developed a parallel view with respect to character formation in America. Conquering the horizontal frontier – the West – is presented as the seat of character. In contrast, twentieth century accounts of personality (appearance) tend to divide status that follows from property ownership from status that derives from attention capital. Van Kriekan's (2012) concept of attention capital holds that status derives from social impact. [6] While this may translate into the accumulation of property, the accent is upon the pronunciation of personality in order to achieve the status of a noteworthy person in the sight of others. Social impact is therefore an extension of personality because it rests upon performance rather than integrity. The horizon being challenged is not so much physical space as stratified social expectations in social settings that are understood to be fluid. The tension between character and personality reflects a profound structural antagonism at the heart of modernity. As I argued elsewhere, in order to grasp modernity accurately it is necessary to pay due recognition to its Janus face (Rojek 1995). We need to always bear in mind a distinction between Modernity 1 and Modernity 2. The two faces of modernity were born at the same time. The story of modern development is rooted in the dialectic between them. Modernity 1 proceeds on the basis that modern life can be read and practised as a grid of rational rules. This reflects the Enlightenment tradition which equates power and control with reason and discipline. Character may be said to be the internalization of these rules. That is, the Ego ideal appointed by Modernity 1 is of an individual agent driven by reason and discipline.

Of course, trial and error are recognized as part of the process. Nevertheless, the emphasis on reason suggests that humankind is a learning animal and that the dividend of learning is to produce a society based upon principles of utility and justice. Consecutively, modernity has another face. Modernity 2 proceeds on the basis that the object of eliciting and implanting rational rules in the conduct of life is a fool's errand. Social life always proceeds in a direction that out-paces the legislative capacity of rational thought. Modernity 2 sees humankind as 'interpreters' rather than 'legislators' (Bauman 1987.[7] On this logic, the thrust of social life is that we inevitably become conscious of the partiality of rational rules governing the conduct of life. So Modernity 2 is preoccupied with unmasking reason, revealing the hand of power, showing that the Emperor has no clothes and, in general, operationalizing interpretive capacities of various sorts to demonstrate that a rational grid underpinning the conduct of life is a monstrous conceit, that is, it amputates the potential for genuine human enrichment and eliminates forms of being human that are in conflict with this logic.

Definite social, political and psychological consequences accrue from this way of looking at modernity as a Janus-faced process. To put it bluntly, character is the bedfellow of Modernity 1; and personality is the scion of Modernity 2. What does it mean to state that there is a twinned relationship between character and Modernity 1 and personality and Modernity 2? To answer this question it is necessary to turn to comparative and historical analysis, that is, we need to situate character and personality in social and historical frameworks that illuminate their calibre and burr as effective social agents. By these means comprehension of the relationship of character and personality to the positioning and social dynamics of presumed intimacy may be advanced. This is the task of the next two chapters.

5

Horizontal Frontierism: The Juggernaut of Character

The concept of the frontier is familiar to students of American history and mythology (Billington 1966; Slotkin 1973, 1985, 1992). Insofar as there is a canonical text, it is surely Frederick Jackson Turner's (1893) famous thesis on 'The Significance of the Frontier in American History'. The thesis was always intended to be a bold justification of American exceptionalism. By foregrounding the relationship between the rolling frontier and the efflorescence of American character, it conveniently legitimates pioneer land-grabbing and the organized slaughter of native American populations. Turner does not anticipate Theodor Roosevelt's (1889) frankly racist account, with its overtones of social Darwinism and pioneer triumphalism. For Roosevelt, it is the destiny of the racially superior group (White settlers) to annex the 'wasteland' and by means of 'honest' (White man's) industry and enterprise, build a new Canaan. Turner's account is more firmly rooted in republican political economy with its unflinching belief in the supreme virtue of enterprise and property in the cultivation of civilization. For him, the frontier is won by nourishing and advancing the three central components of American character, namely individualism, dynamism and a sacred respect for democracy. The ideal of conquering the frontier is a rallying point for presumed intimacy in settlers since it invests them with the moral superiority of following a noble quest. Throughout his study the connotation between the Western push and the heroism and vitality of Ancient Greek and Roman precedents resounds, but is never convincingly developed. Turner holds that only in America are the qualities of individualism, dynamism and democracy fully realized.

The surplus land of the American West enables pioneers to skip beyond the barnacled integuments of stratified society on the Atlantic shore and the Old World. Greece, Rome and the Ancient World in general, revered the qualities of masculinity, courage, individual enterprise, dynamism and democracy, but they were blocked by age-old courtly encrustations of deference and servility. Turner's correlation of the flowering of individualism, dynamism and democracy with pioneer communities in America implicitly dismisses the significance of the revolutions in England (1642–9) and France (1789) as failures. Instead of truly overturning the aristocratic order, in the long run, they are discounted for affording a new version of 'Old Corruption'. [1]

The English and French Revolutions end in a revised version of the *ancien regime*. Hence, in 1661 the English Restoration crowned Charles II as the new king, and in France the dictatorship of Napoleon Bonaparte climaxed in the proclamation declaring him Emperor in 1804. It is easy to see why nineteenth-century scholars of Turner's generation took it for granted that the evolution of the qualities of individualism, dynamism and democracy is fatefully stunted in Europe. The vision of individual liberty that they gave birth to is checked by inveterate, tenacious tradition. Old habits may be uprooted, but they are adept in re-pollinating and eventually providing a bulwark for new, parallel systems of hereditary privilege and deference. In contrast, the American pioneer held no idea of a check upon liberty set by tradition or anti-utopian reflection. Instead, human nature was viewed as infinitely perfectible. American liberty was revered as an opportunity to forge a new beginning. This does not mean that the original settlers were free of Old World traditions. It is an error to view them as radicals, antithetical to all the values of the Old World. Many carried strong loyalties to the British throne and respect for social hierarchy across the Atlantic and transported them over the Alleghenies. Hence, the agonized debates and guilt-ridden reactions among loyalists in the thirteen states when the momentum for independence became insurmountable (Bailyn 1976). The pioneers leading the Westward push had to dispense with commitments of this sort. The immense 'surplus' space of the West presented a providential invitation to men and women of character to establish property rights and prosper. It was commonly seen as a fresh slate, or 'virgin wasteland' in Billington's (1958) term. Of course, there are innumerable difficulties with the idea of the West as 'surplus' space. By defining it as such, the settlers both negate the validity of native claims and establish that it is the God-given right of every pioneer, with the requisite habits of hard work, ambition and vision, to become a property holder. The sheer extent of the brutality of the Whites against the Indians is put into context by Madley's (2008) finding that in 1846, California's indigenous population numbered 150,000; less than two decades later only between 25,000 and 30,000 survived. The pioneers held fast to the charm of derring-do and the doctrine that faint heart never wins favour. Pushing West, into the space of abounding civic uncertainties and natural hazards, offered pioneers scope for interpreting morals in their own ways and the abundant reward of land annexation. In the American imagination the West was never merely a quantum of physical space. The 'surplus' land mass was always conflated with the metaphor of a perpetually expanding boundary of hope and ambition. The details were conveniently redefined by successive generations to fit the changing requirements of each successive age. Farmland in one era, the Gold Rush in the next, oil in the next, Hollywood thereafter, silicon valley and so on. What remains consistent is the dream of escaping from the stifling conventions of the stratified societies of the Old World and the Atlantic seaboard. The 'virgin wasteland' of the West was a constantly reconfiguring frontier in which ordinary, as well as privileged, settlers would get a fair shake in the pursuit of self development and prosperity, if only they had the courage to join the wagon-train.

According to Turner, the frontier offered fertile proving ground for the innate strengths of American character to mature and flourish. The fierce challenges of the wilderness and hostile native forces called upon the migrants to mobilize hereditary principles of toughness, improvisation and self-reliance. Closely allied to this was the invention of the Western kinsman as a national model of individualism, dynamism and innate fidelity to democracy. Turner's thesis challenges the notion that the West is ruled by what later came to be called, 'gunfighter logic' (Slotkin 1992). Instead, it portrays the wagon trains rolling out of the East as embryonic democracies in which individual resourcefulness, vitality of and dynamism unlock the American spirit. The West, with its dislike of government and fabled opportunities for wealth creation and advancement to men and women of character, offered Americans not merely vacant land, but a stage for a Promethean new beginning (Billington 1958: 5).

The thesis exerted a huge influence upon generations of American scholars. It became the benchmark for understanding American character. It appeared to demonstrate nothing less than an evidence-based set of propositions that the fit reward for individual enterprise and dynamism is property and influence. The Western kinsman became a benchmark of courage and strength of character for urban Americans living in the cities of the Eastern seaboard and Southern states. Bloody conflicts, like the famous Battle of the Alamo (1836) fought between the Texan army and the army of Mexico, projected Jim Bowie, Davy Crockett and William Barret Travis into the front rank of American folk heroes and contributed to the mythology of the frontier as a place in which the human spirit can be decisively enlarged. Despite its influence, the thesis has been subject to cogent criticism and revisionism. The pioneers were not embryonic democrats. Many represented mercantile interests or were bound to Old World trading companies; they differed markedly in wealth and power (by 1860 the richest 20 per cent of households owned 64 per cent of the wealth (Pessen 1971; Wright 1978)); and they were faithful to the imperatives of global capital, which meant that commercialization, land speculation and the quest for monopoly power quickly asserted themselves (Slotkin 1992: 57–8; Ford 1993).

Turner's portrait of the frontier as a rolling boundary of enterprise and virtue has also been challenged on etymological grounds. The English word 'frontier' derives from the classical Latin root ('front' or 'forepart') via the medieval Latin term 'fronteria', meaning line of battle. In America the earliest, most common usage designated the frontier as a 'fortress' or 'fortification' (Juriceck 1966: 10–11). It is this association that the Tsarnaev brothers and more sophisticated critics of American imperialism today seize upon. On this logic, the frontier does not mark the achievement of a new beginning but the cold hand of a superior power seeking to impose the American version of character upon an unreceptive world.

On this reading, Turner over-amplifies the connections with 'expansion', 'liberation' and 'opportunity' and under-values the links with 'containment', 'defence' and 'domination'. The metaphor of the frontier becomes redefined from triumphantly expanding space to the horse whip of domination. Notwithstanding these reservations, Turner's thesis continues to exert considerable influence in debates about American character. In part, this reflects the condensation of rich associations and representations embodied in the concept. Psychologically and symbolically, 'the frontier' is more complex than it appears at first sight. *Inter alia*, it stands for perennial rebirth, creativity, mobility (social and geographical), freedom, escape, promise, opportunity, daring, resourcefulness, restlessness, purification, redemption and conquest. As Turner (1961: 205) put it, the frontier 'breaks the cake of custom' and makes the Western kinsman an emblem of all that is most permanently worthy and honourable in American character.

Mythical West

To view Turner's thesis as only, or even in the balance, a commentary on the perpetually evolving spatial boundary is to misconstrue its true significance. Turner presents the frontier above all, as a matter of evolving American character. In fact, there are two interrelated dimensions to the thesis that Turner did not fully recognize or separate. The *spatial* frontier refers to the rolling back of the boundary, over the Alleghenies and the Plains and on to the Rockies and the Pacific coast. The *social* frontier refers to wrenching apart, or 'breaking the cake' of the conventions of the stratified societies of the Old World, the creation of the new kinsman (the Western pioneer) and the presumption of new relations of intimacy between conquering pioneers against both native Americans and Eastern stick-in-the-muds. The conflation of space with psychology works through the metaphor of the frontier which Turner conceives of as a perpetually shifting horizon. The move through the Alleghenies, across the Great Plains, over the Rockies, to the Pacific seaboard opens the spatial expanse in which American character is decisively forged and magnified. Turner locates pioneers as positioned midway between the Old World – typified as a repository of productive resources imprisoned in a complex of inhibitions and restrictions – and the emerging New World of perennial rebirth, re-invention, redemption, purification and all the rest. Symbolically, the spatial frontier denotes an imaginative expanse where individual character and social being may be tested, reinvented, reframed and, crucially for our purposes, admired and rewarded. The stage in which character is forged may initially have been fragile and provisional, but, in Turner's view, what emerged was unquestionably solid and awesome. Unlike his cousins on the Eastern seaboard, the Western kinsman is seldom anxious, indecisive or confused. In vanquishing the natural elements, and what were conveniently regarded as primitives ('savages'), he realizes national prospects and hopes through the qualities of character notably, courage, competence, self-discipline, physical prowess and integrity.

Turner's logic on frontier character is, it must be said, very orthodox. For him, character is produced and defended through the confrontation with wilderness and subduing natives. It was through this titanic struggle that American character achieved apotheosis. Moreover, he depicts the process of self-making in relentlessly progressive terms. What emerges from the defeat of wilderness is the re-invigoration and re-invention of American character. Consecutively, he implies that the Western kinsman offers Americans the image of an American everyman. This image, with its glorification of initiative, forbearance, valour and skill, operates as the inspiration of the nation and holds a mirror up to would-be pioneers from around the world. America is portrayed as the great hope of the subdued, the mauled, the oppressed.

The essential components of the thesis were faithfully transferred to popular fiction dealing with an idealized frontier, notably in the enormously popular novels of Zane Grey, Ned Buntline, Owen Wister and Max Brand. [2] With the arrival of film, the symbol of the frontier was ravishingly revised and elaborated. The cowboy was fetishized as a progressive hero (Slotkin 1992). The leading Wild West stars of the silent era, such as W. S. Hart and Tom Mix, were portrayed as stereotypes of resourcefulness, fearlessness, decisiveness and rugged plain speaking. They are bardic retellings of the legend that Turner consecrated in which a lone man, with nothing to gain, acts by dint of a sense of innate justice and courage, does his duty, and achieves retribution and justice for others. This is a rebuke to the love of mammon displayed by the robber barons and scheming politicians back East (Kleinfeld and Kleinfeld 2004: 49). The Cowboy Silents bequeathed the formula for subsequent actors like John Wayne, Gary Cooper, James Stewart and Clint Eastwood and the film directors behind them like John Ford, Anthony Mann, John Sturgess, Sam Pekinpah and Sergio Leone, to shape and re-mould. The standard Western plot-line is a monument to Turner's (1920) thesis. It relishes the values of individualism, dynamism and respect for the common man. By the 1940s, John Wayne became the iconic American cowboy. Congress even authorized a medal honouring him as the embodiment of American heroism and prowess. In doing so it ignored the inconvenient fact that he was (controversially) exempted from service during the war and never fought a day's military conflict in his life (Wills 1997). What mattered was the *image* of Wayne and the frontier as symbols of freedom, watchful vigilance, steely responsibility and self-effacing competence. This was the foundation of popular presumed intimacy around the seductive notion of the Western kinsman.

Revisionist accounts of Turner's thesis highlight the mythological foundations of the qualities of individualism, dynamism and democracy that he extols (Slotkin 1973, 1985, 1992). For a start, take the question of individualism. Contemporary historians show that 'winning the West' and spreading ranch settlements were supported by massive public expenditures. [3] Settler ranchers survived and prospered through subsidized access financed from Washington and Eastern banks and robber barons (Wilshire, Nielson, Hazlett 2008). They supplied the infrastructure of transportation, state educational institutions and military protection against Indians. Of course, there were countless tales and examples of personal heroism, but the ethic of individualism was cushioned by finance in the so-called stratified societies of the Atlantic seaboard and the Old World. Turner's account of the individualism of the pioneers was based in the principle that they were doing something liberating and bold that the Old World could not do. Conversely, one might observe that the frontier was hardly 'regenerative' for native Indian populations. Properly speaking, exterminating them and annexing their traditional rights over land was not a case of American exceptionalism. It has the odour of old style European colonialism (Slatta 1990, 2001; Vandervort 2006). Furthermore, the operation of finance capital and the establishment of a legal basis for land rights followed European precedents. The ranches of the West were based in principles of private ownership. The entire annexation process was conceived and executed as a massive, irrevocable extension of private property. This brings me to Turner's second proposition, namely that the frontier permitted hallowed values of democracy to prosper in a fashion that was without precedent in Europe or the Eastern seaboard.

Pessen's (1971) famous work on *antebellum* property ownership, variable capital differences and social structure knocks a huge dent into any notion of egalitarianism among pioneers. Even a respectful critic like Gallman (1994: 195) estimates that in 1860, 96 per cent of America's wealth was owned by 30 per cent of American families.[4] It is safe to assume that inequalities were less severe among settlers pushing West because they would have included a greater proportion of young, marginal people seeking their fortune. Older people with property may have participated in Western speculation, but because of the risks attached, it is probable that comparatively few ventured to become full blown settlers. Pessen (1971: 1026) himself maintains that on the eve of the Civil War the maldistribution of wealth in Philadelphia and in a number of Southern and Western cities was 'quite similar'. In numerical terms, the wealthiest one per cent in Philadelphia owned fifty percent of the city's wealth. In New Orleans and St Louis the richest five per cent owned about 66 per cent of each city's wealth. In Chicago in 1860, 80 per cent of the wealth was owned by ten per cent of families (Bubnys 1982: 105). Moreover, prior to the Homestead Act (1862), which the populist newspaper editor, Horace Greeley, did so much to achieve through his powerful *New York Tribune*, pioneers had to pay the government $1.25 an acre for land. Billington (1958: 7) puts the additional cost of land clearance, fencing and erecting homes, feeding cattle, buying farm machinery, while paying taxes, building roads, supporting schools and churches, at $1,000. This was far beyond the means of most Eastern factory hands and adds a further coat of scepticism to Turner's sentimental picture that 'beyond the Alleghenies' lay freedom for the poor, the discontented and the oppressed. Speculators were more evident in the march of the pioneers than this picture allows. Even poor pioneers who clubbed together, required significant finance to prosper. True, the Homestead Act (1862) passed by Lincoln during the Civil War, permitted any citizen or intended citizen to select surveyed, unclaimed land of up to 160 acres and, after five years residence, enforcing prescribed improvements, to gain title to it. But significant capital investment implications were connected to the phrase 'prescribed improvements'. Legal land annexation was regulated from Washington and financial prerequisites were assumed.

Billington (1958) applauds the boldness and originality of Turner's thesis. But even he grants that the proposition of Western egalitarianism is vastly exaggerated. Wealth levels were highly skewed, and differences became more concentrated quite rapidly, thus undermining the romantic notion of the frontier as a place where the poor and ambitious would receive the same fair shake at the hands of providence. Initially, wealth maldistribution may not have been as divided as among the Eastern city states, but once land was annexed, ranches established and trading centres founded, the Western frontier revealed patterns of 'increasing inequality' and 'social rigidity' (Pessen 1971: 1030). With wealth inequality goes more political influence in opinion formation and law making. It is in the nature of financial advantage to offer behind the scenes contacts with law makers, law enforcers and the organs of public opinion. Given the levels of inequality in America identified by Pessen (1971) and Gallman (1994), it beggars belief to cast the West as some sort of embryonic pure democracy. It was stratified, unequal and conflicted from the start.

As to Turner's third proposition concerning the dynamism of the West, it pitches the push West as the apotheosis of American character. For example, he is breezily dismissive of French traders because he sees them as 'ambivalent capitalists' who resist the American model of expansion and retain strong ties of loyalty with their culture of origin. In contrast, Gitlin's (2010) research into French traders and American expansion paints a more subtle and persuasive picture. *Contra* Turner, he maintains that French merchant settlers built the so-called 'Creole corridor' that stretched from the Great Lakes, through the Mississippi Valley to the Gulf of Mexico, as a zone of French dominated trading and political influence (Gitlin 2010: 11). This space emerged after 1763 as 'a new profit-driven frontier', beyond the Anglo boundary. Far from being 'ambivalent capitalists' the dominant French families in the region invested heavily in constructing the urban and communications infrastructure and speculative Indian land clearance (to create space for settlers from the East). Gitlin's (2010) account of the Creole corridor depicts French merchants as cosmopolitan power brokers playing off the land interests of native Americans against the opportunities for profiteering provided by White pioneer migration. Turner's unlinear thesis presents American expansion as the product of mountain men, fur trappers, traders and farm folk who unlocked reserves dormant in American character to tame the wilderness. Gitlin's analysis reveals a more complex picture in which strong family based webs of Old World culture, with deep loyalties to the patterns of taste and discrimination that obtain in the homeland, played a key part in the Westward push. His study leaves readers in no doubt about the political subtlety and economic dynamism of these formations. By extension, it challenges Turner's argument that American settlers were the only 'unambivalent capitalists' pushing West. The French merchants had strong ties to France, but consecutively they saw themselves as genuine and distinctive settlers. Their property interests and the finance capital at their disposal derived from tenure and husbandry in the Creole corridor. Yet culturally, economically and politically they remained a distinct formation. It took many decades before they began to succumb to normative coercion and abandon their language and national codes of behaviour. In Gitlin's view then, there is not one frontier, but many. By implication, Turner is accused of being wide of the mark in implying that they could all be neatly reconciled beneath one intoxicating, propulsive imperative: the revelation of the true, unfolding soul of America.

All Hail the Horizon

The conflation of spatial and social dimensions in Turner's concept of the frontier equates the enlargement of character with the annexation of land in the West and its transformation into apportioned, alienated, private property. Subduing the native population was part of the drama of annexation. However, in securely colonizing the West it was secondary to the elevation of private property as the new standard of spatial composition, with enforceable, legally demarcated territorial boundaries. Turner conceives character as ultimately founded and extended through private property ownership. It was contractually bonded acres, not Indian scalps that truly won the West. Nominally, throughout the 1800s and early decades of the

1900s, a legal basis of egalitarianism was established in the federal recognition of split-estate interests in water rights, rights of way, improvements and grazing values (McIntosh 2002). These were matters of expedience designed to facilitate the secure procurement and prosperity of enclosed ranch land. The Western push was fundamentally about the multiplication and advance of capital. The property base was the foundation of what Turner understood by self-development and character enlargement. In using the 'bounty' of the virgin wasteland to propel Turner's claim that the formation of American character enjoyed material conditions that were unparalleled in Europe, he proposed too much. It is more accurate to hold that the logic of capitalist accumulation and colonization was not re-invented in the American West. It was repeated on European precedents. Along the whole breadth of the constantly moving Western frontier, White settlers were perfectly free to ply a grotesque version of eugenics in equating land-grabbing and butchery of the native population with progress. *Contra* Turner's insistence upon American exceptionalism, the same principles of land grabbing and expropriation applied by the Europeans, in the salad days of Empire-mania, obtained in the conquest of land and native peoples in America. The concentration of the means of production into fewer and fewer hands, the policing of private space, the creation of a labour force with scarcely any recognized rights of employment, the undue influence of the wealthy over a so-called 'independent' judiciary and the establishment of a reserve army of labour (eventually drawing on Mexican and other Latino sources), all followed in short order.

The character formation of the Western kinsman that Turner outlines is based on the supposition that the spatial engagement of the frontier is the catalyst for robust individualism, discipline, courage and responsibility. It fuses expansion of character with spatial conquest. This is further attached to a questionable cultural proposition. Since the space beyond the frontier is defined as either vacant ('virgin wilderness') or the preserve of barbarians ('savages'), land annexation and the subjugation of the native population are ennobled as an inherently progressive initiative. Turner portrays American expansion almost wholly as an engagement with the spatial horizon. Advancing the Western boundary is associated with the enlargement of self-reliance and the accumulation of wealth. Leaving aside ambiguous zones in which cultural traditions were observed and honoured, like the Creole corridor, the settlers' decision to forsake the stratified societies of the East and the Old World sundered ties of loyalty and magnified opportunities for appropriation. The ideals of robust individualism, discipline, courage and responsibility are firmly built upon a material base. Land acquisition is positioned as the seat of character because annexation is understood to subdue wilderness and repel barbarian interests. In terms of the psychological balance of power, it is probable that there was a good deal more in the nature of emotional ambivalence among migrants than was allowed in Turner's speculative concoction of Western character. Feelings of guilt, self-reproach and shame must have gripped many pioneers as they violently seized native land and decimated the indigenous population. For Turner the consequences of these matters never became symptoms of American character because he believed that the frontier, namely 'the line of most rapid and effective americanization', forces upon pioneers a 'forest philosophy' in which pragmatism and re-invention prevail (Turner 1893: 3–4, 2). This affords a convenient pretext for aggression. Forget the bad that you do today for the sake of the greater good that you will accomplish tomorrow. In addition, the abundance of natural resources gives rise to the careless 'waste' to which Turner often refers in his thesis. The pioneers remain steadfast to the bible, but this prudence does not extend to the management of resources of soil, water and, even animals, since the bounties of the frontier are held to be limitless, thus giving credence to the holy grail of God-given American expansion without end. Indeed, it has been rightly observed that Turner's thesis is partly a eulogy for the frontier (Billington 1958; Coleman 2003). Since the seventeenth, eighteenth and nineteenth centuries, he tells us , the warm, welcoming frontier, has momentously and irrepressibly rolled back to the sea. Turner, who originally delivered his paper on the significance of the frontier in 1893, wrote at a moment in which the realization that the expansion of the Western frontier was at its conclusive end. Once the Pacific shore was reached there was, practically speaking. nowhere further West to go on American soil. Coleman's (2003) ingenious suggestion, is that 'the primal frontier' offering 'limitless space' for the improvisation and improvement of American character, could only be replaced by representational culture and a representational frontier. Here the possibility of growth and redemption was transferred to the boundless domain of symbols and codes rather than physical space. As the open space of the physical horizon closed, the conception of an enduring ever-renewing space in America was transferred elsewhere: to 'ad space' and new boundaries of commercialization and property accumulation. The 'Mad Men' of a later generation of satellite TV watchers replaced the Mountain Men, fur trappers, farm folk and virtuous traders of Turner's frontier fantasy. Coleman's (2003) link between a commercial activity that compulsively follows the imperative of commodification and the frontier thesis is appropriate. Read in the correct light, it exposes Turner's study for unwarrantably celebrating the enlargement of American character in the

West by opportunistic land annexation and cavalier accumulation. Far from enlarging American character, it blistered whatever good came from Westward expansion with *faux* ennoblement of relentless acquisition, casual racism, buccaneer land adventurism and pioneer supremacy. The pioneer advance had its moments of heroism, but at bottom it was a horrible mixture of blood, bullets and clay.

In looking West, Turner completely missed the mould-breaking changes in mobility and aspiration that were taking place around him in the settled East and Midwest. Age-old boundaries were breaking around Turner's head, but he remained oblivious to them. This did not take the form of a charge against a Western horizontal frontier just waiting to be conquered by pioneer fortitude. Rather, it looked upward, to the heavens, which it beheld to be festooned with rope ladders to the stars. The mobility in the pioneer trail that Jackson failed to notice was a vertical ascent, not a horizontal surge. Its coinage was not character formation but the staging, exchange and daring extension of personality to build attention capital and achieve social impact. A parallel revolution in America (to the conquering of space and construction of character) was the re-invention of personality and the revision of presumed intimacy. This was not a rural victory over an inhospitable physical terrain, but an urban, cultural revolution. The people who clasped and scrambled up the rope ladders to the stars hailed from the urban crowd. The stars that they looked up to, and wished to reach and, if they were lucky, surpass, were only too mortal and originated from the same stock. They emerged from the same towns, and sometimes even the same streets. The message that their success, in the expanding, lucrative world of entertainment, gave, is that anyone can make it if they possess talent and pluck. Pushing back the vertical horizon, and seizing upward mobility, was not a matter of acquiring acres and building fences. Rather, it reflected increasing cultural literacy, the enlarged ambitions and fantasy lives of soaring urban populations who were enjoying modest, but rising real incomes, the growing importance of commercial, professional entertainment in lifestyle and magnified opportunities to access the new, revolutionary technologies of mass communication (especially radio, film and recorded music). The enlarging political profile of the public, which followed the reform movement and the creation of effective political parties representing propertyless labour, provided the essential resources for these trends. Suffrage increased the political power of propertyless labour and counterbalanced the weight of property in politics. It made working class and immigrant life proper objects of representation the dramatization and popular culture (Gundle 2008; Inglis 2010).

6

The Accentuation of Personality

The thesis that a distinctive feature of the present age is the supplanting of gravitas and esteem with approval, a search for acceptance and social impact does not want for champions. Beginning with Schmitt (1919), through to *The Lonely Crowd* (Riesman, Glazer and Denney 1950), the work on the ascendancy of therapy culture (Rieff 1965; Furedi 2003), the culture of narcissism (Lasch (1979), the dynamics of Reality TV (Turner, G. 2009) and the study of 'cold intimacies' in the present day (Illouz 2007), a keen appreciation of the relationship between social impact, mediation and the construction of personality has been advanced and refined. Investing attention capital in social settings may take the form of dress, deportment, verbal intervention, psychological manipulation, seizing the occasion, or a combination of all these elements. The object is to attain social impact through self-promotion and exposure management in order to generate and accumulate attention capital. Some critics regard the issue as the continuation of orthodox processes of compliance and domination. For example, Riesman, Glazer and Denney (1950) hold that modern society produces 'Other Directed' personality types whose agency is piloted by cues and prompts from peer groups and the media. For his part, Lasch (1979) directly attacks the ideology of acceptance and approval in society by dismissing it as mostly superficial, serving hidden 'narcissistic' purposes. He contends that being emotionally open, confronting issues frankly, appearing to be connected to the world in its entirety and keeping pace with trending events, often conceals an inner urge for nothing other than plain old fashioned egocentric domination. For Lasch (1979), personal revelation carries high attention capital, reticence is scorned, and openness, relaxation and frankness gain high approval.

The argument echoes Schmitt's (1919) pioneering discussion of the connection between political leadership and personality. One need not go the whole hog with Schmitt and hold that narcissistic egocentricity is rife. Indeed, to do so would be problematic. For one thing it would involve denying the presence of altruism and trust in social relations. It need hardly be added that an explanation of social existence that has no place for altruism and trust would be a poor thing indeed. Lasch (1979) is on to something in noting the colossal post war increase in the need for approval and acceptance and relating it to a more old fashioned drive for egocentric domination. But the ferocity of his attack on narcissism has a distorting effect on analysis. While his intent is to demonstrate the relationship between consumer culture and prosaic personality it miscarries by implying that personality has won the day. To be sure, Lasch's (1979) account is a testament to the power of character in imposing itself upon social order. He is right to propose that the social order in which we are enmeshed demands personality games. Narcissism and presumed intimacy are part of what makes society tick. [1] We can agree with adherents of the proposition that the frank display and exhibition of personality are pivotal to achieve social impact, acceptance and approval. That granted, personality and character abide in a balance of power relationship. Just because personality is presently ascendant does not mean that character is either a negligible force in society or a lost cause as a foundation for social reconstruction.

The gadfly characteristics of personality are remarked upon by Schmitt (1919). Personality thrives upon the visibility of self promotion and opportunism. His account will be taken up and examined in more detail later. At this juncture, it is important to explore a question implied in Schmitt's (1919) analysis, but only decisively formulated by Strathern (2000: 310): 'what does visibility *conceal*'? If the content of display and expression were to be generally seen as the products of some hidden inner demon, madly directing outward appearances, they would quickly possess little credibility with others. Attention capital is most effective when it is advanced and accepted as the sincere reflection of inner life. At the same time, Strathern (2000) is properly wary of transparency in social institutions as bona fide. Personality is inherently partly adventitious, that is, its display and expression are heavily conditioned by social settings and circumstances. If this is granted, in what sense can we attribute transparent integrity and constancy to it? It might be said that the display and expression of sincerity based around personality are subject to inevitable laws of attrition. People and settings change. The person who is the love of your life at one moment becomes someone from whom you must escape at another; the town that you thought of as so charming and welcoming ten years ago, now seems like a claustrophobic dungeon. To be sure, some well-respected commentators hold that change is now so chronic in the human condition that we live in 'liquid' times where next to nothing can be taken on trust, and chronic uncertainty is the hallmark of life with others (Bauman 2000, 2006). A good deal from the postmodern debate of the 1990s is no longer accepted, but this notion of living in an age of uncertainty, ambivalence and appearance, perseveres. Here, it should be observed that the consequence of this line of thought for understanding how personality operates is that acceptance, approval and social impact are not eternal. What works in one setting at a given time, is not timeless. What I say and believe about statistical men and women today, may change next month or next year. To be sure, it might be observed that, the more I elucidate about this social category, the more I am setting myself up for a fall. In an age when information gathering is as ubiquitous and sophisticated as today, the volume of data in the world about statistical men and women always expands at a rate exceeding the capacity of my consciousness to encompass. I am always going to be left behind by the flood of new information. In that case, why say anything at all?

The question is pertinent because it raises the issue of personality *type*. The interest in social impact, the inexhaustible appetite for acceptance and approval, are not essential features of the human species. I submit they started to become paramount in social life from about the 1870s. The onset is not accidental. It coincided with the rise of commercial popular entertainment, at first in the music halls and vaudeville, and later with radio, film and television, the growing concentration of urban populations and new technologies of mass communication. These forms of entertainment became more insistent in social consciousness not only because there were more outlets for them, but because they drilled home a set of equations between personality, presumed intimacy and upward mobility. The link between following achieved celebrity and identifying with the emotions revealed was made and refined. The public became intrigued, and some elements became obsessed, by the notion of what it means to be in the public eye. Under ascribed celebrity, this question was not insistent. Stratified society conducted itself on the principle that everyone knows his place. It is appropriate to claim that achieved celebrity exerted an unplanned, unintended, informal pedagogic effect upon popular culture. What the forms of amusement offered were crash

courses in the value of effective self-promotion and exposure management. They taught that to get ahead requires applying personality to
acquire social impact. Presumed intimacy as a generalized feature of
para-social relationships was born. There is a romantic kernel to this
shift, since it assumes that every barrier, all conceivable impediments,
may be overcome with determination, discipline and a little talent.
Further, the successful are role models that can be emotionally *known*
even if we never directly encounter them face-to-face. In addition,
vaudeville and the music-hall tradition made no bones about anchor-
ing attention capital with sociability. The intoxicating seduction of
social consciousness by the new *means* of mass communication is not
insignificant. In his pioneering, semi-forgotten contribution to the
sociology of celebrity, Leo Lowenthal (1961) was right to give
advanced profile to the consequences of cheaper print technologies,
radio, film and the phonograph in turning some entertainers into stars
with mass appeal. Achieved celebrities in the field of popular entertainment, at this time, rivalled the traditional popularity of the central
pillars of stratified society: monarchs, politicians, military leaders and
writers. This success was not merely a matter of talent and accomplishment, but of symbolically representing the forward march of
ordinary people in pushing back the vertical horizon of mobility. By
the term vertical horizon I mean the aggregate of impediments that
stratified society produced and reproduced against significant upward
mobility. Consecutively, popular entertainment arranged around
achieved celebrities made the urban crowd comfortable with the idea
that they comprehended the inner emotions of the personalities that
became famous. Further, in appearing to make these emotions visible,
achieved celebrities brought the urban crowd *into confidence*. Intimacy worked on the presumption that the achieved personality in the
public eye and the urban crowd hailed from the same emotional position and followed common emotional goals.

Carl Schmitt: The Charm of Romanticism

One of the best guides for understanding the form of presumed intimacy involved here is Carl Schmitt. [2] Ostensibly, his (1919) book,
Political Romanticism, is about German romanticism in the nineteenth century. However, its real aim is to expose the role of personality in the politics of the revolutionary movements of his own day,
especially Marxism. Much of what Schmitt has to say about the
hectic movement from episode to episode and tumultuous romanticism
of remaking the world in one's own image applies to the non-political,

upwardly mobile personality type of the day. How could it not? The shaking of the foundations of stratified society that allowed radical transformative politics to emerge also created the space for personalities who truly believed that they could be anything they wanted to be and do whatever they wanted to do. Schmitt's (1919) discussion of the characteristics of this type is highly illuminating. To begin with, he maintains that those who want to change the world, even if the aspiration extends no further than revising the dimensions of *their* world, are not driven by principle, but by ambition and opportunity. They are moved by the 'emergency', 'the event', 'the incident' or – to use Schmitt's (1919) term – 'the occasion', because it affords the chance to shine. Their conduct is defined by a search for excitement. Cometh the hour, cometh the man. There is a strong element of 'excessive sociability' about this urge. It is not enough to act, one must come to the attention of others as a noteworthy person and exert emotional influence over them. Because the development of personality is opportunity based, romantics often slide between contrary positions without recognizing or acknowledging contradiction. The psychological mechanism that permits this is the substitution of God with what Schmitt (1919) calls 'transcendental ego'. Consequently, romantic achieved celebrities behave as if they only have themselves to answer to. For Schmitt (1919), political romantics tend to possess neither integrity or constancy. That is, they are not men and women of character in the Hegelian sense of the term, i.e. of an 'unfolding' set of principles. Rather, they are adept at having things every which way, and embracing and discarding positions willy nilly, because they operate under the dual discipline of unrestrained ego and 'the occasion' rather than lode stars of principle and consistency (which are the hallmarks of character). Their self-confidence is misleading, since it relies upon the attention, preferably the admiring applause, of an audience. They spurn barriers and impediments to self-promotion and mobility, but, once they have assumed positions of power, they have a habit of letting things not go too far. They put a brake on social change to protect the perpetuity of their ascendence. Their outward radicalism belies their inherent conservatism. What really excites and absorbs them is gaining and holding attention for themselves, not achieving a grand collective cause.

Why should we object to romanticism in political and non-political personalities? Surely, it brings a dash of colour into our experience. For Schmitt (1919) the orientation to romance is incapable of rising above gesture and affords a licence for caprice and double dealing. Romantics are seldom trustworthy. They really do believe that all obstacles are arbitrary, including the obligation to remain faithful to a chosen course of action. Everything can be abandoned, ditched, switched or revised when 'the occasion' demands. Moving on is not seen as a defect of personality, but as evidence of exercising selective advantage. By being ready to change colours, the romantic personality is more adaptable and relevant to changing times. By the same token, the man of principle (character) tends to be dismissed as obsolescent. For principle goes with phlegmatic resolve and seeing the course through doggedly to the end. The romantic personality seizes the day and stakes all on generating attention capital. It is a contrast that Isaiah Berlin captured in another context, in the analogy of the fox and the hedgehog. [3]

According to Schmitt (1919) the romantic impulse is, in the long term, a spoiled asset for productive action. This is because it views all questions and opportunities through the spectacle of adventurism. The business of being seen to tackle a problem, seeming to adopt the right attitude and appearing to do the right thing, is more important than achieving tenable solutions to problems. Virtue lies in being seen to rise to 'the occasion'. Playing the game is the thing.

Nowadays, Schmitt's (1919) academic discussion would be uncannily familiar to any publicist or celebrity gossip columnist. On a number of points it touches directly on how achieved celebrities (not just in the sphere of politics) behave, both in 1919, when Schmitt published his book, and in our own day. The search for excitement, the privileging of the occasion, an opportunity-based orientation to personal development, excessive sociability, transcendental ego, are prominent themes in the literature on celebrity (Schickel 1985; Gabler 2000). I am attributing some weight to them here because, to return to a point made above, I maintain that, from the 1870s a variety of factors coalesced to produce celebrity culture as a major front along which the vertical horizon of stratified society was stressed and challenged and presumed intimacy between an audience of watchers and physically remote but emotionally close apparitions, projected through the media, was formed. Achieved celebrities were not merely understood to be glamorous, talented individuals. They began to operate as informal life coaches providing the crowd with invaluable pointers to how attitudes, grooming, forms of presentation and types of ambition could breach the walls of ascribed culture. [4] In an unplanned, unintended way a cultural pedagogy was developed which showed the urban crowd how to get ahead. The techniques of self-promotion and exposure management that achieved celebrities applied in pursuit of social impact, acceptance and approval were transferred to everyday life. After the 1870s, the selective advantage of personality over character became indisputable.

The triumph of personality did not come without costs. Self-promotion and exposure management were certainly recognized as being capable of creating a stir. Conversely, it was also understood that their content and success were bound by setting. It is in the nature of personality to be *provisionally* approved and accepted. This brings us back to Strathern's (2000) question, of what is concealed by the transparent aspects of personality? With the intimation that circumstances are provisional comes the disturbing undertow of suspicion that defines personality-based forms of social order. At one moment the force of personality may create an apparent kaleidoscope of stability, in the next instant, everything is thrown up in the air bringing confusion and uncertainty to the fore once again, and creating 'the occasion' for a new personality force to seize the day. In a period when truth and reality are genuinely regarded to be indeterminable, it goes without saying that social order is perceived as a permanently provisional, vulnerable kaleidoscope. This accounts for the state of precarious stability that, experientially speaking, surrounds the whole business of personality-based social impact. What has been gained can easily be taken away by events over which the individual has no control. For Schmitt (1919), latent authoritarianism is a hallmark of romantic politics. As the positive fellow-feeling that accumulates around someone who appears to have seized the day dissipates, sheer brutishness is too often, the resort to buttress and bolster attention capital.

Everyone would accept that the foundation of attention capital is trust. Few would maintain that personality-based trust is copper bottomed. It comes with the suspicion that the setting of trust may not endure because the visibility of personality is nothing but a paper clip holding social order together, which conceals inner aspects of presentation, as well as separate features in the setting, that permit trust to obtain in the first place. Only extreme postmodernists would push this further to maintain that trust is no longer a sound category in any form of human relations because media representations of reality expand virally, erode our perception of reality by mixing it with illusion and fantasy and, in general, enfever reason. Nowadays, hardly anyone would follow Baudrillard's (1986, 2004) infamous hypothesis that we live in an era of hyperreality. That is, a time in which media representations of reality and illusion have become so entangled that social consciousness flees from respecting anything as real or lasting. *Contra* Baudrillard, most of us get along very well, understanding that what we see and hear in the media is not necessarily true and that our views about the real state of the world may be subject to decay by events which overtake it. This hardly invalidates the proposition

that we live in an age of chronic uncertainty. In some ways it strength-
ens the proposition because it suggests that the type of social consciousness that believes in items in culture and society as unreservedly
true is actually somewhat cranky. We live in an imperfect market of
knowledge about reality. As such, it is better to be a doubting Thomas
than a purveyor of conviction.

Now Strathern (2000) submits that personal display and exhibition are properly understood as presenting information in public
about the private life of the self. The fact that we automatically
harbour suspicions that the information displayed and expressed by
others may not necessarily be truthful speaks volumes about the form
of social consciousness elicited by a society built around personal
disclosure and transparency. The buck does not stop with being open
and transparent. The state of suspicion requires disclosure to be
monitored and audited. The form of social consciousness that obtains
cannot simply accept things as they appear to be. Independent
evidence-based corroboration is required, generally with a salaried
back up of administrators who guarantee due process. Yet, as soon
as evidence-based monitoring and auditing are introduced into the
mix, disclosure and transparency cease to be matters of naturalistic
exchange. They respect the face of what it is supposed that the cor-
roborator wants to hear. For this reason it is by no means axiomatic
that disclosure and transparency clarify. The act of making private
behaviour public and accountable often raises more problems than
it solves.

At first sight, this sounds like a form of reasoning that is decidedly
back to front. In ordinary social life great store is set upon being open
and transparent. The unflinching candour of the present is automatically understood to be preferential to the repression and witholding
that characterized so much in human relations in the past (Furedi
2003). As mobility challenged the vertical horizon of stratified society,
the successful upwardly mobile personality had reason to maintain
that they were shedding light on how society really worked. In as
much as this is the case, achieved celebrity might be said to be an
heroic form of upward mobility. Part of its force lies in the claim that
it is a phenomenon that makes the cogs and wheels that run society,
transparent. By extension, this tacitly and often directly, challenges
the inveterate power of vested interests. We know that, after the
1870s, the established stratified classes took, more openly, to deplor-
ing the vulgarity of achieved celebrities (Gundle 2008; Inglis 2010).
Yet the challenge that new power laid at the door of old power is
now widely accepted to be significant. According to Cooper (1997)
'making society visible' was a crucial part of modern democratic

nation-state building. Yet it is in the nature of new light to fade. The replacement of heredity and obligation as the central pillars of trust with transparency and evidence-based inquiry is not made without a price to pay in the quality of relations with others. Audit culture is based in the unstated assumption that individuals engaged in the everyday work of the organization cannot be fully trusted (Power 1994:13). If uncertainty and ambivalence are characteristics of modern times, covert suspicion is their bedfellow.

A marked response to this state of affairs, which is a palpable force in the buoyancy of presumed intimacy, is the development of the urge to appear 'relevant', 'caring' and 'knowledgeable'. These are identifying characteristics of the 'virtuous' citizen. They afford approval and impact in social circles. Yet they often rely upon posturing and gesturing. On this reckoning, part of presumed intimacy goes further than a benign commitment to be emotionally open and to care for others. It is a type of personality attention-seeking, that purports to be 'clued in', 'on the ball' and 'empathetic', but conceals 'raw ego' (MacCannell 2011: 24; Schmitt 1919). Here, the emotional labour spent in ontological identification is really directed at enhancing the interpersonal pronunciation of the virtuous citizen in social settings in order to accumulate attention capital and build social impact. Personality operates as a message board communicating the signs of an appealing, integrated, empathetic person who recognizes that the walls of culture are arbitrary and appears to take seriously the maxim that 'we make us'. The accent is upon being recognized, accepted and achieving social impact. Affecting ontological identification with the lives of others through self-promotion and exposure management is a vehicle for gaining this. Acceptance and approval are therefore interpreted as strategies of will designed to acquire competitive advantage. Hence, Illouz's (2007) formulation of 'cold intimacies' to describe a notable characteristic of emotional relations today: calculation. This will be familiar to anyone who has said 'I love you' without meaning it (or had it said to them by someone else). The accent upon social impact, approval and the search for acceptance underscores the importance of personality as the keystone of social relations. Nowadays, nearly everything revolves around personality (rather than character), but personality is a cruel and untrustworthy task-master.

Personality Cult

The term 'cult of personality' was introduced by the Soviet leader, Khrushchev, at the Twentieth Congress of the Communist Party of the USSR (1956). It was aimed pejoratively at Josef Stalin, who died in 1953, and was now publicly condemned for installing and prosecuting a form of rule in which monstrous political power and authority are concentrated in a leader who behaves as if he is unaccountable to the dictate of civil society. In his heyday, the PR/Media hub around Stalin presented him heroically and sentimentally as a courageous, unflinching leader and 'Uncle Joe' to his people. This form of autocracy disguised the imprisonment and extermination of rivals, critics and 'nuisances'. However, it is too limiting to see the cult of the personality simply as the creation of Soviet rule. On the question of propaganda, Stalin's *apparatchicks* would not have been immune to the technologies of personality promotion and exposure management developed by the Hollywood studio system. In the business of managing public expectations Hollywood adopted and overhauled the advertising and market research policies developed by General Motors, Woolworths, Sears and other American corporate giants (Gomery 1986). The implacable heart and indifferent facets of society were softened by personality, depicted in advertising and general celebrity culture, which made modern life more than bearable, novel and exciting. In other words, the construction of personality has its roots in consumer culture. This system was dedicated to present the public face of leading contract players to the urban crowd in a positive, appealing light. Long before Stalin hammered his way to power, it explored finessing the public image of silent film stars, such as Mary Pickford, Charlie Chaplin, Rudolf Valentino and Douglas Fairbanks by building cultic identification with a public schooled to dream and fantasize about climbing rope ladders out of meagre existence into the stars. After the late 1920s, as the Hollywood studio system consolidated, film moguls such as Samuel Goldwyn, Louis Mayer, Daryl Zanuck and Jack Warner became celebrated for mastering the public image of the stars under contract to them. The techniques of personality promotion and exposure management that are integral to the cult of personality may have been custom-built by Stalin's *politburo* to suit the power needs of the regime, but to a considerable extent the essentials were pioneered by the Hollywood dream factory, which, in turn, borrowed much from corporate industrial production and retail organization.

The social construction of a public face designed to court acceptance, approval, empathy and identification reflected and reinforced bigger changes in society. Urbanization, economic growth and the development of mass communications provided new, wider opportunities for social mobility. Erstwhile social hierarchies and attendant conventions of behaviour, long thought to be fixed and immovable, began to wobble. There was not, exactly, a complete about face in the structure of stratified society. Studies of class, gender, race and disability through the twentieth century to today, demonstrate the persistence of organized inequality and predetermined life chances. [5] For all that, from the 1870s onward, popular awareness of the discernible loosening of chains and reference to the erosion of power hierarchies became commonplace. It was dramatically elevated in the popular media. Narratives of mobility from the log cabin and the moody tenement to the glorious pinnacles of power, in the worlds of politics, business and entertainment, were regularly communicated by the media. In America, the template, of course, was Abraham Lincoln, who was promoted as moving from being a brawny, rail-splitting frontiersman to the most noble president who in effect, died for the country by forging the nation. Yet it is easy to miss the immense power of the general parable of personality and upward mobility in the entertainment industry and popular culture. Figures like P. T. Barnum, born in 1810, was the son of an innkeeper and rose to become an illustrious entertainment impresario; Tom Mix, born in 1880, was the son of a stable master who found fame in many American westerns; and Charlie Chaplin, born in 1889 into poverty and hardship in South London, rose to become arguably the biggest star of the silent screen era. Many other names can be added to this list, such as Harry Lauder, Marie Lloyd, Dan Leno, George M. Cohan, Rudolf Valentino and Clara Bow. What they shared was lavishly documented upward mobility from sometimes, the depths of the urban crowd to the zenith of the popular entertainment industry. Their embodied *habitus* signified the dramatic changes available to people in modern, industrial society. They were unapologetic about many of the traits of their disadvantaged origins. To be sure these traits were now given public acclamation. This acclamation reinforced relations of presumed intimacy between achieved celebrities in the field of entertainment and the urban crowd. An essential component of the American dream was the hypothesis that anyone with talent and a readiness to engage in hard work, can make it. Achieved celebrities personified this and provided informal role models for the population to emulate (Sternheimer 2011). It was not so much the reality of new mobility chances that mattered. It was the image of an *achievable* elevated world, filled with glamorous, colourful personalities from the humble, shabby streets, mingling, without deference, indeed with a tangible certainty of justified belonging, with the great, the good and the well to do. Celebrity was redefined from an ascribed characteristic to a capacity in the reach of those eligible by virtue of talent, discipline and ambition.

Self-promotion and exposure management were, and are, predicated in emotional labour. After the 1870s a new type of persuasive
power, attached to readily identifiable people skills, began to perme-
ate society. The accumulation of attention capital was a full time job.
Achieved celebrities, and the upwardly mobile in general, were
obliged to develop new forms of presentational skills that reflected
and reinforced their sincerity, when they were 'in character', and 'out
of character'. [6] In the theatre, on stage, naturalism became prized
and admired. The celebrated British actor, William Macready (1793–
1873), who regularly toured the USA, became famous for developing
a style of acting that reflected the authentic, natural self. Before him,
artificial portrayals, relying heavily on well understood dramatic
mannerisms and facades, were dominant. Against this, Macready
acted naturally, such as in turning his back to the audience and, when
writing letters or notes on stage, putting their full content down on
paper. Such attempts at naturalism were considered ground-breaking
(Downer 1966: 75–7). By implication, they eroded the conventional
dichotomy in celebrity culture between the public and private face.
Indeed, Macready's willingness to ride roughshod over this division
and present himself in private and public life in 'what you see is what
you get' terms, further alloyed the sense of a radical departure in
theatrical celebrity.

At the same time, the premium in out-of-character exchanges
became affixed to disclosure. The more candid and apparently
unguarded the achieved celebrity might be about personal emotions
in public, the greater public credulity in the absolute sincerity of the
personality. In our day, the para-confessional stands, above all, as the
setting in which disclosure maximizes attention capital (King 2008).
By addressing the TV presenter and sharing intimate secrets with the
audience, the credibility of the celebrity is put on the line. The impression of a face-to-face exchange between the celebrity in the hot seat
and the audience is bolted into social consciousness. But is it right to
take disclosure on trust? When we think about it, we know that
staged naturalism in the theatre or in film and television, is an act.
Naturalism and disclosure both involve emotional labour.

So why should we believe that what is disclosed in the para-
confessional is true?

Lifies

The social and psychological consequences of the insertion of the
details of the private lives of celebrities into popular culture has been

widely debated. Gabler(2000) has coined the interesting term 'lifies' to refer to media portrayals of the real lives of the famous as soap operas. By this is meant the public dramatization of the private lives of celebrities through the media. The *mediated* character of celebrity became the acknowledged route of communication. Photo-play, the memoir, the candid interview and the para-confessional are among the means through which this is accomplished. Yet what exactly is being accomplished here? The life displayed in the lifie is an exercise in self promotion and exposure management. In moving 'out of character' the individual presents a picture that is supposedly a reflection of reality. Whatever we may feel about the veracity of what is disclosed, we are aware that a picture is being presented. Nothing is what it seems in mediated culture. For example, Philip Seymour Hoffman declared in 2006 in '60 Minutes', a television interview on CBS, that he quit drugs and alcohol abuse when he was twenty-two. All of that was behind him. Barely eight years later he was dead of a heroin overdose. Now it might be said, there is nothing remarkable about this. People change and settings change. But in a small way it illustrates that the 'what you see is what you get' style of self promotion and exposure management is unreliable. Sincerity with an audience needs to be taken with a pinch of salt. For it is built upon techniques of staging and persuasion that aim to build naturalism and presumed intimacy, but conceal more than they reveal.

Commentators have identified three motivations and consequences for the rise of celebrity culture and 'lifies'. Firstly, personal stories provide an axis of identification that can overcome some of the prejudices of disapproval relating to celebrity wealth. Secondly, life data operate as product placement exercises in which the commodities and consumption choices of stars are emulated by their fans. Thirdly, celebrity scandals can be turned into morality tales designed to reinforce compliance and the work ethic (Gamson 2001; Sternheimer 2011: 229).

Lifie culture received a shot in the arm with the rise of television, but historians of celebrity have pointed to its pre-TV origins in fan clubs, gossip columnists and 'real life' interviews in newspapers and magazines (Studlar 1996; Sternheimer 2011). Part of the glamour of the new achieved celebrities in the arts and entertainment after the 1870s was their readiness not to beat about the bush and to call a spade a spade. It is upon this basis that audiences, divided from them by wealth and experience, could affect to develop relations of presumed intimacy. This goes hand in hand with the personal and social drives for social impact, acceptance and approval. In the culture of achieved celebrity sharing and coming clean about private life is ritually revered and rewarded. Today, in talk shows, the para-confession is the gold standard of attention capital (King 2008). All of this moving between being 'in character' in the stage, on television and in film, but also 'out of character' (in mediated ways) through magazine interviews, chat shows and adverts spins around the public dramatization of private issues. It purports to use disclosure and natural exchange to clarify relations. But it leaves the public with the nagging suspicion that it is being sold a pig in a poke.

Part of this reflects the over-determined character of celebrity disclosure. It is important to recognize that contemporary celebrity culture, embracing in-character and out-of-character encounters, is at one and the same time 'a commodity system, an industry, a set of stories and a participatory culture' (Gamson 2011: 1062); further, that the culture promotes dualistic narratives of fame. In one, namely the narrative of achieved celebrity, fame is presented as the reward for talent, application and discipline. In the other, an expression of what Graeme Turner (2004) calls 'the demotic turn', fame is an artificial, commercially motivated construction, produced by investors, to cultivate attention capital around ordinary people (Gamson 2011:1063). The overdetermined character of celebrity culture makes slippage in interpretation unavoidable. Yet there is widespread agreement that interpretation is not just a matter of keeping in touch with celebrity. Rather, it involves the transfer of elements from this culture to everyday life. The strategies of self-promotion and exposure management developed by cultural intermediaries working for achieved celebrities are socially emulated (Gabler 2000; Maltby et al. 2006). The ideology of using self-promotion and exposure management to accumulate attention capital and social impact produces a 'mirror effect' (Pinsky and Young 2009). Stars became objects of popular fantasy. Obviously, not all believe that they can emulate them, but the existence of a highly public stratum of achieved celebrities who have successfully climbed the rope ladder to the stars legitimates the popular belief that stratified barriers are not impregnable and that celebrated strategies designed to achieve, impact, acceptance and approval are transferable to everyday life. In short, the vertical frontier can be penetrated.

By the term 'social mix' is meant not only greater physical contact between strata, but also greater intelligence of the lives of others through multiple media channels. After the 1870s, emotional projection and management became pivotal because their value in achieving social impact, acceptance and approval was communicated, and frequently championed by the press, magazines and later radio, film, television and the web. In the process the 'distant intimacy' that divides the urban crowd from the firmament of media celebrities was re-wired. Of course, stars remained at the top of the social ladder, seldom directly encountered in everyday life and the object of sultry fantasies and outright daydreaming. But now distant intimacy was brought down to earth by making the global urban crowd the object of nothing less than its self-referring social consciousness (Lambert 2013). If achieved celebrities hailed from the urban crowd, the milieux, personalities and exchange routines of street and suburban life became hunting grounds for personality truffles that might be used in the never ending quest of self-development and the achievement of social impact. For did not the media teach that it is reasonable to propose that these truffles might be turned into prized assets in the construction of personalities fit to acquire approval and fame? Self-promotion, exposure management and presumed intimacy became prosaic features of the classroom, the workplace, the local bar and other urban settings. In addition to immediate resources, they engaged with symbolic references from film, radio and other types of media culture. Life with semi-invisible multitudes, all caught up in a medley of social rhythms that defy the powers of any single imagination to encapsulate or decisively influence, became more entwined with a mixed ball of celebrity references provided by the media. Informalization begat personality types based in what students of the media, call the dance of 'mediation' and 'mediatization' (Couldry 2008).

Mediation and Mediatization

Formally defined by one of the leading pioneers in the field, the late Roger Silverstone (2002: 761), mediation refers to

> the fundamentally, but unevenly, dialectical process in which institutionalized media of communication (the press, broadcast radio and television, and increasingly the World Wide Web) are involved in the general circulation of symbols in social life. That circulation no longer requires face-to-face communication, though it does not exclude it.

Mediation is central in explaining how individuals manage their lives and how institutions organize and reproduce social ordering. It is the vein between first-order (face-to-face relations with family, peer groups, communities) and second-order (media) constructions of social reality. It is at the heart of presumed intimacy since it translates characteristics that are *remote*, in Simmel's sense of the term, into emotions that are recognized as *near*. Crucially, it describes a mutually referring, *conversational* process. Embodied habitus ceases to be a matter of narrow materiality – the family, the home, the community. The dimension added to the pot was the huge and unfolding field of symbolic initiatives and references supplied by the media. Silverstone (2002: 762) is at pains to insist upon the dialectical and uneven nature of mediation. The emphasis upon dialectics is designed to capture 'the continuous creative engagement' that listeners and viewers have with media output. He was intent on conditioning this engagement as 'uneven' because he understood that the power to work with, or resist, the 'dominant' or 'deeply entrenched' meanings in media output is unevenly distributed within, and between, societies. The insistence upon qualifying the process of mediation as dialectic and uneven is a useful counterweight to the concept of mediatization and its relation to everyday life.

Mediatization refers to the linear colonization of association, identity and practice in everyday and public life by the conventions or 'logic' of the media (Hjarvard 2004; Schulz 2004). In other words the form of everyday and public life is held to converge to precedents and protocols developed and transmitted by the media. Real life becomes more like film and television. Schulz (2004) postulates four stages to the process: *extension* (in which the conventions of the media spill over into everyday life); *substitution* (in which media conventions supplant local traditions and become part of what might be called *embodied habitus*); *amalgamation* (the gradual fusion of media conventions into the routines of everyday exchange); and *accommodation* (the assumption of the core elements of cultural or social activity around a media form). Nowadays the concept is propelled by strong headwinds. One can see why. Jeffrey Alexander's (2011) study of presidential political campaigning convincingly argues that nowadays, campaigns borrow liberally from the performative scripts and technological effects that have their highest technical expression in Hollywood. On a more mundane level the digital recording of graduation ceremonies, christenings and wedding celebrations routinely imitate the conventions of media forms.

In his thoughtful account of the question, Nick Couldry (2008: 376, 378) strikes the right note of justified caution in welcoming the clarification that the concept of mediatization brings to the analysis of contemporary society and culture, while at the same time, warning that Schutz's account of the logic of linear colonization is faulty. The concept cannot encompass uneven, conversational, dialectical qualities of exchange, which is why Couldry (2008) prefers Silverstone's (2002) concept of 'mediation'. Intrinsic to the latter is the notion of media exchange as a non-linear, 'multi-fronted, reciprocal process'. That is, the conventions of media forms effect society and culture and in doing so produce a plethora of feedback loops that change the conditions through which media forms operate. As Couldry (2008: 381) observes in addition to matters of heterogeneity and multiple layers of exchange, the question of blank spots which are either intentionally or unintentionally isolated from the mutually reinforcing conversation must be acknowledged.

Mediation then, is at bottom a process in which personality formation adopts cues and routines developed and transmitted by the media and, in doing so, alters the conditions through which media representation operates. It is the extension of the argument made by social critics that ours is an age dominated by the search for approval, acceptance and social impact (Riesman, Glazer and Denney 1950; Rieff 1965; Lasch 1979; Furedi 2003; Illouz 2007). It would be rash to claim that these social forces are unique to our times. There is just more exposure to issues of approval, acceptance and social impact through the relentless onslaught of digital communication and the formal requirements of civic virtue. The subtitle of Lasch's book is 'American Life in an Age of Diminishing Expectations'. Rosen's (2005) witticism that, were it written today, a more telling subtitle might be 'The Overpraised American', hits the mark. The accumulation of attention capital is not just a bid for social impact, it is also a cry for acceptance and approval. In the age of therapy culture, with its hallmarks of acute sensitivity to the other, diversity awareness and fierce imperative to be politically correct, this often results in dubious recommendations.

The outflanking of what Riesman, Glazer and Denney (1950) refer to as the 'gyroscope' of (inner directed) character with emotionally flexible, approval seeking, attention acquiring, personality is the product of multitude forces. Commentators nominate as primary influences, bureaucracy, pscyhoanalysis, therapeutic counselling ideologies, advertising, media images and consumer culture (Rieff 1965; Lasch 1979; Furedi 2003; Illouz 2007). One factor that bears traces of all of these, but which has not been given its due, is celebrity culture and the relations of presumed intimacy that it encourages and perpetuates. In the last third of the nineteenth century a variety of factors combined to augment the scale and variety of commercial entertainment in the distribution of time among the urban crowd. In the 1870s, apart from cheap theatres, dime museums, music halls and 'concert saloons', commercial leisure territory was dominated by the wealthy and the sporting crowd. The expansion of cities, the multiplication of workers in the white-collar sector, the gains of the labour movement in reducing work time and the relative rise in real incomes, created a demand for new types of commercial entertainment targeted at the urban crowd. Cultural impresarios satisfied this bourgeoning demand with the development of mixed gender, mixed-class cultural institutions such as vaudeville, amusement parks, basketball, dance halls and motion pictures (Nasaw 1993; Butsch 2008). Before the age of radio and television, relationships of presumed intimacy were being actively formed via the para-social manoeuvrings of impressarios and nascent PR/Media hubs. In these settings, social conventions and orthodox power hierarchy were frequently lampooned and ridiculed, developing widespread impressions of emotional nearness, shared history and common interests in the human molecules that compose the urban crowd. Take the British male impersonator, Vesta Tilley. She developed a successful career on both sides of the Atlantic playing dandies and tops on stage. Her turns as 'Burlington Bertie' and 'The Piccadilly Johnny with the Little Glass Eye', saved no male blushes in revealing the audacity and eccentricity of patriarchal power. Appropriately, she was lionized by women who saw her as a symbol of free thinking and independence. Music Hall and vaudeville entertainers like Tilley used personality, exposure management and self-promotion partly to reveal the arbitrary character of gender and class power. The refusal to know your place, and hold your tongue, may have been dramatically played out on the stage, but it reflected and reinforced the wider erosion of hierarchy and stultifying deference.

Consecutively, and by no means accidentally, parallel developments in fiction, music and art combined to inflate the cult of personality in popular culture. The distinctive nineteenth-century man of letters chased the dragon of fame by proposing to expound a panoramic view of society in which character and personality clashed and fought a ferocious battle of wills against implacable nature and indifferent society. Independent thought and self-making challenged the strictures of religion and gender inequality. Perhaps the most insistent theme in nineteenth-century literature is the mutability of social order, the seemingly perpetual violation of custom and the presumed intimacy between the author (who expresses these insights) and the urban crowd caught up in the same maelstrom. Naturally, protagonists drive the narrative. Yet the overwhelming impression from reading the narratives is of an engagement with the imagined urban crowd in which appearance and reality constantly blend, clash and stubbornly refuse to be disentangled. The integrity of behaviour given by men and women of character is buffeted by the scene-changing opportunities for personality to make waves. This is true of Thackery in *Vanity Fair*, Trollope, Balzac, Wilkie Collins, Flaubert, Thomas Hardy, Henry James and, of course, Dickens. In the works of these writers self promotion, staging, illusion and posturing, tirelessly raise questions about the validity and security of character. The novel that exemplifies this, *par excellence*, is Herman Melville's *The Confidence Man*. Set aboard a Mississippi steamer, the *Fidele* (appropriately a vessel named for truth, resting on liquid foundations), the cascade of appearances, the constant movement between stating and subverting facts and the suspension of authorial judgement, leaves the reader with the great problem of identifying the novel's central character. In Melville's hands the discipline and habits of action that are the foundation of our general understanding of character are portrayed as a mixture of loam and wet cement (Chabot 1976: 573). A sense of order is maintained only via artful bluff and diligent sleight of hand. Social impact is entirely a matter of self promotion, exposure management and engineering presumed intimacy. Personality is presented not only as the axis of change and development, but the only rational way to get ahead. Character is too plodding in the principles of custom and unable to adapt swiftly to changing conditions.

In painting too, mutability and the violation of trust and custom became prominent themes. For example, Gustave Courbet's paintings rejected the standard nineteenth-century symbols of noble, religious and historical themes. His work eschews moralizing sentiment and unequivocal meaning. It addresses ordinary culture, and was maligned by many critics for so doing. Yet what Courbet, and other painters, like Honore Daumier and Jean-François Millet, who thought like him, were doing was to break with the idealism of academic painterly traditions to plough a furrow of realism. Their canvases and drawings make a virtue of ambivalence and begin to expose the arbitrary character of boundaries that is later, more adventurously, seized upon by cubism. The foregrounding of bluff, ambivalence and sleight of hand in inter-personal relations reveal the depth of the shifting balance of power between established time-worn precedent and the shock of the new.

By the 1870s, in the metropolitan centres of the Old World and the New World, fresh routes of upward mobility based on the acquisition of renown were boring through the crystallized accumulations of power that characterized stratified society. In pushing back the vertical horizon, achieved celebrities inevitably challenged established boundaries of social identity, encrusted rules of deference, established norms of respect and the whole set of precedents and restraints attached to knowing your place. At the levels of experience and social impact, what seized the social imagination of the day was the cult of personality. This displayed frank, new forms of emotional candour, personal disclosure and public intimacy that mirrored the transformations in popular culture and proved immensely appealing to the public. The drama of frankness, and a refusal to apologize for upward mobility and the confidence that it bestowed, exhibited in vaudeville, the music hall, fiction and art, mirrored structural transformations in the power hierarchy of stratified society. Achieved celebrity loosened the threads of the established social fabric. It made it more difficult for established power to bask in the light of the cosy assurance that age-old systems of ascribed renown would persist in perpetuity.

The new struggle for renown was not confined to celebrity culture attached to the realm of entertainment. The extension of suffrage contributed to the development of new political parties and new trade unions representing the conditions and interests of propertyless wage labour. In Britain, the figureheads of these movements, such as Keir Hardie, Ben Tillett, John Burns, Tom Mann, Willie Gallacher, Mary Barbour, James Henry Thomas and Philip Snowden, became political celebrities. They were 'romantic role models' in Schmitt's (1919) sense of the term. Keir Hardie, worked as a 'trapper' and miner in the coal mines, and was the first Labour Party leader. Philip Snowden, the son of a weaver, who worked as a lowly Excise officer in Liverpool, and later in Scotland and Devon, became the Labour Party's first ever Chancellor of the Exchequer after the victory of Ramsay MacDonald's Labour Party in 1924. For the rising working class in Britain, these were inspirational political celebrities. They were stars to look up to and admire, not least because their origins lay in the urban crowd and their mission took the form of reforming this crowd's conditions and life chances. And yet, despite the cultural upheaval that their public presence signified, they did not somehow, truly represent the unique character of the times. Because the roots of their political personalities lay in a rational political creed that demanded behavioural discipline and moral rectitude, their popularity with the urban crowd took the form of the appearance of reinvigorated character rather than an extension of the cult of personality. The appeal of these political figures finally rested in believing in them as messengers of a more just and equal world in which all would have a chance and be valued. There are strong parallels with Turner's frontierism, in the notions of the rolling back of barriers, conquering disadvantages and liberating the latent talents and energies of the people. These were representatives and advocates of Modernity 1;

that is, they believed in the rational mastery of structures and processes so that events, episodes and incidents would, in time, lose their capricious, apparently random form and become *governed*.

What was happening with the emergence and growth of the cult of personality was something quite different. At the heart of the matter was the recognition of the provisional nature of commitments, undertakings and actions of every sort. Turner looked forward serenely to the Western kinsman as exemplifying, and eventually solidifying, the best in American character. He failed to notice that in the urban settings around him on the Eastern seaboard, the Midwest, and even in the deplored, stratified societies of the abandoned Old World, self creation was being adventurously redefined by the *polis* as self promotion, which, moreover, was passionately understood to be a perpetual process. While there were rational, principled aspects to this, the engine behind it was letting the emotions out of jail. The cult of personality, and the various propulsions of self promotion and personal preening, that went with it, were ultimately understood to be situational matters. The fact that they were frequently presented as pointing to consistent habits of action was of no relevance. No impediment was recognized to respecting the public traits of character. But the appearance and performance of character was very different from the heroic vitalism asserted by Turner in respect of the Western kinsman. Since character was tacitly acknowledged to be a respected, but obsolete ideal (since the nature of the changing times undermined its foundations), social advantage lay in the persuasive performance of traits that would accumulate attention capital and achieve social impact. The gain rested in judging situations shrewdly and becoming an appropriate chameleon when circumstances warranted.

In cultural production, self promotion and exposure management became more dependent upon cultural intermediaries, although, in the most epic cases, it was boldly presented as the labour of genius. The stress upon personal genius reflected the strong ideology of individualism, demanded and buttressed by *laissez-faire* conditions.

Artists portrayed themselves as being in a relation of exalted presumed intimacy with the *zeitgeist*. As such, the urban crowd was prevailed upon to believe that it possessed the magic of divination or prophecy. Writers, musicians and painters went about their business on the pretext that they were summoned by drives and urges that were beyond their comprehension which they could not fully control.

This was the demo-urge of Modernity 2. It acknowledges all order to be a masquerade and the contingencies that bring success or failure to life to be objects for dramatization and the mere assertion of governance. Being in the grip of this emotional demi-urge was used as an excuse for all sorts of questionable and downright bad behaviour. The public exchange and reception of their works gradually succumbed to assumptions about the craftsman as Artist. This depended upon demonstrable changes in the social positioning of public personality *viz-a-viz* the urban crowd. By the mid nineteenth century, for the publicly accepted man of letters, composer or artist, uncompromising vision became acknowledged as a revelatory force in the revaluation of life. When one examines its claims, uncompromising vision turns out mainly to be bound up with complex, inter-related social transformations that render the social horizon more elastic, flexible, mediated and – to return to a term already used – mutable. The most admired forms of cultural production became celebrated not only as capturing the spirit of the times, but as offering a haven of intimate identification for sections of the urban crowd who felt adrift and vulnerable from heartless Nature and the scene-changing transformations of the urban-industrial onslaught.

In a word, achieved celebrities were developing strategies and employing specialists to render them *mediagenic* personalities. The emphasis was upon creating a public image that accomplished impact and afforded the *mediation* of sentiments of presumed intimacy. Emotional manipulation was, and is, at the heart of engineering relations of presumed intimacy because it permits strong and automatic identification with mediated spectres. The para-social relationships that began to develop with the print culture of the late eighteenth and nineteenth centuries produced concealed italicized data captions around achieved celebrities. Public encounters were prefigured with accumulations of knowledge about the celebrity personality. Through the media people developed acquaintance with private details of the public life. Literacy with the private lives of achieved celebrities became a mark of distinction, certainly among fans, but, more generally, among the cognoscenti of public life. We began to live a counter life in which we became watchers scanning, filtering and filing details of the private lives of others. If this were a matter of relating to achieved celebrities to begin with, it transferred without too much difficulty to quotidian exotic apparitions communicated via the media. The condition of knowing about the private details of public lives and accepting that there is much that can be usefully learned from them is the seedbed of presumed intimacy.

7

Vertical Frontierism: Four Case Studies

It is time to bring these matters down to earth by examining some actual historical personalities, who expressed and developed the rising cult of personality, strove to accumulate attention capital to conquer the vertical frontier, and around whom relations of presumed intimacy flourished. The assault on the social (vertical) frontier was every bit as momentous for the transformation of society as the challenge to the spatial (horizontal) frontier. Indeed, in weighing the scales of frontiers in relation to their effect upon identity, association and emulation, there is good reason to submit that the vertical assault is of greater significance. For it directly involved a much larger demographic and successive generations inured to meagre existence, with a single focus of upward mobility in mind: look to the stars. The historical examples I have chosen to illustrate this personality type are Charles Dickens, Richard Wagner, Eva Tanguay and Mae West.

I have deliberately selected examples from 'the Old World' of Europe and the Eastern seaboard in order to counter Turner's proposition that pushing back social boundaries is compromised in so-called 'stratified societies'. The quartet of celebrities based in Western Europe and the seaboard cities of America pioneered methods of self promotion and exposure management to push back vertical boundaries in the social hierarchy. They made their mark via exploiting and developing the cult of personality in a European and quasi-European field of power that Turner tacitly dismissed as unpropitious to social mobility. They did so in very different fields of activity.

Dickens was a popular novelist who, we sometimes forget, enjoyed almost instant success, but his fiction and public image challenged social convention and the establishment in the field of cultural production and criticized key aspects of the field of power. In the field of culture, the establishment accused him of vulgarity and melodrama, especially in the early stages of his career. What this failed to recognize is the determined manner in which Dickens used self promotion and exposure management as accessories to his fiction in order to imprint himself upon social consciousness as a signature personality of the age.

Wagner was initially located in the marginal, *avant garde* of music, and began as a political revolutionary to boot. His career trajectory is particularly noteworthy because it invented and applied what has been called 'the Wagner industry' to curry favour. It culminated in his music becoming a powerful high-culture symbol of national identity and his personality being recognized as personifying national and racial characteristics (Vazsonyi 2012). Wagner's inexhaustible fondness for mixing up elements of high culture with fragments from low culture was symptomatic of the cultural transformations of the time. Mediation made the low popularly equivalent in prestige to the high. This compromised so-called authoritative readings of cultural significance because it implied that ontological identification with the low was as valid a variant of modern experience as affecting exalted comity with the culturally rarefied and high. The cases of exposure management and self promotion in the careers of Eva Tanguay and Mae West bear this out more fully. Both achieved fame from the position of representatives who are commonly seen as specimens of decidedly low, arguably *the lowest*, form of urban-industrial culture, i.e. the umbraceous, spit and sawdust, 'new', uneducated, industrial woman.

Tanguay (now a semi-forgotten figure of the 1920s) was the biggest music-hall star of her generation (Erdman 2012). By her own admission, she was not glamorous or richly talented. She turned her ordinariness into attention capital. She developed a deliberately contrived *arriviste* stage personality. She mocked high Victorian ideals of feminine reserve, beauty and deference. Before the term was invented (and applied to film star, Clara Bow), Tanguay was the 'it' girl.[1] She combined an assault on the vertical barrier of class stratification with street-wise female emancipation. Tanguay stood up for working people and saw herself as a 'new' woman. She used techniques of self promotion and exposure management to boost attention capital and accumulate approval and eventually, acceptance. The importance of 'the occasion' was well known to her. She personally supervised advertising campaigns to build her fan base and planted false stories about being kidnapped, being a victim of theft and being fined for a fight with a stagehand to build attention capital. Her costumes celebrated her frank sexuality and unbridled materialism. Her outrageous reputation was enhanced by wearing a dress made of pennies and another consisting of dollar bills. She used the press to communicate a public image of confident achieved celebrity and triumphant, unapologetic upward mobility.

Mae West borrowed much from Tanguay. Indeed, it has been suggested that at the beginning of her career she studied and copied Tanguay's stage act (Erdman 2012: 164–6). As with Tanguay, West's stage and screen persona is independent, sexually emancipated, unapologetic, hard-boiled and bawdy. She is seldom deferential, except as a gestural means to get her own way. Men are treated as *her* sex objects (Mellen 1974: 577). Unlike Tanguay she developed a career beyond vaudeville in writing, producing and staging *risqué* plays, films and managing real estate. West used camp to demystify and parody established feminine stereotypes. Camp is the colourful, playful aesthetic sensibility associated with metropolitan gay culture. West added camp to innuendo and transgressive desire in her treatment of heterosexual relations (notably in her frank portrayal of female sexuality and her no-nonsense acceptance of the inevitability of prostitution and rejection of the mumbo jumbo of sanctimony). Commentators have referred to her as a 'sex symbol, a camp idol and a female grotesque' whose values challenged mainstream culture (Robertson 1996). West self consciously *performed* Mae West. Her creation of a confrontative female sexual personality provoked industry and civic disapproval. Her stage, film and even, radio, performances were subject to censorship. She served a brief prison sentence for offending public morals. Hers is a particularly clear case of using personality to challenge the arbitrary conventions of the vertical horizon and stratified society.

All four used their personalities to create public images that challenged the habitual traditional, conservative view that society imposes a ceiling or vertical perimeter that bestows for the good of all an encompassing sense of time-honoured order and meet and just emplacement. Very publicly, they seized upon social barriers not only as arbitrary, but as cumbersome. They refused to obey the edicts to know your place and to defer to your social superiors. Their social impact and financial success contributed to the erosion of long-established hierarchies of power based upon ascribed characteristics of birth and inherited influence. In these and other respects, which will become evident below, they provide a touchstone to social

transformations of the day whose consequences now form the immediate context of the social order in which we live.

Each generated a global audience of watchers who professed to
know something of the private lives behind the public image. Presumed intimacy was part of the strategy of fame seeking applied by
Dickens, Wagner, Tanguay and West, and the specialist, cultural
intermediaries that they appointed to represent their interests. The
financial and cultural remoteness that divided them from their audience was counterbalanced by an economy of emotional nearness that
made each of them seem like part of the family.

The Inimitable

Dickens regarded himself to be an artistic comet of such singularity
that he often referred to himself as 'the Inimitable'. He rather made
a habit of encouraging others close to him to follow suit. Whether
this was in earnest or play, remains a moot point. The degree of
reflexivity in a public personality built around social impact is a nice
point of debate.[2] Leaving this aside, it is beyond doubt that the
continuing popularity of his fiction partly reflects his triumph in
emblazoning his personality as one of the leading lights of the
Victorian age. What has not been noticed so often by commentators,
is the pioneering role that he played in self promotion and exposure
management. Dickens would of course, have been conscious of actor
managers in the theatre because, from an early age, he adored the
stage. In his career he adapted the same role to forge his own career
and public image. He drew on a sort of ensemble of amateur cultural
intermediaries, consisting of close friends, who included John Forster,
Wilkie Collins, William Macready, Thomas Beard and Edward
Bulwer-Lytton, to give career advice. Yet in the end, with the aid of
his editorial assistant in the office of *All The Year Round*, William
Henry Willis, and the phlegmatic secretary and tour manager of his
readings, George Dolby, he understood that he must consciously steer
the course of his own affairs in public, that is, that part of the responsibility of celebrity is effective exposure management and optimal self
promotion. Sometimes he got things very wrong. For example, the
public statements he made in the midst of the ugly emotional separation from his wife, Catherine, were widely regarded, even at the time,
to be cold and heartless. His adroit skills of impression management
successfully secluded his mistress, Ellen Ternan, from public view.

Dickens regarded himself as the working man's friend. In part, this
reflected his relatively humble origins and the much cited period that

he spent as a boy working (against his will and to his eternal distress and shame) in a blacking factory. Despite this, he was no shrinking violet when it came to the proclamation of his talent and achievement. When he gave his successful public readings (often to audiences numbering thousands), he requested the crowd to imagine that they were present at a fireside chat. The homely image of the hearth immediately suggests family bonds that the social and financial divisions, between author and readers cannot dispel. Unquestionably Dickens staged himself as the ring master. The public readings were exercises in the manipulation of emotional relations based in the inversion of cultural remoteness with emotional nearness.

Dickens rocketed to fame at the age of twenty-four, when *The Pickwick Papers* (1836) was published. In the years that followed, until his death in 1870, he was never viewed as anything less than a beacon of achieved celebrity in the Victorian age. This extended from his fiction to his vigorous campaigning for social reform. Despite the image he cultivated as an 'inimitable' author, Dickens was, in fact, part of the radical broadsheet tradition that began in the 1820s. As a journalist he learned many lessons from the verbal and visual (cartoons) satires directed against George IV and his ministers after the Peterloo Massacre. Unequivocally, his sympathies lay with 'the People' (Ledger 2007: 232). On their behalf, specifically in the name of acting as friend to the underdog, he fought for what he regarded to be centuries of engrained prejudice and grating belittlement from on high. His fiction and campaigns for reform challenged the lumpy conventions of the gentry and deflated the plump and shiny certainties of the self-made, pious bourgeoisie. Pecksniff, Gradgrind and the Veneerings are odious characters in Dickens's novels because their pomposity makes them cocksure and unable to identify with contrasting perspectives. However, for all his acute awareness of class inequalities, the picture of human life that emerges most strongly from his fiction is of individuals propelled by implacable social and economic forces in directions that are sometimes against their best interests and conscious will. It is a perspective that rests easily upon an engagement with the contradictions between subjective agency and objective force (especially the money economy). In this respect, it resembles many aspects of Marx's (parallel) analysis of the forces of political economy in *Capital*. Marx was, of course, aware of Dickens. In a *New York Tribune* article he praised him and 'the splendid brotherhood of fiction-writers in England, whose graphic and eloquent pages have issued the world more political and social truths than have been uttered by all the professional, politicians, publicists and moralists put together' (Marx 1854: 4). It has been speculated that,

methodologically, Dickens's fictional accounts about the human condition constitute legitimate 'data sets' for the elaboration of social
theory, that Marx and others utilized in their political economy
(Stearns and Burns 2011: 2). In *A Christmas Carol*, Scrooge has
grown rich by hoarding and refusing to donate to the poor. Pecksniff,
Gradgrind and the Veneerings convey the embodied habitus of
acquisitive capital, either in the sense of expressing it or aspiring to
achieve it. In *Great Expectations*, Pip finds himself suspended between
'the world of "respectability" and the world of "ignominy"; of
oppressors and oppressed; of the living and the dead' (Hagan 1954:
177). Like Marx, Dickens understood the unbreakable relationship
between capitalism and violence. *A Tale of Two Cities* pulsates with
a cogent appreciation of the revolutionary crowd and the conditions
that gave rise to it. In addition, both Dickens and Marx were alive
to 'the redemptive power of violence' (Stedman Jones 2008). In a
Tale of Two Cities, a book heavily indebted to Thomas Carlyle's
account of the French Revolution, he provided an indelible discussion
of the elements of power, rage and imbecility in the urban crowd.
Dickens disapproved of 'the mob'. But, like Marx, he appreciated the
pressure-cooker effect of lives held down by violence and the waste
of talent and aptitude that this historical situation entails. In this
respect, both Marx and Dickens can be said to be true children of
the Enlightenment.

Dickens has been situated in the sentimental tradition of Fielding,
Richardson, Sterne, Sheridan and Goldsmith (Purton 2012). The
evidence for this assertion is fourfold: his belief in the basic goodness
of human nature (an inheritance from the Enlightenment); his faith
in reason as the master of emotion; his belief that part of the nobility
of the species is to care for others; and his commitment to the primacy
of social virtues (Purton 2012: 18). These are, above all, qualities of
personality. Character may include all of the qualities in question.
But it does so blindly, out of habit rather than through reason and a
sense of fair play. Joe Gargery, the simple, good-natured, steadfast
blacksmith in *Great Expectations* (1861) believes in the basic goodness of human nature, care for others, reason and the primacy of
social virtues, because these are the folk values of his background.
Joe is suspicious and mistrustful of the money and the metropolis
that his young brother-in-law, and charge, Philip Pirrip ('Pip'), enters
via a mysterious inheritance. It is Pip who, in encountering the hurly
burly of London, learns how to shape and project his personality to
acquire social impact through dress, acquaintance and deportment.
It might be objected that the novel demonstrates Pip overcoming the
deceptions and flatteries of personality by learning the true worth of

character demonstrated by his real benefactor, Magwitch (the convict who escaped and made good in the New World), and the steadfast nature of Joe. In making Magwitch the benefactor, Dickens exposes the cant of establishment claims to behave responsibly and generously to the poor. For Magwitch recognizes the responsibilities that his new fortune affords, whereas the establishment exercises the right of serene indifference. Miss Havisham, the rich old maid who does not discourage Pip in his mistaken belief that she is his benefactor, is ultimately portrayed as warped and spiteful. Pip's encounters with Magwitch and his presence at the death of Miss Havisham make the scales fall from his eyes. He seems to grasp the shallow nature of using position and personality to achieve approval and social impact. Yet the novel ends by his putting himself in the hands of the untrustworthy and damaged Estella, who claims to have turned over a new leaf following the dreadful death and pointless years of melancholy and mourning endured by Miss Havisham. In the original ending Dickens leaves Pip estranged from Estella, who, following the death of Bentley Drummond, has remarried. Following objections from Bulwer-Lytton that the original ending left the reader disagreeably downcast, Dickens revised the manuscript. The book now ends with Pip venturing that, 'I saw no shadow of another parting from her.' This is ambivalent since it suggests that the proposition may be nothing more than a delusion. Estella's history of bad judgement and wilful, enigmatic behaviour offers no firm basis for lasting security and prosperity.

Using self-promotion and exposure management as a means of accumulating attention capital is, of course, a characteristic theme in the sentimental tradition. In the fiction and public life of Dickens it is applied with gusto. Only in the monstrous *bonhomie* that he insisted on applying in his domestic life is it remotely accurate to describe him as a traditionalist (a patriarch). In all other respects he sees himself as an alpha male of the new age challenging boundaries. As he states many times in his writings, this means seizing the mantle of progressive thought and casting a defiant snook against humbug. He took it upon himself to paint a celebrity image that would appeal to the public. In addition to the more or less constant avowal of discipline and the work ethic as cardinal virtues of success, after his first visit to America, he cultivated public disdain for many aspects of American life (where his public was wide, but his royalties low, due to organized piracy). He took great pains to protect his halo of respectability and rectitude after his separation from his wife in 1858, and his affair with the actress Ellen Ternan (Slater 2012). Dickens knew and practised the arts of constructing the public face in a context of mass communication where whispers and innuendo were a-plenty. He approached the business of capturing public interest along many fronts. He wrote, directed and acted in six stage plays, including *The Frozen Deep* (with Wilkie Collins). Between 1853 and his death, he performed some 472 public readings in Great Britain and America (Collins 1975).

The readings merit a moment's closer consideration because they unintentionally reveal his determination to imprint his personality, rather than just his art, upon public consciousness. Contemporary accounts comment on the stripped-down nature of the stage sets. They consisted of a small reading desk, a book and, sometimes, a jug of water, a glass, gloves, a handkerchief and a paper knife. There were no costume changes. The lighting arrangements were plain and avoided ornamentation of any sort. Dickens simply faithfully read from his writings and dramatically acted out central scenes. It was a performance designed to bring the author before his adoring audience, but also to remind them that they were in the presence of a phenomenon. 'Dickens's performances', writes Ferguson (2001: 731), 'were not simply of *his* characters, but of *himself*, or, more accurately, of his public persona' (emphasis in the original). The trans-Atlantic schedule of public readings, delivered in large theatres, without modern benefits of amplification, dominated the final decade of his life. The considerable financial rewards were counterbalanced by physical costs on his health. He was aware that the public readings were physically damaging, but he seemed unable to fully abandon the lure of the 'affective aspects' of public performance (Andrews 2006: 11). The distaste that Dickens felt for 'emotionally frigid' audiences and his relish for 'openness', the 'immediate', 'spontaneous reciprocation' of the crowd, and his dislike of 'ceremony' and 'formality', are familiar traits of achieved celebrity (Andrews 2006: 18; Bevis 2001: 332). Dickens appreciated the urban crowd, from which he hailed and took care to emphasize that there were strong relations of presumed intimacy between him and them. He consciously saw his fame as challenging the privileges of ascribed celebrity and stratified society. He was embodiment of the new man, the *Novus Homo*, who seized the new technologies and forms of presentation of the day and the opportunities for attention capital that they afforded, to maximize impact upon the urban crowd and shake the stratified foundations of the establishment. He saw no reason to be apologetic for his success or falsely deferential to inherited privilege. Instead, he wanted his talent and industry to speak for itself. Yet he was far from being above building attention capital and positioning himself to achieve what he regarded to be the right sort of social impact.

The Sorcerer

Much the same applies to Richard Wagner. The son of a clerk and a baker's daughter, he consistently portrays himself as scrabbling forth from an unremarkable background and winning the admiration of the public by overcoming huge obstacles. His humble origins; his political radicalism with the German *volk* (which cost him thirteen years in exile after 1849); his war against the indifference and hostility of music critics and envious musicians; the poor health that plagued him; the relentless, highly adept courting of supporters and backers to finance his chosen (very expensive), art form; the reactions of audiences that he often deemed to be 'superficial' because, he believed, they failed to grasp the truly, revolutionary significance of his work – all of this he recounts with Pharaonic disdain. It is the counter-piece to the ideologies of race, blood and redemption that he notoriously propagated elsewhere in his work. Wagner was intent on using his music and projecting his personality as a means to both recover passions, dulled and lost in the industrial and commercial regimentation of life, and to be a portent of a new stage in human relations. Sensuality in Wagner's music was designed to carry the message that the societal norms of stratified society must be overcome to permit real social change (Harper Scott 2011: 57). His music and public life were predicated in making emotional relations of presumed intimacy with an audience of fellow travellers who were schooled through self-promotion and exposure management to regard him as their idol.

Dickens and Wagner believed that great art could not speak for itself. New technologies of communication and the rising tide of cultural literacy had combined to change the rules of the game. In order to fully connect with the audiences of the day, self-promotion and exposure management were required. The public craved personalities larger and more breath-taking than the denizens of the urban crowd – celebrities fit to rival the ascribed figureheads of the establishment. Against the stratified pomp of ascribed celebrity, they became increasingly fixated upon pioneers from their own streets and settings, who challenged the vertical ceiling that traditionally assigned (and mostly confined), fame and influence to the nobility. It was the conceit of self-promotion to present this process as spontaneous and autonomous. In fact, Dickens leant heavily upon his trusted ensemble of advisers to construct a winning public image. They helped mitigate the negative consequences for his reputation that followed his separation from his wife and his extended, furtive liaison with the actress, Ellen Ternan. Wagner also worked with cultural intermediaries, like

Theodor Uhlig and Franz Liszt, to manipulate the press and achieve social impact with the public. Commentators have referred repeatedly to his megalomania. He insisted upon being 'the centre of attention' at all times (Kroplin 1989). Uhlig has been called 'Wagner's first publicity agent', although of course, he worked in an amateur capacity (Vazsonyi 2012: 109). Together they planted influential notices and articles in publications such as the *Neue Zeitschrift fur Music (NZfM)* to promote Wagner's music and revolutionary status. The editor of *NZfM*, Franz Brendel, was also enlisted to the cause. Liszt's long essay, 'Lohengrin und Tannhauser von Richard Wagner', was in part the product of a campaign for public acclaim schemed for, and agitated for, by Wagner himself. Liszt proclaims Wagner to be an 'extraordinary genius' who 'introduces a totally new system' not only in music but in the art of social impact (Vazsonyi 2012: 116). The effect on the culturally literate public was sensational. Praise from a composer of Listz's standing was gold-dust in advancing Wagner's reputation and public stature. Wagner also poured forth torrents of prose writings dealing with his early life, his current struggles, the uninspiring state of music produced by his peers, the revolutionary character of his composition, the need for new forms of relations between people and a variety of social, economic and political questions. Its purpose was designed to educate the public not only in all things Wagner, but to the notion that Wagner's opinions counted in society at large. Anonymously, tirelessly and lovingly, Wagner promoted his own work.

In this he was spectacularly successful. He became one of the most famous and controversial artists of the nineteenth century (Vazsonyi 2012). We remember him as much for his gusto, flamboyance, 'fabric fetish' (Dreyfus 2010), anti-semitism and scorn for Victorian values, as for his compositional brilliance and ground-breaking reforms of the theatre. Artistically speaking, he sees himself occupying the loftiest peak of the *avant garde*. Yet he mixes this up with an unapologetically populist demeanour. He submits that his art is the most complete expression of the German spirit. 'I am the most German of all', he (1975:86) wrote in a diary entry of 11 September 1865. 'I am the German spirit. Just look at the unparalleled magic of my works; compare them with all of the others.' Nietzsche refers frequently to the 'magical' qualities of Wagner's music. A contemporary doyen of Wagner Studies repeats the claim by describing Wagner as 'the sorcerer' (Millington 2012). Without doubt, Wagner saw himself as a phenomenon of the age and, like Dickens ('The Inimitable'), portrayed this as the central message in his public image. By the term 'phenomenon' here, is meant a figure who hails from the people but magically clarifies their essence and so unifies them, by dint of sheer personal brilliance. Through his writings, whether acidly commenting upon the music scene and the associated fastidious rituals of musical composition or the social and political questions facing the German people, he contrives to create an image of iconoclasm and exclusivity from the herd mentality. Nowhere is this more transparent than in Bayreuth.

Wagner conceived the Bayreuth Festival as a major cultural event. Now, music festivals were not unprecedented. In 1784 a festival to commemorate Handel's music was held in London, and Birmingham commenced the Triennial Music Festival, which became something of a kite for cultural events of this sort. By the early years of the nineteenth-century music festivals were starting to emerge in Germany. Inspired by idealized representations of Ancient Greek traditions and fuelled by the quest for German nationalism, the most prestigious was the Lower Rhine Music Festival (1818). This was largely organized and performed by amateurs. It rotated its venue around a group of cities including Dusseldorf, Cologne and Aachen. The Bayreuth Festival (1876), founded by Wagner, was intended to take the festival into an entirely new, exalted realm (Vazsonyi 2012: 169–75). Adorno (1981) saw in Bayreuth the authentic beginnings of the culture industry. Wagner intended it to be a permanent cultural and spatial monument, not only to his music, but to the genius of his personality (Trippett 2010). Attendance at the Festival was made synonymous with 'individuality' and 'prestige'. Both characteristics are reminiscent of another of Adorno's (1992: 222, 226) signature concepts, 'pseudo-individualism'. That is, the cultivation of a social reaction to a standardized commodity that is calculated to convey the *faux* personal impression of discernment, taste, distinction and individuality. Bayreuth was an event and monument that was planned to communicate a semi-religious bond with 'the creator', namely Wagner (Sennett 2003). It drew on support from the network of 'Wagner-Verein' (Wagner Societies). The piano manufacturer Emil Heckel founded the first Wagner-Verein in Mannheim in 1871. Its statutes provided for recognition of Wagner's national significance, a personal commitment to his art and, crucially (for fund-raising purposes), dedication to the goal of realizing a permanent home for the *Ring* in Bayreuth. These provisions formed the template for cognate national and international Wagner Societies. Within eighteen months, outposts were founded in Leipzig, Munich, Vienna, Dresden, Berlin, Weimar, Nuremberg, Mainz, Darmstadt and Cologne. Wagner mania was not confined to Germany. In 1872 a Wagner society was founded in Pest. It was succeeded by similar organizations in London, New York, Basel, Prague, Zurich, Paris, Riga, Florence, Milan, Boston, Cairo, Warsaw, Amsterdam, Copenhagen and Stockholm. Outwardly,

Wagner professed to be uncomfortable with the adulation of this social network made up of presumed intimates. He stressed their separate origins and on the whole, publicly distanced himself from their activities. Simultaneously, he privately took a keen interest in their business, especially in the matter of fund-raising. To this end, his close friend Carl Tausig and his wife, Cosima, were delegated to perform monitoring and surveillance roles. Despite Wagner's high hopes, the fund-raising efforts failed and in the end, he was forced to negotiate a loan from Ludwig II to build the theatre in Bayreuth. However, after 1876, the Societies provided seed money to develop the Festival programme. Bayreuth was brought into the world as the temple for all things Wagnerian. It remains so to this day. Other significant artists have Festivals in their honour. The Shakespeare Festival in Stratford, Ontario is a world-famous example. But this was inaugurated centuries after Shakespeare's death. Conversely, the Bayreuth Festival was founded as an annual, quasi-sacred tribute to a living artist allowing fans to make pilgrimage to their idol. In Bayreuth, Wagner often adopted the public persona of a humble German worker, gratified at the blessings bestowed upon him by a grateful public. In the same breath, he resolved to impress upon the world that he has touched the hem of the immortals and is part of their company. 'For Wagner, everything is personal', contends Vazsonyi (2012: 124). This 'theatricality' extended into 'making a production of himself' in every walk of life (Vazsonyi 2008: 195).

Wagner deplored the commercialization of music and the efforts of promoters to turn it into an industry. But his lifelong energies devoted to image-building, product-branding and advertising make it hard to see his disavowal of commercialization as anything other than a pretence. Through a complex battery of networking, iconography and social positioning he sought to etch his exclusivity and immortality upon the public. 'Great masters' of music had been proclaimed before him, and the techniques of merchandizing and public elevation that he employed were not invented by him. However, nobody before produced such a tireless assault on so many fronts – in composition, essays and public speeches – calculated not only to avow the birth of a new category of musical communication, but to emblazon the light of his star on the public horizon.

The 'Cyclone'

Few people who read this book will have heard of Eva Tanguay. A century ago in the Anglophone world she was a super-star with the same, instant public recognition as Harry Houdini or Charlie Chaplin. The entry for Eva Tanguay (1878–1947) in the *Cambridge Guide to Theatre* describes her as the 'Oomph' Girl – neither 'beautiful', 'witty' or 'graceful'. She was of average height, prone to portliness, but with obvious athleticism. In most respects she was perfectly ordinary. But what makes her noteworthy is that she turned this quality into attention capital at a time when the ordinary was being historically transformed into an acceptable and frequently absorbing focus of public attention. She personified, celebrated and enthusiastically engaged in the mediation of the attitudes of blue-collar females and succeeded in making them objects of attention and pleasure for the white-collar class and the strata above them. Her stage persona and pioneering role in Lifie culture made a virtue of accelerated intimacy. Discretion and reserve were dismissed as symptoms of the emotional immobility that clouded stratified society. She saw sexual candour and class opposition as no basis for admonition. Unless she wanted to gain her own way in social exchange, she would have no more tugged her forelock to a person of outwardly superior rank, than place her savings on a table and set fire to them. Tanguay dramatized the application of personality as an instrument to accumulate attention capital and acquire social impact. There was no guile about this. It was a partnership between her and her public. She and her audience knew that she was breaking boundaries to accumulate attention capital. Her frankness and indiscretion were exaggerated, dramatic forms of the loosening of social relations taking place more widely. The normative emotional structure built around stratified society was evidently loosening. The great and the good had, in their pig-headed, unbending way, steered the world into the horrific inferno of the 1914–18 war. As a result they were widely seen as being out-of-touch with modern realities. They clung on to power, and through Woodrow Wilson's championing of the League of Nations, grandly gave a blowhard image of creating a new world order. Yet, while there was widespread gratitude that the bloodshed was now over, it was soon outdistanced by cynicism and opportunism. The 'Jazz Age', which reached its height in the era after Tanguay's stage success, but was obviously influenced by her example, 'broke the cake of custom' all right. Yet it revolved around insubstantial personality, excitement highs, the rapid, tempestuous exchange of emotions, the bliss of successful self promotion and constantly new 'occasions'.

Tanguay's immense popularity symbolized the beginnings of a new settlement in society in which the ante of social impact had passed from character to personality. What was undeniable is that she, 'the cyclone', could only have risen to be one of the highest-paid entertainers of the age without the benefit of ground-breaking change in the whole social order around her. Tanguay's mass appeal derived from 'the force of her personality' (Wilmeth and Miller 1996: 374). That is, it produced a social reaction to personal qualities that possessed high attention capital. In Tanguay's case, this involved challenging time-worn sexual boundaries and inveterate forms of class deference. She has been called the forerunner of Madonna and Lady Gaga, and in her brazen public posturing and self promotion, comparisons have been drawn with Kim Kardashian (Erdman 2012 :5). Before the advent of Reality TV, she offered no special talents or inherited claims to greatness. Yet, as with Reality TV stars, her quirky, daring and carelessness resonated.

Her theme song, *I Don't Care* (1904) captures the spirit and some of the main features of the rising personality type which she projected that pitchforks itself against stratified society:

> You see I'm sort of independent
> Of a clever race descendent,
> My star is on the ascendant -
> That's why I don't care.
> I don't care
> What people say or do,
> My voice, it may sound funny
> But it's getting me the money,
> So I don't care

'Ultimately what appealed to theatre goers again and again', writes (Erdman 2012: 20) 'was Eva's commanding and unique self-presentation. She was able to project individuality and personality in a way few had ever done and at a time when audiences longed for something striking and highly individualistic.' This was especially bold because it debunked conventional female stereotypes of the demure woman. In her stage act, she dressed in *risqué* costumes that flaunted her buxom figure and muscular legs. Her stage presence communicated a new type of power that drew most of its inspiration from the urban crowd and vaudeville rather than the conventions of theatre and its patrons. Critics of the day commented upon her 'cyclonic energy' and 'animalistic' abandon (Rosen 2009). At her peak, between 1908 and 1918, she was the biggest and best-paid star in vaudeville (Eichenweld 2001: 26). She has been described as the 'first American popular musician to achieve mass-media celebrity'; Edward Bernays, the father of public relations, called her 'our first symbol of emergence from the Victorian age' (Rosen 2009). With the guidance of publicists, she launched public relations stunts designed to create a sense of drama and accumulate attention capital. These included threats to retire, stories of being kidnapped and brawling with stage hands, which triggered apparently unadorned confessions, greedily consumed by show-biz magazine editors. Staged crises and frank disclosures played to the public need for change and candour in public life. Through them the urban crowd formed the opinion of equivalence. That is, the intimation they really knew what was going on in the hearts and minds of achieved celebrities, because they recognized that what they said and how they behaved were dramatically realized versions of working class habitus. The discrete silence favoured by figureheads of ascribed celebrity was regarded by the public as a sign of emotional paralysis which disguised more fundamental defects in how the ruling class conducted itself. Disclosure was held to be more emotionally honest and healthier to boot. Through these *success de scandales* Tanguay carved out a reputation for self promotion, emancipation and bolstered ties of presumed intimacy with her public. Her very ordinariness provided a point of identification for girls and women trapped and stultified in their factory, office work and domestic settings. She provided a benchmark of female, blue/white-collar upward mobility. Tanguay let her hair down on stage, made suggestive sexual utterances and relished outrageous and *risqué* stage costumes (notably, her 'abbreviated' costume for *Salome* and her '$30 dress' which consisted of 4,000 pennies stitched together). She acted out the dreams and fantasies of people from humble walks of life and perhaps, also attracted fans from the ranks of the wealthy who felt likewise thwarted by hierarchy. Her magazine interviews strongly implied that her colourful public life spilled over into her private life. Instead of the artificial style of performance and superior private bearing of the generation of achieved celebrities in the world of entertainment that preceded her, she oozed the vulgar naturalism of the urban crowd.

Tanguay then, came from an era in which the ground of popular culture was shifting, and the hierarchy of stratified society that, for so long, appeared to be secure and unruffled began to be treated as arbitrary and rickety. Forms of public presentation anchored by deep chains of tradition and habitual passive observance were being tossed in directions that threatened the stability of the general social order. Polite society may have deplored the noise and vulgarity of the urban crowd. However, to paraphrase the lyrics from Tanguay's theme song. the ascent of the latter 'may sound funny' but it 'gets the money'. Suddenly it was all right to be acquisitive, materialistic, vulgar and unapologetic. The counter-weight to this, namely the complacent, slumbering inertia of stratified society, was fatefully shattered by the Great War. It was the start of the age in which anything goes.

The Sex Symbol

In many ways Mae West carried on where Tanguay left off. She was a spikey, controversial cultural icon in the Jazz Age and Depression years. She symbolized access to the steamy, seamy side of American underworld life, which the cascading columns of stratified society were opening up to public scrutiny. West played the role of a knowing amanuensis to larger, emancipatory social and cultural forces. This made her walk a thin line between public acceptability and social disapproval. While her later career dissolved into self parody, the heyday of her stage and film work affronted respectable society and was important in breaking down cultural phobias, prejudices and intolerance. In the Jazz Age and Prohibition era, West treated every 'occasion' as an opportunity to insinuate the transgressive, alternative edge that lurked beneath the veneer of American straight society. In the 1950s she toured her stage act in Vegas, backed by a troupe of muscle-bound, camp, young hunks dressed in shorts and body oil, and ended up playing an octogenarian sex bomb in the film *Sextette* (1978). We know that she was a studious, revealingly respectful, disciple of Tanguay's performances (Erdman 2012). She poached the wry, ribald, shameless aspects of the older vaudevillian's public persona. *Prima facie*, it might seem that she simply appropriated the latter's *risqué* personality as a straight-talking 'new' woman and modernized it. But West was 'new' in ways that Tanguay had been reluctant to explore. She learned the craft of sexual innuendo and self parody from female impersonators like Bert Savoy and Julian Eltinge (Curry 1996). Transposing a *risqué* personality of more or less publicly acceptable identity with a beckoning counter-identity that hinted at outlawed pleasures was her trademark. Tanguay was naughty. West was downright dirty. She displayed familiarity and ease with the taboos of prostitution and camp culture. Two of her plays were raided by the vice squad, and a third was 'dissuaded' from opening in New York (Hamilton 1990: 384). Her scandalously successful stage plays *Sex* (1926), for which she received a ten-day prison sentence (for allegedly corrupting the morals of youth), and *The Drag* (1927), dealt with controversial subjects of sex workers, homosexuality and cross dressing. *The Drag* employed openly gay actors and freely used slang from gay culture to ears in Broadway audiences that were not accustomed to this sort of thing. West wrote, produced and starred in these productions. Unlike Tanguay, who relied heavily on management guidance, at this point in her career, she exerted direct control over all aspects of her image. At the peak of her popularity she was an unerring judge of self promotion and exposure management. She knew how far to go in both stressing and titillating public morals. Very visibly, she defied social and sexual conventions. Indeed, her plain-speaking style parodied these conventions as the hypocritical bastions of a discredited social order. Her self-proclaimed assault on 'Victorian censorship', and garish sexuality did not make her an outcast. Instead, she became an enduring sexual icon for the gay community, as well as a symbol of the transgressive metropolis, the hidden, under-world, in the Prohibition era.

There is no question that Tanguay made a virtue of independence, but West levered this to another level. 'In most of her films', writes Mellen (1974: 576), 'she reduces herself to a sexual object in quest of economic security while she is, simultaneously, defiant and self-sufficient, seeking mastery over her life.' The wisecracks, the (frankly still) dazzling *double entendres*, the take-it or leave-it attitude she adopted with her stage and on-screen lovers, cemented the public image of a hard-boiled, mould-breaker. Her film work discards the respectable idea that the relationship between the sexes is one of politesse and decorous reserve. For West, the only possible relationship between the sexes is the endless see-saw between dominance and submission. There is an aggressive and unapologetic sexual *realpolitik* in her attitude. 'When women go wrong', she has her character Lou say in the film *She Done Him Wrong* (Williams 1975: 120), 'men go right after them.' This would have been deplored as coarse, vulgar and offensive by strait-laced, stratified society, but ordinary people applauded it as refreshing 'straight talk'. In West's hands it turns into something more knowingly disruptive that further weakens the foundations of a social order based upon the character ideals of transparency and accountability. For West, stratified society plays a deceiving game of rational, sedimented, settled order. 'By rejecting the divisions between Black and White', writes Watts (2001: 317), 'man and woman, rich and poor, self and the other, she continues to challenge a society that thrives on fixity and certainty.' This life-long interest in role play, counter identity and visible concealment, led some writers to call her 'the first female leading man' and 'greatest female impersonator' (McCorkle 2001: 48). For her, attention capital and social impact was like a second skin. Her provocative public appearances represented 'premeditated abandon, calculated for maximum shock or show-stopping effect' (Wortis-Leider 1997: 4). It all boiled down to projecting personality – deployed artfully in different settings – to be noticed, publicized and craved. West was not interested in being a role model or providing lessons in character. Her object was to use personality and the occasion to achieve social impact in popular culture and to be recognized as a mould-breaker. All of this disguised a shrewd, hard-headed business woman who built a substantial and lucrative property portfolio in California.

When she left for Hollywood in the 1930s, her films were said to have saved the studio that hired her. Not accidentally, she lost control of the persona that she created. To begin with, the calculated ambiguity of her film roles was too clever for censors to notice and stifle. However, as the moral majority vocalized unease with her sensationalist plots, in-your-face wisecracks and *double entendres*, the studios clamped down on her risqué, sexual persona (Hamilton 1997). West's response was to make a gaudy caricature of herself – a part that she played in public for the rest of her long life. It was an act of revenge against a studio system that sought to barricade and corral her. But it was also built upon relations of presumed intimacy between the urban crowd who were also barricaded and corralled by the conventions of established power.

Head Tennis Among the Union of Watchers

In match-play tennis the ball that races and spins from one side of the court to the other is followed by a sea of bobbing heads in the stadium. One thinks of the heads bobbing in the famous tennis sequence in Alfred Hitchcock's film, *Strangers On A Train* (1951). This is a type of visible relation of what might be called, head tennis. The latter is mostly private, unaudited and unremarked. As the tennis sequence in Hitchock's film brilliantly prefigures, by counterposing the bobbing heads in the stadium eagerly following the flight of the ball with the adjoining, bobbing heads of the invisible cinema audience, head tennis is not restricted to match-play tennis. Why the scene dramatically succeeds is that only one head in the stadium refuses to follow the flight of the ball. It belongs to the leading protagonist, Bruno Anthony (Robert Walker) who stares intently at one of the players on court, Guy Haines (Farley Granger),whom he plans to implicate in a murder. I've called it 'brilliant prefiguration', because metaphorically, in a society dominated by electronic and digital visual culture this movement of to-and-fro bobbing is what occurs daily through villages, towns, cities, nations and entire continents in various processes of mediated communication. Head tennis is how we track the significance of national and world events, incidents and emergencies. This is often the first, and in many cases, the final, stop in filtering and 'interpreting' the real state of the world around us. The moves made in celebrity culture involve no history of direct communication with spectators. They are modestly based in principled non-communication. But subconsciously we track and absorb them without necessarily meaning to, or even wanting to. If you ask anybody about celebrity or statistical men and women it is astonishing how much they purport to know, simply by virtue of reading a newspaper, watching TV, surfing the net or just gossiping. The knowledge may not be accurate or tested, but it is extraordinarily co-present with the details of their own lives. The presence of these representations in the social landscape and in our lives is inescapable. So familiar strangers become the permanent residents of mental speculation and fantasy life in ways that Milgram (1971) could never have anticipated. They can be placed anywhere in our social landscape. They can bolster this or that position. They do not answer back. In head tennis there is no umpire who adjudicates on point scoring. The media supplies watchers with data but it does not pursue a continuous narrative. As befits an age organized around personality, they convey 'the occasion' through dramatic reports of 'incidents', episodes', 'events' and 'emergencies'. The watchers follow the flight of those data, but can switch off autonomously at any point. They may make up their minds about the state of play, but they are under no responsibility to do so. They track movement without necessarily being obliged to develop any big picture. They are called upon to observe and identify, but not precisely to do anything that will alter the environments set out before them. When the media try to make sense of what is going on, the watchers are free to accept or discard what they see. They are encouraged to change channels if they want to. In a febrile world of monstrously divided interest, transparency and accountability possess little in the way of universal validity. These are portrayed as hang-ups from an obsolescent world in which character ruled the day. The lesson of cultural relativism is that truth is merely a point of view. We are divorced from choice by the choices that we make. The watchers are omnipotent in the sense of having the capacity to exercise complete judgements about the reality and truth of the representations that they access. Consecutively, they are powerless in being unable to prove that what they believe is either real or true and lacking the effective power to do anything about it. Doing bears no connection to watching. Indeed, for most intents and purposes, it is entirely secondary to it.

I contend that the roots of this important structural shift in social order go back to the 1870s. The surge against the vertical horizon of stratified society, in which achieved celebrities play a privileged role, and the plight of statistical men and women became widely observed. At one important level, society was turned irrevocably into a union

of watchers. There was no membership fee or common political programme involved. Union was properly democratic, in that anyone
who could pass the time of day gossiping with someone about stories
in the press, buy a newspaper, browse a magazine or – as new mass
communications technologies were invented and brought within the
reach of ordinary men and women – access a radio, a cinema screen,
television, a computer etc., was already joined up. Just as in match-
play tennis, where the personality of the game is set by interplay with
the stadium audience, in rising celebrity and news culture after the
1870s, the inquisitive eyes of the crowd watch the countless trajectories of others who they never meet and, in respect of which, possess
only a second-hand knowledge. The ubiquity of news culture is
relentless. The incidents, emergencies and episodes that the media
transmit are so plentiful, granular and contradictory that the effect is
akin to throwing sand into our eyes. It over-informs us, blinding us
to what is really going on. Not surprisingly the search for escapism,
transcendence, instruction, daydreaming, rumour-mongering and
scandal has emerged as a human interest element in the news that
allows us to grasp something that we can immediately understand.

   Immediate understanding is important because it conveys the
impression of communicating competitive advantage. In the challenging business of seizing the initiative, being seen as convincingly understanding things is as important as really understanding things.The
emergence of this global news culture transformed the social order.
It offered new standards of upward mobility, based in the self-
promotion and exposure management, and enlarged the scope of
moral density to embrace statistical men and women. This carried
over into civil society, having significant effects upon how mobility,
ethics, civic virtue and attention capital were scoped and interpreted.
The high born and well-to-do still possessed social impact by coming
from the right families and having the right education. But after the
1880s, the chains binding the cultural imbalance that concentrated
attention-capital and social impact in ascribed celebrity began to lose
their grip. Ideals of character, earthed around the principle of property, started to be challenged by sheer *chutzpah*, stridently claiming,
as a right, that which had been debarred by the vertical horizon
of stratified society. Commanding social impact was no longer
mainly a matter of being born with a silver spoon in your mouth. It
became more widely associated with efforts and aspirations from
representatives of the economically disadvantaged, politically and
culturally marginalized to translate their labour power into high-
profile visibility. Upwardly mobile achieved celebrities at this time
(and later) applied the drama of indignation, effrontery, audacity, gall

and seduction to appropriate some of the scarce economic and publicity resources for themselves. In doing so, they provided ordinary people with resources to pursue a variety of new ends. Some consumers of celebrity culture fantasized about escape and transcendence; others modelled themselves on versions of the public face of selected celebrities; a few began to worship selected celebrities; others exchanged rumours and gossip about stars to widen and strengthen their social networks, or simply comment on the dreadful emptiness of commercial entertainment culture.

The complex set of relationships we have with selected celebrities is a microcosm of principles of presumed intimacy formatted by cultural intermediaries in relationships with the PR/Media hub. However, a broad-brush approach to this is misleading. The celebrity relationships that we pursue are positioned firstly, and often go little further, than watching. How each microcosm of attention capital works depends partly upon the visual data that each individual brings to the para-social encounter. But the fact that it is interaction with formatted, pixillated familiar strangers in which there is no history of communication is significant. Stephen Greenblatt (1991: 4) comments on the 'immense transformative power' of mass communications and their 'ability to diminish difference by initiating relatively isolated and autonomous cultures into the imagery and values of the world system'. Visibility of celebrity positions consumers everywhere in the role of watchers and laid the foundations for relating to statistical men and women through the same emotional goggles. Our knowledge is necessarily imperfect. We cannot be everywhere all of the time, nor can we rely on the media to provide a complete, perfect reflection of everything. So we volunteer to demand and assimilate lines of mediated information which render emotionally close and intimate social predicaments and personalities, who are transmitted to us from media producers, but from whom we are divorced by the magnitude of cultural, spatial and economic distance.

In view of this, the fact that the ordinary is now fetishized in Reality TV should not come as a complete surprise. The ordinary and the exceptional have been twin staples of our media diet since the 1880s. The social business of watching, whether it be focused on celebrities or familiar strangers at the local subway station or *Facebook* site, is utterly prosaic and banal. The immediate access that we have to this level of everyday experience disguises its social importance. As we have already noted, Gamson (2011: 1063) points to two often competing consecutive narratives in celebrity culture. Firstly, that which is affixed to what is defined as the extraordinary, i.e. the world of the achieved celebrity, which is a magnet for popular attention. Secondly, that which is attached to the ordinary, elevated from obscurity by media programmers and deliberately turned into an object of attention capital. Each narrative revolves around forms of para-social interaction which, in this study, have been called Category A and Category B relationships. For Gamson (2011: 1063), Reality TV is the epitome of this; it turns ordinary people into 'factory products'. The distinction is shrewd because it implies that motifs from each narrative are constantly swapped, modified and interchanged. For example, interviews with celebrities of extraordinary achievements often take pains to assure consumers that the stars are really ordinary people just like us. Consecutively, the exercises in self-promotion and exposure management on Reality TV borrow from the practices and scripts of achieved celebrity. There is no necessary integrity to either category A or B para-social exchange. So why should we believe that the celebrities who populate these channels possess integrity themselves? In celebrity culture, watching is central. But that which is visible is always understood to be something other than transparent, since in para-social interaction the predicate of visibility is concealment. The cultural intermediaries behind the celebrity are divided from the viewer. Likewise, the viewer is concealed from the celebrity. Consuming celebrity culture means entering a no-man's land in which things are neither entirely extraordinary or wholly ordinary. Yet the technology and socio-technics of television create an ethos in which the line of resistance to believe what is really going on is weak. We do not exactly believe all that we see, but our background expectations are that what we see is only worth being communicated to us because it is valid.

However, it is too limiting to restrict the narrative around the ordinary in celebrity culture to Reality TV contestants. It extends to the gigantic, realm of statistical men and women. We do not get a balanced picture of how statistical men and women live, because their existence is mediated and generally reaches the public eye only when an incident, emergency or event pushes them centre stage. This has consequences for how data are conveyed. Above all, it means that it is often communicated *theatrically*, with drama accented, in visual frames that purport to convey reality to us. Yet the presumed intimacy that we automatically display with respect to their conditions of life, their predicaments and their plight is remarkable. In abstract form, the poor, the beleaguered, the hungry, the disabled and the oppressed are part of the visual (and verbal) vernacular of our daily existence. So, when the media transmit representatives from this hazy, imprecise statistical multitude into our living rooms or onto our portable devices we often encounter them as familiar strangers, i.e.

as people with whom we have 'knowledge' and recognize 'a connection'. Ordinary people are pursued to generate attention capital by more than the moguls of Reality TV broadcasts. Watching them is a staple of a form of civic culture in which the media have replaced religion and class as the decisive moral force. Thus, Gamson (2011: 1068) refers to 'an increased expectation that we are being watched, a growing willingness to offer up private parts of the self to watchers known and unknown, and a hovering sense that perhaps the unwatched life is invalid or insufficient'. This is supported by Rhodes's (1998) work on panoptical intimacy in institutionalized settings that we referred to earlier, where counselling and monitoring are applied to engineer behaviour modification. Gamson's (2011) study implies that the applications of counselling and monitoring techniques cannot be confined to institutionalized settings. Ordinary life is balanced with pressures that make us want to disclose. Those who 'withold' or are glib about their inner feelings are instantly suspected of being damaged or shallow. The caveat is that disclosure is not necessarily about unlocking blocked emotions. Rather, it is often more centrally about acquiring attention capital. Public disclosure has values that private life lacks. High among them is the power to generate empathy and trust. But why should 'the unwatched life' be 'invalid' or 'insufficient'? What price should we put on the visibility of emotions? If things are concealed, what might they really be, and why do we conceal them?

8

Cracks in the Mirror

We are at our most intimate when we are most vulnerable. This is one reason why celebrities turn to the para-confessional in times of career turbulence. By coming down from the pedestal of stardom, and re-entering the realm of the human-all-too-human, with its endless parade of rash conduct, ill judgement and outright folly, they seek to re-connect emotionally with ordinary men and women (King 2008). But what about our emotional interaction in para-social relationships with statistical men and women? One emotional response to images of vulnerable people is certainly to empathize with them (Batson, Chang, Orr and Rowland 2002; Miron, Branscombe and Schmitt 2006). But how deep do these emotions go? You might think that our reactions are solely driven by empathy. Of course, it is commonplace to say that we 'feel' for victims or 'grieve' for their relatives. But is it more common to display these emotions so as to promote a reaction than to wrestle with them ourselves, in private, absent from the culture of observation and auditing? As we noted with the Boston Marathon bombing (2013), it remains an open question whether publicly disclosed emotions are based on genuine empathy with strangers, the visceral recognition of our own vulnerability and mortality, or constitute an exercise in impression management. It goes without saying – but should be said anyway – there is no necessary correlation between emotional exhibitionism and genuine emotional connections (Katz 1999).

We cannot assume that presumed intimacy is a reflection of genuine empathy or altruism. In some cases empathetic display has more to do with emotions built around self-preservation and *amour propre*, i.e. the positive self-image that we wish to project as credible and appealing to people in the sight of others. Identifying with vulnerability is often a good way of acquiring and amassing approval because it automatically conveys the image of *noblesse oblige* and purity of the soul. However, the purity of emotion is mediated through the social filters that help us represent ourselves to others, and for others to represent themselves to us, as valuable, decent folk. As we know from anthropological research, the gift often comes with built-in, unstated assumptions of restitution and expectations of personal payback (Mauss 1990; Godelier 1999). Now it is no part of the argument to maintain that the world is devoid of pure empathy or altruism. Only that things regarding (outwardly) selfless investment in other people's troubles are often not what they seem to be.

Among the most important variable factors that influence emotional intensity with vulnerable people are *identification* and *visibility*. That is, if we feel that we can put ourselves into the shoes of someone who is suffering, and if that suffering is visually communicated, our emotional identification tends to be stronger (Boholm 1998; Joffre 2008; Bradley et al. 2011). Not unexpectedly, psychological research into social reactions of extreme situations shows that our emotions are most intense when we, or a person from our kith/kin network, are directly involved in an incident or episode (North et al. 2008; North 2010). However, again, the nature of emotional identification and projection is not straightforward. We know that visual material of high-impact incidents elicits strong emotional reactions. It is less clear how long these reactions endure and what effects they have in modifying behaviour. For example, there seems to have been a shadow effect with 9/11. Among spectators, levels of sadness, anger and fear were highest where the presumption of social identity with the stricken exists. That is, where spectators were pro-American or identified with American interests they expressed higher levels of emotional identification with victims (Dumont et al. 2003: 1512). Adolescents in post 9/11 studies conducted in London and India reveal unequivocal stress symptoms (Ray and Malhi 2005: 220; Holmes et al. 2007). Again, it is important to stress that our emotional reactions to extreme events are complex. Empathy with the vulnerable cannot be assumed. One-fifth of respondents in the Indian survey reported that the main cause of their anxiety was that a similar fate to the victims of 9/11 might befall them or their country. Similarly, when wider samples of Europeans were shown footage of the 9/11 attack they expressed feelings of fear relating to the threat to self-preservation, especially if they were located in nations openly allied with the USA (Dumont et al. 2003). Their reactions were governed by a 'for whom the bell tolls' moment. They were motivated by the worry that it might be their turn next (if American foreign policy and its effects on Arab militantism are not checked).

Other studies have shown that when nationals are asked to respond to the suffering of foreign victims of national aggression the reaction is often one of distress. But it is not so much distress at the plight of foreign victims or covert fears for themselves as discomfort or disapproval about national policy decisions. When adult Americans were given visual information about the maltreatment of Iraqis at the hands of American and Allied personnel during the occupation, their dominant expressed feelings were guilt and shame about the actions of their country (Iyer and Oldmeadow 2006). This did not translate into the sort of personal anxieties and fears associated with a perceived threat to self-preservation. It came closer to the discomfort of shame. Research among 335 well educated citizens in Sri Lanka – a country with a bloody history of terrorist events – is sobering. Among high levels of sympathy with the USA (91 per cent) and less strong (52 per cent) condemnation of the bombers, nearly three-quarters responded that the United States brought the attack upon itself (Dundes and Rajapaksa 2004: 42). Similarly, visual research has shown that some in the Arab World rejoiced at photographs of the stricken World Trade Center in 2001, on the grounds that it is what the Americans, who are the helmsmen of global policies inimical to Arab interests, deserve, while most Westerners were appalled (Joffre 2008: 85–6). Generally speaking, research into social reactions to 9/11 show that sympathy with the victims and commiseration with the bereaved are part of the mix, but not necessarily ascendant. Intolerance, discrimination, prejudice and indignation directed against the perpetrators, anger, fear, helplesslness, figure prominently in research findings (Argonick, Steuve, Vargo and O'Donnell 2007; Morgan, Wisenski and Skitka 2011; so do greater anxieties about personal safety and security, enhanced patriotism, an increased desire to participate in civic engagement, sadness, fear and victimization (Traugott et al. 2002; Peek 2003; Woods 2011).

The role of visual communication appears to be significant. A study of responses to news reportage of the tenth anniversary of the Chernobyl disaster across five European countries found that emotional engagement and personal concern were appreciably higher when people looked at visual images rather than written texts (Boholm 1998). Researchers speculated that visuals of extreme situations elicit 'positioning power' in the mind of watchers. That is, visual images have the capacity to make risks that are indirect to viewers, by virtue of the magnitude of geographical space or social difference, become 'subjectively relevant' (Boholm 1998: 127). The presumption that there is a uniform reaction to visuals of extreme situations should be firmly resisted (Cohen 2001: 279). In a study of respondents exposed to photographs of people suffering acute trauma and victims of violent death, strong physiological responses, including cardiac deceleration and skin conductance, were registered (Bradley et al. 2001). The responses were found not to be primarily reflections of care and empathy for the victims. Rather, respondents appeared to feel fear arising at the imaginary prospect of what it would be like to find themselves in the predicament of the victims. The concept of positioning power needs to be extended and refined to embrace social variables of identity based in social background, religion, politics and other imbalances of power and influence.

Positioning then, is a matter of recognizing situated actions filtered through sub-fields of cultural capital. It is unclear whether there is any solid relationship between positioning and assuming responsibilities to act. In primary relationships with kith-and-kin networks there are strong pressures and impulses that push individuals into acting to alleviate pain and suffering. In sum, research conclusions show that the empathy displayed in social reactions to extreme situations appears to involve a mixture of empathy, self-preservation and *amour propre*. Certainly, a universal spirit of altruism must not be assumed.

Oddly, there has not been much detailed research on how people translate the expression of strong emotions to representations of extreme situations into the personal *obligation* to do something. Circumstantially, there is reason to maintain that personal obligations do not stretch very far. The expression of emotional sympathy for the pain and suffering of victims is mostly contingent and temporary. Researchers have speculated that the vulnerability of young people renders them especially susceptible to the traumatic after-shock of high-impact events. In the overwhelming majority of cases, behavioural symptoms were of limited duration (Eisenberg and Silver 2011). Among people living close to the attack site, post-traumatic stress symptoms were more intense (especially if they suffered bereavement or belonged to kinship networks where friends had suffered bereavement) (Corner and Kendall 2007; Rosen and Cohen 2010). However, in general, behavioural symptoms subside with time (Shalev 2004: 174).

Comparative research on the psychological consequences of high-impact events mirror the findings on the reactions to 9/11. Work on post-traumatic stress syndrome among survivors of the Wenchaun earthquake, China (2008), the Chi-Chi earthquake (1999), Taiwan, and the Izmit earthquake in Turkey (1999) discovered a concentration of emotion in the immediate aftermath of the event. Among survivors, stress symptoms began to fade after a year. As for those with indirect involvement, the rate of decline was much steeper (Jiuping and Xiaocui 2011; Yang et al. 2003; Livanou et al. 2006).

In the face of the suffering of statistical men and women, people appear to have a strong capacity to get on with their lives and adopt a bystander mentality (Cohen 2001). For the subject of presumed intimacy this issue is significant, since it raises the questions of the moral solidarity or gestural content of social reactions representing emotional identification. On one side, solid identification and presumed intimacy might be expected to translate into an acceptance of the obligation to act. On the other side, emotional identification and presumed intimacy is gestural. That is, it has more to do with exhibitionism and issues of social acceptance and group approval. It draws the line at the obligation to act directly.

Although one common instrument in the gestural repertoire is to articulate votive behaviour, i.e. the strong, but vague undertaking to do something at some unspecified time in the form of donating to charity relief operations. As we saw in Chapter 2, risk and chimerical risk management correlate strongly with high levels of moral density in which the socially included define themselves against the supposed risk posed by the socially excluded. However, the previous discussion strongly suggests that the assumption of a linear, top-down effect that presupposes strong emotional identification with victims in visual images of suffering is unsafe. When we explore concrete forms of para-social interaction with statistical men and women, the range of emotions is very considerable. As with most things pertaining to presumed intimacy, face value is not a reliable guide to what is really going on.

The Ordeal of Kenneth Bigley and the Psychology of Torture

One attempt to examine the under-examined relationship between identification and obligation was researched by social psychologists at the University of Exeter into visuals of a high-profile event involving a media figure in a real life and death predicament that unfolded over a three-week period (Iyer and Oldmeadow 2006). The case in question was heavily featured in the media. At the time it was a matter of intense controversy. On 16 September 2004, British citizen

Kenneth Bigley was kidnapped by the Tawhid and Jihad while working as a civil engineer in Iraq. The kidnappers demanded the release of women prisoners from Iraqi prisons in return for his release. If these demands were not fulfilled, they threatened to execute Bigley and other American hostages. During the twenty-one days of his ordeal, he was videoed, chained in a small cell pleading for the British government to comply with the kidnappers' demands. To millions of watchers he became, so to speak, a familiar stranger. The footage was broadcast extensively on network television and stills were front-page items in national newspapers. The media coverage of the story was not distinguished by its objectivity. Scarcely any attention was devoted to the motives of the kidnappers or the conditions that gave rise to them. Instead the focus was on Bigley's horrifying physical, emotional and psychological predicament. As far as can be judged, the general public reaction seemed to consist of a mixture of indignation and horror. The media amplified this by making strong representations to Tony Blair's government to intervene. The official government line was to repeat the state-approved *mantra* that in no circumstance will the British state negotiate with kidnappers. Bigley's captors tested this resolve by releasing further video footage of him pleading for his life. After the media coverage of the second video, the British government appeared to modify its position. Blair suggested that he might be willing to enter personally into negotiations. In fact, we now know that clandestine attempts were made to negotiate Bigley's release, notably by the Sinn Fein leader, Gerry Adams. They proved to be futile. Bigley was decapitated on 7 October 2004 and the video of the gruesome event was shortly released on the world wide web.

The general reaction of public horror implies strong emotions of presumed intimacy with Bigley and frustration with the position of the government. A good deal of media coverage implied that the public regarded Bigley's predicament as obligating the government to act. However, research into the social reactions in two control groups of students at Exeter University discovered stronger correlations between visual representations of the ordeal and the drive for self-preservation (Iyer and Oldmeadow 2006). Emotions of anger, fear and sympathy were stirred up by the visual material. But they related to one another in contradictory ways. This finding strongly militates against interpretations of presumed intimacy as a uniform relation between representations of a figure at mortal risk and social reactions to the incident.

Questionnaires were distributed while Bigley was still assumed to be alive. Two research groups were established. Group 1 was given a written summary of Bigley's ordeal and a list of options for the British government. Group 2 was provided with the written summary and a series of photographs of Bigley in captivity. The summary was confined to factual data describing his kidnapping, identifying the group who were believed to be responsible and what their demands were reported to be. The gravity of Bigley's situation was made clear by noting that the kidnappers had already killed two (American) hostages and set out their undertaking to execute Bigley if their demands went unheeded. Next, the statement noted that, following the release of recent video footage, and media and public reactions to it, the prime minister indicated that he might be prepared to negotiate. It was explained that this had triggered divisions in the media. The pros and cons of intervention were noted and explained.

Group 1 went straight from the summary to the questionnaire, with no exposure to photographs. Group 2 was supplied with a colour transparency from the *Daily Mail* (30.9.2004) showing five photographs of Bigley in captivity. The first showed him blindfolded, wearing a white-collared shirt. The second showed Bigley and two other hostages, blindfolded, hands tied, sitting on the ground with a masked kidnapper standing behind them appearing to read from a prepared script. In the other three photographs Bigley was shown dressed in an orange, prison-style jumpsuit and chained inside his small cage of captivity. While the photos were not of high quality, they clearly show Bigley to be in a state of acute distress (Iyer and Oldmeadow 2006: 640).

Participants who were shown photographs reported much stronger feelings of fear, rather than anger and sympathy, than the control group who had exposure only to the written summary. This confirms general research on the effect of visual representations of people in extreme situations and emotional reactions to them (Boholm 1998; Joffre 2008). The conclusions are that anxiety for the victim and his ordeal, is a common response. Respondents opposed to war experienced higher levels of fear. Among respondents that expressed anti-war beliefs this was conjectured to be caused by worries that the terrorists will retaliate further against British actions in Iraq. In other words, the fear derives from personal anxieties of risk, not the fate that might befall the captive in the photographs.

Group 2 did not respond with higher levels of sympathy or anger than the control group who received only the written summary of events. This supports general research findings in the field of emotional categorization to extreme events, i.e. that reactions of anxiety and distress are stronger than compassion or sympathy.

Similarly, the control group exposed to the photographs did not express higher levels of anger at Bigley's plight. Again this is consistent with general findings. Anger in social reactions to hostage incidents is directed at photographs of the kidnappers, not the captives. The kidnappers are perceived to be guilty of an injustice or transgression and therefore a legitimate target for disapproval and anger (Iyer and Oldmeadow 2006: 644). Turning to the relationship between visual representation and obligation, reactions of fear and sympathy to photographic stimuli were found to have a marginal effect in enhancing support for negotiation.

What are the policy and strategy implications of the research findings? The force of media moral discipline over the public, especially via the use of photographs of captives in extreme situations, is a key factor in raising support for the obligation of the authorities to intervene. One implication of this is that publishing photographs of victims in hostage situations may benefit kidnappers because it has the effect of expanding public support for the authorities to negotiate. Conversely, the cause of the kidnappers is probably damaged by showing images of the perpetrators, since this correlates strongly with the social reaction of anger (Iyer and Oldmeadow 2006: 645–6). The conclusion that moral violation and injustice in extreme situations is intolerable to public opinion would seem to be comfortably carried.

However, separate research on the psychology of torture draws findings that exist in some tension with the Exeter research (Tarrant, Branscombe, Warner and Weston 2012). It returns to the point that public opinion on questions of moral violation and injustice in extreme situations is heavily influenced by the perception of social identity. When torture is perpetrated by members of their own national in-group it was found to be more acceptable than when it was conducted by members of a group to which they don't belong (Tarrant, Branscombe, Warner and Weston 2012: 513). Moral disapproval of human rights violations seem to be inhibited if torture is conducted in 'the national interest' or for the welfare of the 'in-group' (Opotow 1990: 1). In such cases, 'empathy avoidance' or removed intimacy seems to be mobilized. Some of us reconcile the torture conducted by people with whom we subjectively identify as morally tolerable (Haidt 2001: Nordgren, McDonnell and Loewenstein 2011). Expressions of empathy and intimacy then, are more than matters of genuine altruism, self-preservation and *amour propre*. They are bound up in complex ways with our sense of social integrity and belonging in social groups. The question of moral violation may confirm positive social identity if it is portrayed as justified by the threat that victims pose to the way of life and security of the in-group.

'Sub-optimal' Presumed Intimacy: The Hurricane Katrina Speech

In moments of national vulnerability or global dislocation, we look to our elected leaders to demonstrate that they feel our pain, want to reach out to us and possess a narrative of problem solving that is beyond ordinary citizens to devise or implement. At the heart of this are statements of presumed intimacy by national elected leaders. The *9/11 Commission Report* (2004) makes it incumbent upon the president to declare natural or man-made high-impact events *catastrophes* and take steps to co-ordinate rapid reaction responses to alleviate dislocation and suffering. In the USA the Department of Homeland Security (DHS) (US DHS 2004: ix) defines such incidents as 'an actual or potential high-impact event that requires coordination of Federal, State; local, tribal, governmental and/or private sector entities in order to save lives and minimize damage'. Typically, this involves as a crucial first step, the president expressing empathy and presumed intimacy with those who have died or experienced trauma as a consequence of a high-impact event. This entails the projection of personal emotion through para-social exchange, onto an aggregate of statistical men and women with the purpose of bolstering solidarity and nationalism. The conditions demand that the leader shows resolve, vision in settings that are unstable and grace under duress. This responsibility extends beyond the theatre of American politics. Democratically elected leaders in all countries are expected to grieve over the dead, give solace to the physically and emotionally wounded and provide credible solutions to problems. Their ultimate worth in the eyes of the electorate partly rests upon their powers to marshal compassion in the face of trauma, offer serenity and resolve on cue and steer through viable solutions to completion.

According to Human Relations and Public Relations experts one of the main qualities of successful leaders and opinion makers is establishing empathy and presumed intimacy with the electorate. Of course, since the days of the Ancient Greeks and Romans, the value of spinning intimacy between the leader, the opinion maker and the crowd has been well understood. However, whereas in the original versions of Greek democracy leaders could appeal directly to the people in the *agora*, the bar is raised in societies where exchange is heavily influenced by mass communications and where para-social interaction is an influential currency of exchange. Doubtless, even in addressing the *agora*, advocates deployed tricks of emotional familiarity and supposedly shared sentiments to sway the crowd. In minatory democracy, where, to repeat, the data communicated by the media create a surplus of information and points of view that is beyond the capacity of society to absorb and reconcile fully, the challenges facing elected leaders and the PR/Media hubs around them to achieve consent are precipitate. Para-social relationships with elected leaders constantly brush upon strangers who refuse to regard themselves as 'familiars'. It is not just a question of denying official accounts. It is a matter of millions of statistical men and women who regard themselves as essentially living in different worlds to the pictures framed by the centre. Evidently, for elected representatives to make public claims to speak 'truth' in post-truth democracy concentrates the mind. Showcase emotion proclaims public intimacy on the basis of the absence of firm or even superficial personal contact. Immediately, questions of agenda, tone and purpose arise. How plausible is it for leaders to speak of the victims of high-impact incidents as if they are truly familiar with the personalities and conditions involved? What are their motives in doing so? By familiarity, I do not mean the recognition of the status of fellow citizenship, but the altogether more obscure presence of an affirming recognition of presumed intimacy. That is, the presumption of kinship between the leader and the victims of a high-impact incident, and beyond that, those who identify with the casualties. For the PR/Media hub this produces daunting challenges of exposure management. The deployment of face, sentiment, reputation and formal status can build accelerated intimacy between a leader and the people (Scott and Lyman 1968; Ware and Linkugel 1973; Seeger, Sellnow and Ulmer 2003). It can also go badly wrong. Consider the following recent example, of the leadership response in the USA to Hurricane Katrina (2005).

Generally, it is now acknowledged that President George W. Bush's response to the disaster was 'sub-optimal'. This Category 4 hurricane led to the loss of 1,833 lives and the destruction of nearly two-thirds of coastal housing on the Gulf. The Federal Emergency Management Agency (FEMA) reported that 900,000 households received assistance and 400,000 applied for transitional housing (Olshansky 2006: 147). To put the scale of the disaster in perspective, the area affected stretched for 90,000 miles, roughly the size of Great Britain (Forgette et al. 2009: 32). The crisis exposed fundamental errors in Local, State and Federal provision of hazard mitigation and disaster relief. For example, of sixteen hospitals in New Orleans, only three remained open (Manning 2005). City officials feared that drinking water was contaminated, but lacked effective means of communication to warn remaining residents about potential health risks (Parker and Frank 2005). Some commentators allege that the catastrophe was exacerbated by the desertion of sections of the city's police force (Levin 2005). The ordinary presumption, that is the bedrock of civil society, that reliance upon all ranks of city and state officials is taken for granted was not fulfilled. While it was common for city and state officials to behave impeccably, it was not universal. Katrina produced a social atmosphere in which many felt abandoned and poorly treated by the authorities.

President Bush was on vacation when the disaster struck (Meehan 2006: 85). His initial response was condemned as sluggish, too casual, under-informed and lacking in appropriate levels of compassion and sincerity. Two weeks after the disaster, a combination of media criticism, public disquiet and the threat to Presidential ratings compelled him to make a public statement aimed at damage limitation and repair. The venue selected was Jackson Square in the heart of the French Quarter and one of the most photographed tourist sites in the city. The Presidential PR/Media hub clearly appreciated the political capital at stake by presenting Bush as directly present and active at the scene of the relief operation. The television broadcast was timed at night with the President dramatically backlit by the Disneyesque facade of St Louis Cathedral.

Bush starts by reassuring viewers of his good character and deep faith. He continues, that 'we're tied together in this life, in this nation – and that despair of any touches us all'. The utmost importance is allocated to producing the appearance of compassion and sincerity. 'You need to know that our whole nation cares about you', emotes Bush, as if speaking directly to the homeless and the relatives of the dead. 'In the journey ahead you're not alone.' He pledges $60 billion Congressional aid and reassures viewers that the worst effects of flooding on power supplies, health provision and welfare relief have already been vanquished by decisive Federal, State and Local action. Further, he commits to long-term urban reconstruction. He pledges that the Federal government will 'help the citizens of the Gulf Coast to overcome this disaster, put their lives back together, and rebuild their communities . . . we will do what it takes, we stay as long as it takes'. He proposes providing up to $5,000 for job training, education and child care in the form of 'Worker Recovery Accounts'. Supplementing this, he promises to pass the 'Urban Homesteading Act' to give federally owned property to low-income groups to build properties. In addition, he commits to creating a 'Gulf Opportunity Zone' offering tax breaks, loans and other incentives for job creation. Finally, he undertakes to learn from the disaster. 'We're going to review every action and make necessary changes, so that we are better prepared for any challenge of nature, or act of evil men, that could threaten our people.' The conflation of the risk posed by 'natural disaster' with 'evil men' is a blatant attempt to equate the dislocation produced by Katrina with 9/11. The speech portrays Bush as a rider in the storm, restoring order in New Orleans with the same spirit of dedicated conviction and resolve as the earlier stated undertaking in his Presidency (after 9/11, to make terrorists pay).

Public relations experts argue that the speech used three well established strategies for image repair: bolstering, defeasibility and corrective action (Meehan 2006; Benoit and Henson 2009). These terms require a little elaboration. *Bolstering* refers to displaying companionship with the cause. By delivering the speech from Jackson Square in the stricken city, Bush served notice of his indignation, sincerity and fellowship. Leaving aside the question of the depth of these emotions for a moment, the speech strenuously aimed to identify with the relief process and reach out to victims.

Defeasibility refers to the magnitude of the high-impact event. The ideological object is to establish that the scale of catastrophe is beyond the register of normal human experience. It does so in order to purport that the organization of relief could not have been expected to cope with such unprecedented incidents. 'Hurricane Katrina', explains Bush, 'was not a normal hurricane, and the normal disaster relief system was not equal to it'. So any defects levelled at him for not dealing with it 'optimally' must be unreasonable. *Corrective action* refers to the transparent commitment to relieve distress and reconstruct damaged communities. Bush's commitment to bring in mobile homes, doctors, nurses and welfare provision, and the 'Worker Recovery Accounts' programme and 'Urban Homesteading Act' were designed to make a pact with people to provide a solution from the state-corporate nexus to solve the problem.

Subsequent research has revealed major problems with each of the three pillars of Bush's defence. Bolstering was adversely effected by Bush's casual response to the crisis. The delay in cancelling his vacation and flying to the site of the disaster was regarded by many sections of the public to reveal incompetence and perhaps worse, i.e. Presidential indifference. The suspicion deepened when it was revealed that Bush began cutting funding for the Southeast Louisiana Urban Flood Control Project (SELA), which funded the building, maintenance and strengthening of levees, floodwalls and pumping stations, as early as 2003. In 2005, Bush is alleged to have allocated only $3.9 million of the $20 million requested by SELA for the Lake Pontchartrain and Vicinity Hurricane Project (Meehan 2006). The effect of these revelations was to redefine Hurricane Katrina from a natural, to a man-made, disaster. More damagingly, Bush's policy of under-investment in flood defences and the slow response of the administration to suffering were widely identified as the main culprits.

These charges also eroded the plea of defeasibility. It is now widely accepted that Federal, State and Local authorities failed to respond to warnings from the National Hurricane Center of an impending severe weather front on the Gulf coast before the Hurricane struck. The disaster *was* anticipated by scientists but their counsel was not appropriately heeded (Martinko et al. 2009). Similarly, criticism of the worthiness of the flood defences was in the public domain *before* Katrina hit landfall, and appears to have been brushed aside by all levels of government. It is alleged that Bush's re-election campaign, obsessed with 'the war against terror', diverted federal funds from environmental disaster protection (Parker et al. 2009: 210, 216). Support for FEMA was reallocated to the media-friendly objectives of the DHS (Waugh 2006). In short, between 2001 and 2005, evidence of the vulnerability of the Gulf coast was well established. Under the Bush administration, natural hazard mitigation management appears to have been in serious default, with a clear funding focus on the priority of fighting terrorism (Cigler 2006/7).

Coming to the question of corrective action, this raised issues of entrenched inequality and injustice that required a more vigorous response than mere cash investment. The Black population of New Orleans was most adversely affected by Hurricane Katrina. They suffered the biggest loss of life and the greatest devastation to property. Bush's commitment to corrective action was glib about enforcing positive discrimination to assist them. This led some commentators to submit that inadequate provision of flood defences and the general disaster relief programme were blighted by tacit racism (Levitt and Whitaker 2009). One-third of the population of New Orleans is Black (CensusScope 2006). Most of this population (68 per cent) is concentrated in low-income metropolitan boundaries, especially the low-lying areas most devastated by the floods. It has been pointed out that many Black households were relatively uninsured against flooding. Of the people living below the poverty line at the time of the storm 83 per cent were African-American (Katz 2006). Residents stranded by the floods were portrayed by some sections of the media as potential looters and criminals (Dynes and Rodriguez 2007: 31). Bush's speech did little to correct this. A large percentage of the displaced Black population could not afford to return to the city (Henkel, Dovidio, Gaertner 2006: 105; Miller 2011: 126). Five years after the incident, population figures were only 80 per cent of pre-hurricane levels and 29 per cent of housing stock remained blighted (Comfort et al. 2010). Some commentators allege that the land values liberated by the exodus of the poverty-stricken Black population will be inflated by the construction of more affluent homes for White migrants (Lavelle and Feagin 2006: 68–9). Thus, questions of institutionalized racism, having to do with the distribution of Black populations in high risk areas, were not directly addressed. On top of this, public assistance to achieve the pre-hurricane racial mix in metropolitan New Orleans appear to have been a low priority. In the minds of some realtors the enforced eviction of Black populations from 'under-valued' districts was defined as an investment opportunity to 'up grade' inner-city areas and encourage a new, more affluent mix of dwellers.

The $60 billion of Congressional aid to help the relief effort and repair damaged communities was assigned considerable prominence in Bush's speech. Under the Stafford Act, as revised in June 2006, aid to individual households was capped at $25,000. In addition, the Small Businesses Administration (SBA) offers loans of up to $200,000 to eligible homeowners and up to $1.5 million for property owners of businesses. As a result of these provisions, it is estimated that $88 billion in federal aid has been allocated for relief, recovery and rebuilding. The figure is an historical record for federal disaster relief. However, the balance of opinion among commentators is that it falls well short of providing complete restitution for all uninsured losses (Kunreuther and Pauly 2006: 103). Corrective action has failed in its stated objective of rebuilding communities and restoring pre-hurricane levels of order. Outside the damaged Gulf areas, public knowledge of this state of affairs is hazy. Nationally and internationally, Bush's speech fulfilled its main objective of giving the impression (the gesture) of decisive, positive action.

The Jackson Square oration was exploited and developed as a Public Relations opportunity to restore confidence in the authority of the President. As an event, it was front-loaded to convey compassion and sincerity. There was little commitment to engage in public post-Event monitoring of the ambitions voiced and the undertakings made. In this, the speech and the public communications aftermath, are in-line with emotional management practice by national political leaders of high-impact incidents. The aim is to deliver a fulsome, credible, preferably, televised response to a major dislocation in social order, especially if it involves deaths and injuries. The exhibition of heartfelt emotions is extended to the dead and their relatives. Bolstering is reinforced by commitments to corrective action, whether it be upgrading environmental defences or hunting for 'evil men'. Setting aside the jargon of Public Relations for a moment, this is the engagement of a superficial relationship of kinship between an elected national leader and accumulations of statistical men and women. President Bush did not know the names and circumstances of the 1,833 dead or their grieving families on the Gulf coast. Nor did he need to. The flourish of companionship articulated in public, preferably televisual, settings is all that is required.

However, this is problematic since it raises separate questions about the sincerity of relations of presumed intimacy between the President and the public. Statistical men and women are not personally honoured as material beings who have died or who are in pain. Mainly, they are used by political leaders as pieces on a chessboard. The game is to achieve publicity, capture attention in head tennis and electoral advantages to secure the goal of power. This suggests that moral integrity is secondary to political pragmatism. Work by Frank Furedi (2003) and Barbara Ehrenreich (2009) has exposed the insincerity that is often at the heart of Human Relations Positive Psychology programmes. Other commentators have pointed to the widespread use of lies, hypocrisy and the spirit of mendacity rudely abroad in organized politics (Runciman 2008; Jay 2010). The ascendance of 'positive thinking' in politics, management, education and health care owes much to the positive psychology movement (Seligman and Csikszentmihalyi 2000; Snyder and Lopez 2002; Compton 2005). Accentuate the positive may be defensible in prosaic life situations. Failing a class test, getting points on your driving licence or breaking up with your partner can easily be translated into the uplifting and (never ending) task of learning to become a 'better person'. Choosing positive thinking is less digestible in circumstances of personal extremity. As stated, we are at our most intimate when we are most vulnerable. It is a fallacy to assume that at these times we inevitably surrender to the power of positive thinking. Some of us exercise the option to defer and criticize. Ehrenreich's (2009) case is made from challenging personal experience. Diagnosed with breast cancer, she was appalled by the relentlessly positive messages given by counsellors and self-help groups. Her objection to the ubiquitous and inexorable nature of these messages is not that they are wrong, rather, it is that they are unbalanced. Positive thinking is not the right message for everyone. Accentuating the positive with strangers, and acting as if you know what they are going through in their trauma, not only disrespects emotional boundaries, it also raises inflated expectations that create their own psychological and emotional difficulties if they cease to be corroborated.

Institutionalized Intimacy

The discussion has moved from addressing presumed intimacy as an unplanned quality of social exchange to maintaining that it is also often a planned feature of institutional administration. The reaction of some people to utilize visual representations of individuals in extreme situations to proclaim empathy as a masking device to reinforce the drive for self-preservation or display *amour propre*, and the attempt of George W. Bush's 'Hurricane Katrina' speech to bring audiences into confidence, are part of the same continuum. Of course, there is some blurring between the polarities. To propose that Bush exhibited *amour propre* in identifying with the catastrophe in New Orleans as an instrument of mass persuasion is, I think, tenable. Equally, the display of *amour propre* by ordinary folk in the face of visual data of people in extreme (terrorist) situations may be connected to higher state levels of chimerical risk management. Outwardly (for the purposes of public consumption), these are designed to avenge the victims and their families and friends. A quasi-concealed part of this is to bolster the power of elected leaders. Alternatively, declarations of empathy and votive behaviour that pledge, but do not necessarily deliver, may be related to group acceptance and garnering personal approval. Evidently, presumed intimacy is a significant characteristic of emotional exchange orchestrated around para-social interaction. The multiplication of technological data flows by the deregulation, and expansion of mass communications inflates the illusion of being 'in touch' with the world. At times of crises and emergency, votive behaviour is perfectly capable of invoking the shibboleth, 'team-world' to signify active, informed global citizens who are approvingly differentiated from supposed passive, complacent, misinformed others (Rojek 2013). Again, it is necessary to underline that votive behaviour, in which undertakings to be directly active, to donate or, in some other way, to give assistance, does not necessarily translate into concrete action. As we shall see at greater length in the next chapter, votive behaviour is a common feature of the gestural economy in which an interest in acceptance and approval organizes and directs a good deal of social behaviour.

The discussion reveals something of the variable nature of the emotional capital invested in presumed intimacy. It can hardly be said to exhaust the matter. Much more research is needed into the question of how emotions of presumed intimacy operate in different, variable social settings. In particular, the relationships between presumed intimacy and self preservation, *amour propre*, moral inferiority and vulnerability are likely to be fruitful resources in helping us to understand how the phenomenon works in social settings.

Presumed intimacy is part of *artful* social interaction (Katz 1999: 334; Runciman 2008; Jay 2010). In the last twenty years, allied with the longer established growth trajectory of therapy culture, the expansion of multi-channel television, social networking and the internet has greatly contributed to enhancing the significance of self promotion and exposure management in everyday life. Head tennis is the corollary of para-social interaction. The media provide us with an inexhaustible, essentially fractured, stream of data about the private lives of celebrities and the private conditions of life among the statistical men and women of which we are a part. They are 'fractured' because their content is subject to due editorial process which must take the ratings war as part of its essential considerations. Yet sociologically, what is striking is that the old division between private and public life has buckled. At bottom, this is a matter of the radical recasting of popular conceptions of presence and co-presence. To elaborate: Traditionally Western philosophy, and Western life relations in general, are etched deeply with the concept of presence. Heidegger (1978) famously argued that Western culture has privileged metaphysical presence/being. That is, it identifies being human with a self-enclosed, embodied, thinking subject, which is understood to be ontologically separate from other objects in the world. According to Heidegger, this is objectionable on two counts. Firstly, it misrepresents the embedded, interconnected nature of sentient beings with other beings and material objects. Secondly, it perpetuates an orientation to the world which is primarily instrumental. On this logic, the world exists to be exploited and consumed, rather than cherished and respected. Because of this, Heidegger concludes, the metaphysic of self-enclosed presence has been a disfiguring influence on the content and form of human relations. Our concern here is not with the nature of this disfigurement, but with his proposition that the metaphysic of self-enclosed presence is privileged. Supportive evidence to back up the proposition that a metaphysic of presence has been cardinal in Western development, can quickly be marshalled from a number of sources. For example, neo-liberals make no bones about regarding the individual as the primary unit in society. Individual liberty is the central thrust of this philosophy, and the basis for the corresponding principle that free and open markets are necessary to enable individual initiative and enterprise to flourish (Harvey 2007). Similarly, work on therapy culture and cold intimacy leaves readers in no doubt that in caring, healing relationships, and romance, the basic unit of analysis in the West is the individual (Furedi 2003; Illouz 2007).

Yet this work also forcefully suggests that the Heideggerean notion of the metaphysic of self-enclosed presence is out of touch with contemporary life. It is no longer plausible to hold that Western life is predicated in the metaphysic of presence, since so much of our ordinary lives are now lived in the consciousness of co-presence (and absence). We are conscious mostly in a vague sort of way of the conditions of the statistical men and women that inhabit the world with us, but when they are out of sight they are also (mostly) out of mind. At least at a performative level (in the case of celebrity culture), and perhaps at more fundamental levels, private life is now, more than ever before in the modern world, lived in public. To be self-enclosed or self-absorbed is associated with repression and witholding. It is the basis for disapproval and censure. Therapy culture and para-social interaction make a virtue of being open, relaxed about your feelings and willing to share private thoughts and emotions. In the process the logistics of personal disclosure have changed (Furedi 2003). The engagement with the public disclosure of private circumstances makes the union of watchers more willing to yield selected or random private aspects of their lives up to public scrutiny. The unwatched life may indeed be in the process of becoming generally labelled and understood as invalid or insufficient (Gamson 2011: 1068). The move to multi-channel broadcasting after deregulation in the 1990s, and the spread of the internet, social networking sites and webcam has transformed conventional divisions between domestic space, the hermetic self and the outside world. It goes without saying that knowledge and engagement with co-presence (and absence) is variable. The economically advanced nations of the West have technologically communicated data flow about life with others that are of greater density and layering than what prevails in, say, mountain tribes or desert dwellers. Further, within these nations important distinctions need to be made with regard to the relationship of stratification with access to data. It is reasonable to assume that individuals who are employed in the knowledge/information/communication sector will have the self-image of being more 'in touch' with statistical men and women than someone who works in a factory or on the land. Be that as it may, nearly everywhere, individual existence is now mediated through technologically informed relations of co-presence. Watching and being watched through mechanical devices is now an ineluctable part of the human condition.

At this point, it is tempting to recall Rhodes's (1998) concept of 'panoptical intimacies' to bear upon analysis. As we will see in the next chapter, the concept is most useful in the analysis of presumed intimacy in total or quasi-total institutions where the Orwellian over-tones in the concept of 'the panopticon' (that Foucault borrowed from Bentham) are replete. Yet it is fair enough to maintain that the concept can be applied to general para-social relationships that promote social consciousness of co-presence. For in being connected to data flow about celebrities and statistical men and women we are under an obligation to be affected, i.e. to mobilize and exhibit affect. Leaving aside for the moment, the thorny question of the ratio between sincerity and gesture in cases of the exhibition of affect, this obligation is clearly part of the dialectics of watching and being watched that is at the heart of panoptical intimacy. In watching and being watched we look for signs, and strive to give evidence, that reinforce group acceptance and approval. Para-social interaction and presumed intimacy are interlocked. It is the massification of these everyday life qualities in society that is the real target of Ehrenreich's (2009) fusillade against positive thinking, one key aspect of which is presumed intimacy. In her view, institutions codify and managerialize the gestural economy of conditioned, provisional intimacy by com-mercializing and standardizing emotions. They cannot accomplish this task unless presumed intimacy is accepted as a normative feature of social exchange. This is the first step in commercializing and stan-dardizing affect. The second step is devising programmes of manage-ment that enlist the machinery of presumed intimacy and harness it to traditional goals of line management and accumulation. Upon these foundations reside the machinery of panoptical intimacy. This demands that we consider what the gestural economy is, and how it operates.

9

The Gestural Economy

At the outset, we must settle upon the meaning of the term 'gesture'. For in English the term carries more than one meaning. The interpretation pursued here follows the work of Adam Kendon (1997: 109, 204). It treats gesture as a form of social utterance. That is, it is a type of extra-verbal communication designed to convey intelligible cognitive intentions (Gullberg 2006: 104). Some gestures are spontaneous, such as raising the palms of the hand in defence against attack or shaking the head to indicate disagreement. Others, probably the vast majority, are value laden in the sense of using motor activity to signify cognitive intentions. In social exchange they are used to convey a wide range of emotions and social relationships including friendship, admiration, joy, fear, enmity and disapproval. Examples include a series of 'symptomatic movements' such as crossing fingers to represent good luck, the thumbs up sign, a wave, a bow, a wag of the head, the peace sign, eyebrow raising, posture, blushing, blinking etc. (Erkman and Friesen 1969; Bull 1987; Hall 1968). They are also commonly used to refer negatively to something as being regarded as light-weight or insincere (Kendon 2012: 311). As in 'he made the *gesture* of an apology' or 'the government made the *gesture* of helping'. It is this meaning of the term that is of particular interest in a study of presumed intimacy. As a social condition, the latter proposes that we make gestures of emotional identification with people to whom we are directly and indirectly connected, as an ordinary part of relating socially to others. An important corollary of this is the proposition that visible gestures may bear no relation to what the gesture is apparently designed to mark. For example, I may express support for unknown victims of an earthquake in Turkey or Japan. But the gesture is not necessarily based upon genuine emotional identification. My real cognitive intention may be to garner acceptance and approval in the social networks of which I am a member. In usage of this type, gesture refers to an inferior form of communication because it is based in a strategy of impression management in which real emotion and the representation of emotion are disconnected. We might introduce the term *artful presumed intimacy* to refer to this form of agency. This is the sense in which Obama and Bush used presumed intimacy in their respective signature responses to the Boston Marathon bombs (2013) and the distress in New Orleans and Louisana, following Hurricane Katrina (2005). More generally, it is this application that is of particular interest to the subject of presumed intimacy. Manifestly, in cases of artful presumed intimacy what is conveyed is not sincerely intended. Emotional persuasion and aesthetic impact are to the fore in motivation. Typically, artful presumed intimacy applies votive behaviour designed to fabricate underlying cognitive intentions that would otherwise be a source of disapproval or censure in the group. As such, it disguises hidden motivations and objectives. In the business of presumed intimacy, and in our social relationships with others generally, it is wise to appreciate that gesture is no less integral to language, than words, phrases and sentences in communicating meaning (McNeil 1992: 2). Gestures 'fill out', or render cohesive, verbal communication (Gumperz et al. 1984: 3). In order to be expressive, gesture has to be visible and recognized as a meaningful component in communication. The economy of gesture is already apparent. A well-chosen gesture can convey immediately what it would take scores of words to say. Thus, in particular settings, gestures possess high cultural capital. This translates into the value of expediting cognitive intentions in social interaction or disguising them to conceal or dissemble one's real purpose in the communicative act. Extra-verbal communication can reinforce, contradict or sidestep verbal interaction. They can also be employed to advance power over others by means of the display of emotional identification and votive behaviour.

Speech Illustrators and Emblems

Broadly speaking, gestures fall into two types: those that are coterminous with speech and those that are independent of speech. The former are known as 'speech illustrators'; the latter are known as 'emblems' (Matsumoto and Hwang 2013: 2). Speech illustrators and emblems may be further divided into two types. Improvised gestures take the form of on-the-spot visible, extra-verbal utterances (Kendon 2012: 313). These are manifest or latent properties of all social exchange. Their meaning derives from the setting and particulars of the embodied exchange. The second type refers to a common form of sign language that is part of socially shared communication systems (Sandler 2012).

Every culture has evolved a repertoire of symptomatic movements that are partially designed to reinforce distinctions of social inclusion and exclusion, acceptance and disapproval.[1] In this type of extra-verbal communication, it is most useful to think of gesture as an adjunct of culture and power relations. This leads directly to the issue of gestural economy. For although culture consists of representations, codes and values, it is also crucially, a market of meaning. The value of verbal and extra-verbal communication depends upon the setting of exchange and the intentions of interlocutors. Further, it is an imperfect market in which strata of interlocutors have different, variable access to influence outcomes because they apply verbal and extra-verbal communication from positions within a social hierarchy of power. Mention of a power hierarchy, alerts us to the links between verbal and extra-verbal competence and habitus (Bourdieu 1977). In the gestural economy, assets are a reflection of habitus (and therefore power relations). The value of an asset is linked to the field of the gestural economy in which communication occurs. It is in this sense that it is useful to refer to economic, cultural and political parameters in gestural exchange.

This proviso is vital because it directs reflection to the institutional settings and boundaries in which verbal and extra-verbal communication are positioned and unfold. Within organizations and social institutions, gestural economy is an important component in the ratio dynamics of power relations.[2] Gestures set the tone of how people see themselves, how they are viewed by others and how they go about things with each other. Before coming to consider this at greater length, it is important to acknowledge that some gestures appear to be transcultural. For example, Delaporte and Shaw (2009: 39–40) note that crossing index fingers is taken as an injurious gesture in many cultures. According to them, the gesture first appears in a painting by Hans Holbein in the fifteenth century as a sign of hostility addressed to Christ by the Jews. In the twentieth century it has retained the non-verbal meaning of injury. For example, in Alsace, in the East of France, it is considered an insult which is generally accompanied by mockery. In Provence, in the south of France, it is used by children to signify the closure of intimacy. In the Yemen it is a mark of enmity. In Japan it expresses disagreement or negative judgement. Crossing index fingers represents antagonism or negation, while positioning index fingers side by side signifies amity and concord. In Naples, and other parts of Italy, parallel positioning communicates complicity, equality and friendship. In the Middle East it indicates unity. In the culture of the American Plains Indian it means 'same' (Delaporte and Shaw 2009: 40). Different cultures develop different speech illustrators and emblems. These derive from their ways of living and history. They are markers of status, occasion, ritual, bounds and proscribed conduct (Gellner 1988: 206).

Having acknowledged that some gestures are transcultural (even if their meaning is not uniform), it is appropriate to return to the main theme at hand, which is the relationship between presumed intimacy and gestural economies. Speech illustrators and emblems that trigger the presumption of empathy and identification are, of course, not confined to the social relationships that we have with persons. Presumed intimacy also applies to social relationships with animals, positional offices, social processes and commodities. These can be perfectly well expressed through para-social relationships. The sheer scale of relationships with statistical men and women call upon us to devise and exhibit speech illustrators and emblems of presumed intimacy with respect to impersonal social criteria so long as they display due propriety to the standards of equality and fair transactions. We may go further, the application of speech illustrators and emblems to probity, accountability and transparency in impersonal, duly appointed bureaucratic offices and processes is a basic feature of democratic government compared with dictatorial, personal or clan-based types of rule.[3] Congealed and open labour expressed to produce the impression of probity, accountability and transparency is fundamental to the logic of managed democracy (Wolin 2008). I propose to explore this question at greater length via three case studies. To begin with, I will consider speech illustrators and emblems of presumed intimacy in two institutional settings, i.e. where these phenomena are directly inter-laced with recognizable means and ends. The first case study examines the gestural economy and relationships of presumed intimacy in a typical organization of traditional society. It is an ancestor of Goffman's (1961) 'total institutions'. The practice of *kowtow* in the Qing Court in China reveals the roles of central authority in the personalized figure of the Emperor and the rule of precedent in the power structure. In this case, presumed legitimacy is concentrated in the occupant of the highest office in the traditions of the power hierarchy, i.e. the position of Emperor. The ultimate power of the Emperor resides in the lavish respect attributed to his office by the power hierarchy. However, it is his interpretation of his position that influences the ratio dynamics of power in the Court and the pattern of behaviour organized around speech illustrators and emblems that relate to presumed intimacy.[4]

The second case study focuses upon a democratically defined audit process in which strict diligence to the values of accountability and transparency are key undertakings of legitimacy. Here presumed intimacy rests with the purported openness and fairness of due process. The specific case I have selected is the British Research Excellence Framework (REF). In Weber's (1968) model, accountability and transparency are designated benchmarks of legal-rational, bureaucratic rule (founded upon codified rules and strict attachment to impersonal office). The REF sets great store in the virtue of propriety of due process, i.e. peer-reviewed assessment of research outputs. speech illustrators and emblems in the communication process are subject to the ends of value for money and public interest. Some commentators have read them as a facade for the clandestine centralization of academic practice and the retrenchment of traditional rights of academic freedom (Collini 2012; Sayer 2015). Be that as it may, the REF offers great dividends for anyone interested in the undisclosed elements of presumed intimacy under managed democracy, i.e. the hidden political undergrowth behind the shiny surface of transparency, probity and common justice (Strathern 2000). *Prima facie*, the REF is as far away from 'total institutions' as it is possible to get. But this is only a superficial impression. The protocols and procedures enacted in the name of transparency and accountability conceal a fist of iron.

The third case study rather turns things around. It moves from a consideration of presumed intimacy in respect of personal office and due process to another form of the phenomenon, i.e. presumed intimacy with institutions of consumption that hold and accumulate prestige through settings of exchange and types of transaction that are not officially, or legally, sanctioned. In other words, it is a form of presumed intimacy that derives from critically departing from sanctioned protocols and procedures. The point of considering this form of behaviour here is to demonstrate that presumed intimacy is not merely an instrument of managed democracy. It is also a characteristic of social relations that are gesturally located in opposition to managed democracy. There are many instances in ordinary social life in which this type of conduct might be studied. Fiddling, taking illegal drugs, illegal downloading and planning terrorist activity, are all areas of life that deviate from normative rules of behaviour and absorb significant social resources. Presidents who claim to 'feel for' and pray for the victims of a terrorist incident use the same baseless metaphors of belonging and identity as those who see and narrate themselves as pitting resources, or even dedicating their lives, around the war against 'infidels' and 'kaffirs'.[5] Think of society as an intricate landscape of hills, mountains escarpments, valleys and ravines, in and around which people are born, recognize bonds, make emotional commitments and go about their business, shot through with bore holes, caves, ditches and tunnels where a counter life of bonds, commitments and activity is located and perpetuates. There are obvious relations of co-dependence here. The counter life cannot exist without the sanctioned life. The former draws its ends and means from the latter. It goes without saying that the ends of the counter life are highly variable. They extend from resisting order, beating the system, to getting something for nothing. What needs to be emphasized is that they all come with a complex array of gestural distribution, emotional allegiance and status distinction. It is remarkable that in many cases the presumed intimacy involved in this form of conduct has been normalized. Consider the widespread acceptance among office staff of pilfering from the stationery cupboard or the extraordinary social and psychological assumptions made in the polarization of 'the 99 per cent' against the 'one per cent'.[6] To study the range and complexity of these forms of conducts would require a different book. Here I will confine myself to address the world of counterfeit luxury commodities. In this world presumed intimacy is the key to status differentiation among social groups. Under the conventional relations of the general price mechanism consumers that sport *Cartier*, *Louis Vuitton*, *Rolex* etc., affect to command high status in the sight of others. In this study my focus is not upon these strata. I am interested in the experience and rationale of those marginalized by reason of *property disqualification* from legitimate participation in the relationships involving the exchange of luxury goods. The issue here is why individuals whose socio-economic and political servitude is symbolized by the world of luxury goods, should show any interest in exhibiting markers of involvement with this world? And further, what forms of connection or intimacy derive from making these choices? It might be expected that property disqualification will lead naturally to the rejection of this world on the grounds that it relicts inequality and exclusion and further, boosts the super-inflated economic values and pretentious standards of luxury status. An intricate, multi-layered counter culture of speech illustrators and emblems surrounds the consumption of counterfeits. The trade is, in fact, organized around a peculiar moral double-standard. While those who engage in the consumption do not generally believe that they are committing a crime (so their behaviour may properly be described as 'gestural'), they simultaneously believe that the producers and vendors of these goods ought to be punished (Norum and Cuno 2011). Yet why should consumers debarred by reason of property disqualification, develop networks of presumed intimacy around exhibiting imitation luxury goods that, moreover, are very often, obviously fake, rather than produce and develop allegiances designed to overcome the foundations of power that legitimate the inflated values of the luxury goods trade and perpetuate property disqualification?

The three examples examine forms of attention capital, exchanged and invested in relations of status acquisition and maintenance. They constantly pose the question of how social order is produced and reproduced, while also pointing to the issue of how meaningful collective change might be possible. Further, they raise the matter of not only an alternative politics in which the discipline of orthodox relations is either modified or abandoned, but the precise nature of a whole labyrinth of alternative realities that subsist within general, orthodox relations of ontological attachment and identification sanctioned by managed democracy. Gestural economies suggest that to read social relations in terms of the old politics of capital and labour, i.e. engineering compliance and mobilizing resistance, is superficial. Old political slogans based in doubtful premises of ontology now have a hollow ring. Who today really believes that 'workers of the world unite' and have nothing to 'lose but their chains'?[7] Certainly, not workers in the managed democracies of the West. In the UK, most of Europe, the USA, Australia and Canada changes in the labour market since the early 1980s have weakened the role of occupational groupings in the conduct of everyday life. In the US private sector union membership fell to seven per cent in 2009 compared with a high of 29 per cent in the mid 1970s (Stone 2011). In the UK trade union membership peaked in 1979, when it stood at 13.5 million (55 per cent) of the workforce, by 2010 it declined to 6.5 million (26 per cent) (Department for Business, Innovation and Skills 2013a). In other words, nearly three out of every four workers in the UK has nothing to do with trade unions. In Europe, between 1980 and 2008, the steepest rates of decline in Union density were in Austria, Portugal and the UK (Kelly 2012: 354). The casualization of labour has been particularly significant since it has undermined the strength of collective bargaining. In his account of organic solidarity, Durkheim (2013) surmised that occupational groupings are pivotal in building and maintaining moral density. For they constitute a mid-way point between the ontological realities experienced by most people in market society (the experiential and behavioural issues

arising from the necessity to engage in wage labour) and the constitutional and legal summits of the state. Yet nearly everywhere in
Western-type managed democracies occupational groupings organized in the form of trade unions are in recession. Most of them have
insufficient capacity to protect their own sectional conditions and
terms of the labour contract, let alone provide the sort of society-wide
moral cover that Durkheim envisaged as a requirement of organic
solidarity. Yet at the collective level the demand for moral sensibility,
and the collective yearning for moral density, unmediated by the
preferences of the corporate-state axis and the landscape gardening
of the PR/Media hub, remains.

In the rent left by the retreat of union power a variety of multivalent fronts, counter-posed to, and, in some cases, inimical, with
sanctioned procedures and goals have flourished. They are a tribute
to a free society. For only in very extreme cases of incitement to
violence or religious hatred are they suppressed. As Keane (2009)
correctly notes, under minatory democracy, freedom is one of the
central values that is most tenaciously guarded. At the same time, the
freedoms of expression of the many different interests juxtaposed to
the managerial elite of the corporate-state axis constitute a disaggregated mass of interests. Unlike the corporation and the state,
which are defined by composite purposes and acquisitive ends, critically juxtaposed disaggregated interests point everywhere and
nowhere. Being free to be different is entirely compatible with the
ends of the managerial elite of the corporate-state axis because it
produces gridlock. Effective opposition requires leadership, composite administrative discipline and persuasive collective goals that have
the collective force to subsume the divisions of particularism and
convert them into common purpose. Minatory democracy, which is
an adjunct of the greater managed form, makes a *cause célèbre* of
freedom and justice but fails to generate effective oppositional leadership, composite oppositional administrative goals or collective ends
capable of overcoming particularism. It has however, led to a gestural
economy where the currency of multivalent dissent, opposition and
resistance is unprecedented. Digital society has aided and abetted the
process by making connections with people who are geographically
remote seem socially and emotionally near. Never has a 'can do'
approach to life seemed more real or compelling. Arguably, a new,
more artful politics has come to pass. It is distributed along many
fronts which, incidentally, greatly complicates the business of forging
solidarity. It is not concerned with collective organization to transform society, but with mining and tunnelling spaces in society in
which counter lives that represent meaningful critical departures from

institutionalized mores and protocols are lived. At the same time, the global endeavours and interests of the managerial elite remain serenely intact and are openly prospering. It is difficult to reach any other conclusion than that the price for the tolerated gesture of dissent is submission. Many critics of climate change and global poverty resort to the metaphor of a global system that is *out of control*. In fact the endurance of the system is remarkable testimony to the tenacity of privilege and the skill of the managerial elite in permitting freedom to dissent to combine with business as usual.

In some accounts of managed democracy, the concept of hegemony is used to capture this process (Gramsci 1971; Hall and Jacques 1983; Hall 1988). It conveys the contingency and intransigence of negotiating rule under managed democracy very well. Gramsci, in particular, provides an invaluable perspective on how freedom is *positioned* in ways that present no fundamental threat to the system. This perspective also bargains for the logical possibility that in certain historical and social circumstances, positioning may fail to do the job.

Revolution and system change is forever a potential outcome in the compact of hegemony. But so is using celebrity, the temporary occupation of public space and some forms of 'responsible shopping' to expose the misdemeanours of the system. The rub is that gestures of resistance have minimal capacity to wield or promote effective, meaningful social change. You do not fcuk the system by buying your clothing at *FCUK*.[8]

10

Institutional and Counter-Institutional Gestural Economies

In common parlance we think of intimacy as something personal that grows through positive affect. In total and quasi-total institutions, presumed intimacy is administrative and implemented centrally; that is, it is an element in the narrative of corporate 'belonging'. A variety of goals exists in the administrative portfolio. They include loyalty, propriety, deference, *esprit de corps* and compliance. Historically, as the case of *kowtow* in the Qing Court illustrates, accountability and transparency were secondary to the gesture of ultimate obedience. As a general rule, the ideas of equality and openness in presumed intimacy should be handled with caution. Managed democracy may make a virtue of accountability and transparency but it does so to serve hard, often clandestine, veiled organizational motivations. This is one reason why the intimacy that it generates is often personally experienced as spurious and inauthentic. Yet its adhesive quality in allowing business with each other to go on in economically and politically productive ways ought not to be under-estimated. Presumed intimacy is a requirement of effective leadership, composite administration and tenable collective ends. The localized gestural economies that flourish in discrete institutional and counter institutional settings demonstrate how gestures of trust operate to smooth over social relations, even when the article of trust is, as it were, secretly and discretely mistrusted. Perhaps nowhere is this more evident than in the case of the counterfeit, i.e. where a fake is used to articulate supposedly 'solid' social and cultural foundations. The declaration of presumed intimacy is an important element in gestural economies. As with all economies, the open currency of exchange may not bear a sound relation to real value. However, social equilibrium requires the open currency to be respected and honoured. In the gap between appearance and reality an extraordinary complexity of gestural speech illustrators and emblems have gained currency. The three cases here refer to Chinese Court Society, Academic auditing and cultures of consumption based around counterfeit goods. Although localized, all three yield insights into the general mechanism of presumed intimacy in the social order and its role in the gestural economy.

Kowtow

Kowtow (or ketou) refers to the ceremonial practice in the Chinese *Qing* dynasty of displaying respect to an Emperor by kneeling, prostrating and bowing the head to the floor (Hevia 2009: 212). It is a system of codified ritualized gestures designed to demonstrate reverence for the Emperor, elders, dignitaries and ancestors. *Kowtow* is a gestural articulation of the power hierarchy in the Court. In this sense it is a strong example of what Rhodes (1998) later called, panoptical intimacy. For observation and regulation of conduct take place in a total institution centred on the absolutism of Court hierarchy. In addition, the ceremony of transparency is designed both to validate and conceal a system that aims to consolidate and reinforce central, ultimate power. The gestural economy and presumed intimacy that it supports operates on a thin line between transparency and dissimulation. It is best seen as a form of power, since the object of the ceremonial gestures is to require submission to the will of the Emperor *sans* the naked use of verbal aggression or physical force. In the eighteenth and nineteenth centuries, when encountered by visiting Westerners schooled in the values of the Enlightenment (above all, to honour science above metaphysics and dogmatism), *kowtow* was a source of bafflement, indignation and disapproval. Westerners associated it with obeisance, vassalage, tyranny, suzerainty and the so-called 'general backwardness' of the East.[1] Kneeling was equated with submission. Presumed intimacy here rested, and turned, upon knowing your place. Being closer to the earth, was linked symbolically with dirt, and bracketed with decomposition. Conversely, standing upright was immediately appreciated as the hallmark of the hail, free man. John Quincy Adams denigrated *kowtow* because he saw it as violating the right of individuals to be regarded as equals. He deplored the 'arrogant and insupportable' pretensions of the Chinese Court (Hevia 2009: 221). Far from upholding standards of civility, he regarded the Emperor and his Court as adopting the cloak of intrigue with resort to mischief and skulduggery. Adams even speculated that the first Opium war was not about opium at all, but about the *kowtow* (Adams 1909–10). By complying with the *kowtow*, Europeans and Americans berated themselves for compromising Enlightenment values of individualism, freedom and equality. Abhorrence against the practice was also deployed for the conventional purpose of articulating colonial privilege. For example, in 1792 the first British ambassador to China, Lord McCartney, refused to *kowtow* before the Qianlong Emperor on the grounds that his prior allegiance lay with the British Monarch. His refusal is generally thought to have damaged the British delegation's efforts to achieve key trade objectives. *Kowtow* is part of a gestural economy that may be described as incommensurate with the Enlightenment paradigm. But is it right to associate it with submission, backwardness and abject servitude?

In his analysis of the *kowtow* in the Qing Court, the historian James Hevia (2009), reveals it to be a complicated affair. For a start, *kowtow* is not simply obeisance to an Emperor or compliance with vassalage or suzerainty. It is more properly understood as an honorific gesture that consecrates traditional authority. It is made not so much to the individual who is Emperor but to *what* the Emperor *represents*, namely the bridge between the material world and the world of deities. In the culture of the Qing Court, deities are respected as active Gods. That is, they are believed to have direct power to intervene in human affairs. In this respect, some are acknowledged and revered to be more powerful than others, but all have active honorific status. As such, visible gestures of respect and deference to them is a type of presumed intimacy designed to curry favour and invite intervention. The order of the universe was believed to be mirrored in the formal proceedings of the Qing Court. The Emperor, his advisers, other dignitaries and foreign ambassadors obeyed protocols of positioning and bodily comportment designed to symbolize the complex system of rights, duties and responsibilities traditionally distinguished and respected by the power hierarchy. The gestural economy of the Court was intended to ratify the presiding culture and enjoin respect. The strict rules of social positioning and bodily movement, which included correct body posture, respectful movement, dress codes, how and where to arrange letters and papers on desks, that Europeans schooled in the tenets of the Enlightenment found to be so aggravating, were set down to fortify tradition. Acts of communication were mediated through a chain of command. This differed in subtle ways, according to the rank of guests and supplicants to the Court and the Court's interpretation of their significance to the interests of the Emperor and his advisers. The *Comprehensive Rites of the Great*

Qing set down variations in ceremonial protocols according to rank e.g. princes, officials below the Emperor, emissaries and so on. For example, in official Imperial audience, the emissary seldom entered the Emperor's hall, let alone stood before the throne. Instead he was required to kneel at the threshold of the hall, having previously performed three kneelings and nine bows in approaching this space. The Emperor communicated by relaying questions through the director of the Board of Rites and a translator to the emissary. The reply was conveyed along the same route, but in reverse order (Hevia 2009: 217–18). On special occasions, such as tea ceremonies and banquets, the emissary was escorted into the Hall by the director of the Board of Rights to stand before the Emperor. Positioning and bodily movement are again codified by protocols which delimit options and prohibit deviation. In addition to deportment and body posture, questions of spacing between the Emperor and the guest or supplicant were expected to be strictly observed. However, while the codes of behaviour were rigid, they did not debar modification when circumstances required. For example, the Emperor permitted Lord McCartney to waive the *kowtow* and directly deliver a letter from George III into the hands of the Emperor (Lo-Shu 1967). McCartney was allowed to restrict his gesture of presumed intimacy to one kneeling and a slight bow of the head. The Qing Court granted ceremonial latitude because a visit from the representative of the English King was unprecedented. It was judged to portend benefits of trade and military questions that could not be brushed aside.

As the nineteenth century drew to a close, the *kowtow* ceremonial seemed increasingly anomalous before the tide of rationally governed global diplomacy and trade. In international diplomacy the current was flowing in the opposite direction, i.e. towards mutuality, reciprocity and the rationally defined rights and responsibilities of the cult of the individual described by Durkheim (2013). Positioning and acceptable body posture became regularized transculturally by the Congress of Vienna (1814–15). This set the benchmark for polite diplomatic behaviour. Definitions of sovereignty, diplomacy and commercial exchange were delineated and codified. Thus, ambassadors were now required to follow a standard pattern of behaviour. In turn, Courts were expected to honour this order. When entering the presence of the sovereign, emissaries were required to bow three times, be appropriately respectful in verbal communication, place written communications directly into the sovereign's hands, and retreat as they had entered. Kneeling on one or two knees was discouraged. Bowing the head was retained, but only approved when done from a standing position. Increasingly, China seemed out of step with the rest of the world. Eventually, the Boxer Protocol of 1901 (between the Qing Dynasty and the Eight-Nation Alliance) imposed global standards of courtly and diplomatic behaviour upon the Qing dynasty. This undermined the foundations of traditional *kowtow* practices (Hevia 2009: 224). At the same time, some aspects of *kowtow* which had been so deeply abhorred by Europeans and Americans in the eighteenth and nineteenth centuries, such as bowing, were redefined as acceptable traits of polite civil society, for the power base behind them was recognized to be unequivocally crippled. Although negative connotations did not vanish, in some circles gestures of bowing, kneeling and deference were partly redefined as signs of good manners and breeding (Fairbank 1942).

The *kowtow* then, is not an insufferable relic from the days of carts, metaphysics, spears, bows and arrows. It is a nuanced and sophisticated network of power with concrete ends and purposes of social representation and positioning in clearly delineated institutional settings. Although it is hierarchical, it carries real obligations of presumed intimacy between all ranks acknowledged by the Court.

In shifting from the issue of relations of *kowtow* in the Qing Court with emissaries to the significance of *kowtow* in dealings Tibetan Buddhist representatives Hevia (2009: 232–4) introduces a new layer of complexity into the analysis of the phenomenon. All relations between the Qing Court and guests were designed to symbolize asymmetries of power and status. Needless to say, the asymmetries were not of the same scale or intensity. In dealing with trade emissaries, the Emperor and his advisers might assess the scale of appropriate intimacy according to the projected economic benefits to the Court, or the generosity of the gifts from the foreign King or Prince brought by his representatives. In the case of relations with Tibetan Buddhist representatives, a coupling of dual mentorship prevailed. The lamas sought strong patronage from the Emperor so that their community of monks were protected and assisted to go about their business of proselytizing their version of Buddhism to the world. The Emperor was also bound to the lamas by a relationship of mentorship. The lamas were acknowledged teachers of the Emperor. They imparted the 'esoteric tantric rituals' that were meant to achieve Buddahood in a single lifetime and consecrated leaders as universal sovereigns (*cakravartin* kings) (Hevia 2009: 233). Lamas therefore possessed the spiritual power and favoured status that required the Court to acknowledge them as teachers of the Qing Empire. The Emperor sought their loyalty, but stopped well short of acknowledging parity in the teacher–pupil relationship and wider balances of power. The lamas may be worthy of more respect than mere earthly petitioners and guests of Court, such as, say, the Mongol Khans. Notwithstanding this, their proper place was recognized to be that of loyal inferiors.

Reverence and respect in the Qing Court was measured out in ratios according to rank. Guests and petitioners were demanded to exhibit presumed intimacy in mechanical, carefully proportioned measures as if they were beads on an abacus. Presumed intimacy was initially, and primarily, shown institutionally to the *office* of the Emperor and the Court rather than to individual characters and personalities. This did not prohibit personal bonds from developing. However, institutional protocol was the indispensable prelude and immoveable setting for inter-personal exchange. Until the Boxer Protocol forced China to comply with European and American standards of diplomacy and trade, the Qing dynasty operated as a semi-hermetic institution, setting the norms of approved public intimacy. It was an imperfect market form of gestural economy since the value of gestures did not generally obey laws of supply and demand. The latitude given to Lord McCartney was very much the exception to the rule, which is why it became such a controversial talking point in *Qing* society. In general the gestural economy of *kowtow* was based upon the precedent of tradition and the rule of the Emperor and his retinue. In the long run opening up the country to trade was the downfall of the institution. The parameters of Qing gestural economy were revised by commerce, trade initiatives and the accumulation of surplus wealth. Visibility was a perpetual conjuring act against concealment. You might say that it is always thus in semi-hermetic institutions in which panoptical intimacy prevails. Nods, bows and whispers call the shots. What is going on beneath the surface is what counts. This is partly why McCartney, Adams and other emissaries and guests were so tenaciously suspicious of *kowtow* in the Qing Court. That is, they were not clear about the nature of the hidden political and economic agendas that underlay the outward appearance of elaborate courtesy and respect. Yet their discontent was procedural rather than personal. It centred upon the presumed intimacy bound to an office rather than the person who occupies the office. It was not so much the practice of *kowtow* but the institutional machinery that supported and justified it that was condemned as humiliating and obsolete.

It might be thought that this sort of wariness would have no place in institutions that champion independent thought and free speech. What would be the place of nods, bows, whispers and panoptical intimacy in, for example, a modern university? Surely here, intimacy among peers is a respected practice rather than a vacuous presumption. The apparent accountability and transparency of the REF in Britain would seem to confirm all of this. But just as study of the *kowtow* reveals intricacies that are not revealed at face value, examination of the niceties and presumed intimacies of the REF quickly shows that all is not as it seems.

The British Academic Research Excellence Framework (REF)

Without doubt, universities have a long and proud tradition of free speech and intellectual autonomy. While academics are expected to obey the protocols of open discussion they have traditionally been at liberty to ask difficult questions which may be disagreeable to vested interests. The liberty to develop a breadth of vision that is not answerable to power and to bring objectivity to bear upon public issues are the main reasons for introducing and guaranteeing the academic tenure system. In the absence of tenure, the danger is that academics may come under strong pressures to conform to state-corporate requirements and neglect to address issues that are currently defined as controversial or marginal, yet which may turn out to be of great value to society in the long run. Tenure thus supports a particular form of presumed intimacy in which belonging and reciprocity derive from being acknowledged to be located in a culturally privileged public space. Here labour is dedicated to the free pursuit of knowledge and answers to the needs of common interests. As with *kowtow* the relationship of respect resides in the traditions of the post and the social institutions that support it rather than the occupant. Society invests faith in trained, certified strata to pursue knowledge freely and to answer to truth rather than power. A number of social expectations and relationships that can be broadly grouped under the heading of presumed intimacy derive from this principle. In no particular order of precedence, it is linked with elevated collegiality; discretion in the research process; high-trust relations with media and society; respect for principled dissent; a light touch from administrators in planning and executing research; and freedom to communicate outputs in whatever form and whatever location is deemed by the researcher to be fit for purpose. In the bargain, considerable freedom is ceded to academics. In fine, tenure is a relationship of faith through which society offers academics protected space to ask questions that may be embarrassing or difficult for vested interests. By and large, researchers have been permitted to use their own judgement in selecting the subject of their research endeavours and allocating time and other resources to research projects. Under tenure, research that is only of interest to other scholars, or has input to teaching programmes, has enjoyed support. Scholarship is thus, explicitly and unapologetically tied to the goal of the disinterested pursuit of knowledge. Tenured positions allow researchers to go anywhere, subject to appropriate ethical provisos, in the search for truth. As such, academics are assumed to have a greater degree of freedom than say a researcher working for a corporation, a church or a state department. Fidelity to the principle that academic labour is understood to be a professional requirement and research output is regarded to be in the service of society rather than the advance of personal or group ambition.

An entire sub-economy of gestural speech illustrators and emblems has developed around the principle of tenure. It has to do with the rules of behaviour that govern practice and disclose possibilities, informal norms and sanctions of behaviour, unspoken and unwritten reciprocal understandings of productive time-use, the value of reflection, respect for dissent and rigorous, theoretically informed argument. This economy cannot be defined as 'political' in any advanced sense; nevertheless, by the same token, it cannot be counted as 'unpolitical' since it presupposes definite, passionately held notions of the common good. Academics have always understood that research is part of the job. In addition, the traditional appointments procedure has been based on the expectation that part of labour time will be spent in self-determined research activity. The idea that a candidate would be told what to research by an appointments or management committee would be seen as an unwarranted intervention by the employer. The convention is that academics should have discretion in this matter, so long as it remains within ethical protocols.

But what does the disinterested pursuit of knowledge mean in an age of cultural relativism, i.e. where the only accepted designation of 'society' is a collection of mostly disambiguated interests (Furedi 2003)? What price truth when everything is seen as subject to decentring and deconstruction?[2] The attack upon tenure is widely interpreted as a neo-liberal assault against a particular form of state privilege (Collini 2012). Actually, it has more to do with a profound crisis in the status of academic knowledge. Under postmodernism truth is understood not to be independent, but irretrievably entangled with discourse and power. Nor is truth fixed or immoveable. As Martin Jay (2010: 14) puts it, this involves 'a new respect for rhetorical tropes and *hermeneutic suspicion,* as well as the deconstruction of univocal meaning and the liberation of texts from the control of those who had authored them' (emphasis mine). Two consequences follow from this. Firstly, academic research is recast as prey to the same exaggerated claims and power struggles, as every other walk of life. Secondly, since 'univocal meaning' is negated as a meaningful concept, cultural relativism is confirmed. As a corollary the notion of free, independent space in which labour is expended for the common good is subject to the discipline of 'hermeneutic suspicion'. The demand to restrict or abolish tenure follows in short order. For if it is accepted that knowledge is implicated with power, the whole business of tenure looks outmoded, elitist, and those who proselytize it, holier-than-thou. Once this pass is reached, difficult questions of tenure begin to be asked. Why should academics be permitted to maintain that their work transcends interest, when interest is now seen as ubiquitous and unavoidable? What price the concept of 'society' under cultural relativism where only the force of interests is recognized to prevail? It is because postmodernism sees interests everywhere and truth nowhere, that accountability and transparency have emerged so strongly as regulative devices for management. The presumed intimacy, sanctioned by custom, which permits academics to claim that their labour is conducted in the disinterested pursuit of knowledge is now put to the scythe.

Tenure continues to be offered and defended in the USA and Canada. Australia and New Zealand have employment contracts that recognize the right of 'continuing employment'. This arrangement is not as bullet proof as tenure, but it broadly protects traditional academic freedoms. In England, Wales and Northern Ireland, tenure was abolished by the Education Reform Act (1988). Since then, there has been marked intervention from central government and business into teaching and research in British higher education through the Quality Assurance Programme and the Research Assessment Exercise (RAE), (now the Research Excellence Framework (REF)). A number of rhetorical devices, such as value for money, public interest and benchmarking are deployed to legitimate the increase in the ratio of central control. Significantly, state intervention is mediated through academic peer review bodies. This affords the public impression that state influence is carried through an amicable accommodation with academic appointees. In reality, these programmes are state-funded audit exercises designed to achieve 'quality' for consumers and higher engagement in 'user-oriented research'. In this study, I want to concentrate particularly upon the impact component of the REF. I contend that at the level of state funding and state strategy in matters of higher education presumed intimacy has been replaced by hermeneutic suspicion.

The Higher Education Funding Council for England (HEFCE) introduced the REF, which replaced the RAE, in 2008. The chief aim of the new arrangement is to produce robust performance indicators of research excellence that can be applied to assess international benchmarking and guide funding decisions. Attached to this is a commitment to reduce the administrative burden of the research exercise on institutions, and the financial cost to government (compared to the costly RAE) and to promote equality and diversity. Although the REF mirrors the RAE in many respects, one new element stands out and continues to attract a good deal of concern among academics. The REF guidelines allocate approximately 25 per cent of the rating to 'impact'. The latter term is defined partly in terms of *extra-academic* performance results. Impact, in the traditional sense of intellectual influence upon other academics, or the content of teaching, is explicitly *excluded*. Instead the term is confined to the results of research upon 'the economy, society, public policy, culture and the quality of life'. Not surprisingly, within many parts of the Academy, this version of impact is regarded as controversial. Stefan Collini, a leading academic in the humanities, has argued that the REF definition of impact makes research over-dependent upon the requirements of the corporate-state axis (Collini 2012: 168–77). At a stroke, it pre-judges nearly all of the work in the Humanities, and much that occurs in the Social Sciences, as ineligible. For example, it would presumably regard a book on the contemporary political relevance of the poetry of Arthur Hugh Clough or the meaning of metaphysics in the writings of Auguste Comte as something that is of interest only to fellow scholars or teaching needs. But this is to display a capricious logic. To take only the most material element here, books or articles on Clough or Comte's understanding of metaphysics do not appear by magic. They require a publisher to make them available to the public. Academic publishing directly employs editors, marketing staff, production staff and sales personnel. Indirectly, it employs bookshop and online retailers, transport suppliers and warehouse staff. In the UK, it is an industry worth £4.7 billion (academic books and journals combined) (Publishing Association 2014). Conceivably, advocates of the REF might argue that the exercise already covers this by referring to outputs that improve 'the quality of life'. Against this, it is as plain as a pikestaff that this vague, multi-dimensional concept ('the quality of life') is only included in preferred outputs, as a residual category. One can imagine the sort of debates that come up in panel meetings when research of this type is discussed. For the REF, the real meat in output is academic research that supplies the needs of business, society, public policy and culture. Critics would say that the requirements of business and public policy are paramount.

The reason for casting an eye over the REF here, is not to make the case that academic work should be free from audit or accountability. On the contrary, output is a perfectly valid consideration that is of interest both to academics and society. Rather the reason for ruminating upon the REF is to submit that it seeks to replace a culture of presumed intimacy among specialized labourers in knowledge that has proceeded for generations by dint of unwritten rules of 'ambience' and conventions of 'common expectations', with one based in state-defined, codified rules and performance indicators organized around the notions of 'transparency' and 'accountability'. A particular mass evacuation from erstwhile, and hitherto respected conventions of trust is at play here. Funded research is automatically defined as 'good'. For why would anyone wish to invest in activity that is economically or civically unproductive? Conversely, a question mark is inserted over unfunded research. If it is incapable of raising funds, why should it be sanctioned? The Higher Education Funding Council presents the REF as providing a scientific means for assessing the quality of research in UK higher education institutions. The criteria of assessment are purported to be rigorous and measured against internationally approved standards. The exercise is also portrayed as open and fair, since every university has the right to submit, and each department is measured against every other department over which the REF has investigative authority (and panel appointees are peers). Sub-panels, consultation exercises and pilot studies give force to the seriousness and impartiality of the exercise. In theory, no department is excluded, and the public has the satisfaction of knowing that the state is ensuring value for money in the public purse.

Yet the REF also sets a number of other hares running that raise grave doubts about the so-called 'scientific' nature of the exercise. For Strathern (2000), a notable critic of the audit culture, performance indicators designed to achieve transparency produce an unbalanced, distorted picture more suited to the clandestine requirements of central administration than the discipline of science. The outward commitment to acquire an objective yardstick for measuring performance is merely a gesture. It fails to capture the countless, qualitative issues (never formally recorded), that are built up through slow processes of accretion, that are the crux of success or failure in research. For Strathern (2000), research cultures consist of both tangible and *intangible* resources which build cultures of research intimacy in which ideas are allowed to gestate, often in relative silence. The latter are not necessarily intangible in perpetuity. They are intangible *in time*. Not all unfunded ideas bear fruit immediately, or even in the short or medium terms. One might even venture that most come to nothing. But having the ideas in the first place, and allowing them to mature and flourish or perish without external monitoring or testing, is an essential part of the research process. Strathern (2000) goes further. The success of research partly depends upon putting some forms of communication in abeyance, i.e. beyond the reach of auditing. Anyone who has actually done research knows that it does not consist of a hive of perpetual measurable inputs and outputs. A lot of vital research development occurs subconsciously over periods that cannot be pre-determined or usefully measured. To subject them to a discipline of quantified measurement is beside the point. The trick lies in establishing a decentralized ethos of activity that is conducive to producing research energy capable of yielding fruitful ideas and trains of thought. In a word, Strathern (2000) believes that a *Eureka* moment cannot be produced by committee. It requires an ethos of trust and latitude that is conducive for breakthroughs and advances. Most of this is not compatible with audit culture because it occurs tacitly, experientially and internally. The distorting aspects of REF auditing is compounded, because research assessors and civil servants see their main obligation as ultimately lying with the external agency of auditing (the state) rather than the members of the institution undergoing investigation. Extraneous norms rule the process, rather than the particular norms constitutive of the research setting (Furedi 2003: 107). What Strathern drills into them, is the incapacity of the REF to grasp and elucidate the intangible, but indispensable, intimate components of research culture. Outwardly, the REF honours the general, long-standing presumption that effective, creative thought depends upon a union of faith. What the REF tries to do is to make this union transparent by rendering faith accountable through robust performance indicators. In Strathern's view, why this is impossible, and why she describes transparency in this case as 'tyranny', is that productive ideas and outputs cannot be accomplished without *experiential* and *tacit* knowledge built up over extended durations of time. Hence, the REF achieves a misleading view of organizational reality.

What Strathern is getting at is what experts in labour relations used to call the importance of 'trust relations' in settings of labour (Fox 1974). That is, co-relations between labourers in a work setting that are, so to speak, 'beyond contract' and not subject to reliable 'performance indicators'. What Fox (1974) has in mind is not so much the immediate small group issues beloved by work performance analysts that can be measured, such as respect for one's fellow workers, commitment to the goals of the workplace, camaraderie, pride in work, etc. Rather, what he is alluding to is the *perception* or *sentiments* of the relevance of these issues in a context determined in its fundamentals by questions of power, status and privilege that are superior to the norms of the work setting. This assumes that within an existing form of funding arrangement (and society) in which power is perceived to be concentrated in the hands of the state and corporations, the probability is that trust relations in research settings are likely to be skewed. In what way 'skewed'? In the case of the REF, misgivings and objections centre upon the validity of research outputs (books, articles and grants); the imprecise nature of bibliometric indices; the undue influence of the state-corporate axis in determining the selection of research projects; the apparent downgrading of research that is of interest only to other scholars or which is primarily of relevance to matters of teaching; and, more generally, the end of regarding higher education as 'a public good, articulated through educational judgement and largely financed by public fees' (Collini 2012: 178). The notion that the REF gets at the truth of what is going on in research is sullied by the huge administrative burden of panel members to read the full range of departmental outputs (the four best publications of eligible academics), the part-time nature of the work and the relatively low levels of financial reward offered to them. While panel members are selected to represent the full range of specialist knowledge in a discipline, there is bound to be a mismatch between some types of research output submitted and panel expertise. In such circumstances, the suspicion that panels cut corners is surely justified. It is because academics see a disconnect between the claims of competence in panels and the full range of research outputs submitted to them that many see the whole exercise as flawed.

Moreover, since REF submissions are driven by the need to have four measurable outputs over an arbitrary, externally dictated timeline, the value of research is redefined to mean what counts for the REF. Yet it does not follow that what the editorial boards of academic journals or monograph publishers regard to be excellent is, in fact, of value to the discipline or society. Truly cutting-edge research may seem as irrelevant to academic specialists as it does to the public. Derek Sayer (2015) quotes the telling case of the Nobel laureate in Physics, Peter Higgs (2013). Higgs received his prize for his 1964 prediction of the Higgs-Boson particle. In 1964, *Physics Letters*, the prestigious international journal of the CERN, rejected his groundbreaking paper on the grounds that it is 'of no obvious relevance to physics'. Higgs was working at an edge so cutting that the dull vision of expert editors of the journal failed to recognize the originality of what he submitted. The claims that the REF makes to accountability and transparency are indeed, gestural. They would carry more water if the meetings were open to the public and if appeals against the rankings were permitted. But the REF closes its doors to the public and treats panel rankings as final.

What then, one might ask is the purpose of the project? The Research Exercise is legitimated by the argument that investigation is designed to help organizations take stock of the real quality of the research being conducted under their remit. The weighting on measurable research output appears to satisfy the organizational and public requirements for hard data. It therefore makes strong gestures to the broader goals of organizational accountability and state responsibility. Yet because the weighting on measurable output is actually an over-weighting which privileges quantifiable outputs and obscures vital qualitative issues of experiential co-operation and tacit knowledge, it operates as a politically useful fabrication rather than a *bona fide* disclosure of reality. The public is persuaded that something 'scientific' to test the value of academic research for society is being done. This answers to public concerns about value for money in the public finances. In addition, bench-marking provides vice chancellors with a convenient rationale to prune or terminate areas of research that score low ratings and are therefore seen as 'underperforming'. Decisions about the worth of some departments, the value of investment and the wisdom of cost-cutting departmental mergers follow in short order (Sayer 2015).

So there are a number of aspects of presumed intimacy at play here. Most obviously, the intimacy that society has presumed in relation to permitting discretion in academic research is neutralized by supposedly superior claims to public accountability and value for money. One must never forget that the public is not directly canvassed in the crucial matters of goal setting or spending. Democracy requires power to be ceded to elected representatives and contractually bound civil servants. While there is a form of presumed intimacy here, in as much as the public assumes that these mediators will act on their behalf, most of the real decision making is clandestine. This applies directly to the deliberations of the REF itself. To repeat, it is a *closed* exercise and its decisions are *final*.

Further, the guns of 'hermeneutic suspicion' which are turned on academic labour must also be aimed at the labour of workers in the corporate-state axis. Politicians, corporate executives and civil servants are hardly immune from cultural relativism. To be sure, there is good reason to maintain that they are among its most decisive exponents in shaping the climate of national opinion. The obvious antagonisms and immediate objections that these conditions bring to bear on the real inclusiveness and transparency of the exercise are outwardly sublated by the incorporation of academic peers in the assessment process. This gestures to well-respected ideals of partnership and reciprocity, but it also disguises that the agenda of the exercise and its consequences are entirely determined and controlled by the state (in cahoots with what business wants). Moreover, it conveniently side steps the thorny issue that panel members may harbour undisclosed prejudices about the worth of research activities that happen to conflict with their own professional investments. The rather elaborate machinery of consultation exercises, pilot studies, focus groups and scoping-out sessions that the REF supports decorates the cake. They are gestures that play well to the appropriate interest of society in openness and fair play. But the proof of the pudding is in the eating. The real object of the REF is to achieve a stealthy incursion into the academic research process to ensure that resources are diverted and concentrated to comply with business and state interests.

Counterfeit Commerce

Conventionally, the price mechanism under capitalism, and the transactions that follow from it, are understood to be founded upon good faith and trust (Jacoby and Chestnut 1978, Rust and Oliver 1994). Production, exchange and consumption presuppose shared intimacy with the principle of fidelity that purportedly governs all financial transactions determined by the general price mechanism, without favour or deviation. In ordinary transactions trust resides in the copyright of patent of the commodity and the legality of the exchange relationship. It is safe to say that without these shared presumptions commercial transactions would be severely disrupted. Important consecutive factors in buttressing trust are commodity packaging and the setting of retail exchange. Even online purchases have to be conducted through 'recognized' servers if their legitimacy is to be acknowledged. Orthodox transactions then, are predicated in a version of presumed intimacy around the authority of the general price mechanism and probity in exchange relations, i.e. the vendor is trustworthy, the object of exchange is authentic (protected by copyright) and the consumer has resort to acknowledged, independent, regulated rights of redress. Yet everyone knows that a counter world operates in the shadow of orthodox exchange. Counterfeit commerce refers to the illegal production, exchange and consumption of commodities. It maintains a global society of producers, retailers and consumers bound together by nothing less than property theft. The economic value of the trade is considerable. It is estimated that one in ten of all global consumer transactions involves counterfeit goods (Wiedman et al. 2012). By flagrantly flouting copyright and patent laws, you might think that counterfeit commerce renders exchange forfeit. Nothing could be further from the truth. Moreover, it is concomitant with a coherent system of widely recognized, status differentiation, speech illustrators, emblems and a supporting culture of presumed intimacy. Counterfeit goods violate trademarks and also infringe copyrights or patents associated with the brand. The most commonly counterfeited goods are luxury items: cigarettes, alcohol, branded apparel, jewellery, perfume, sunglasses, bags and purses. However, no product is immune. The trade extends to pharmaceuticals, automobile and airline spare parts, electronics and software. Market share is often very considerable. For example, it is estimated that no less than 35 per cent of the packaged software installed in personal computers worldwide is counterfeit (Taylor, Ishida and Wallace 2009: 246). Counterfeit commerce thrives in settings such as car boot sales, flea markets, illegal high street kiosks and other familiar retail settings. It is also a well-established part of the wholesale goods sale, especially (and worryingly) in the market for spare parts in aeroplanes, trucks, automobiles, software and pharmaceuticals (Aldhous 2005; Bird 2008; Guin et al. 2014; Mele 2004). With the rise of the digital economy, the internet is becoming fundamental to the global profitability and expansion of the trade. It is estimated that 'cybersquatting' (using a domain name that capitalizes on an established brand) accounts for 1.7 million websites (Wotherspoon and Cheng 2009: 32).

Counterfeit commodities are illegally produced, illegally retailed and illegally consumed. Yet the trade's producers, retailers and consumers behold this state of affairs as no valid impediment to exchange. A different kind of consumer judgement about the justice of transactions appears to be operational here. It supports an immediately recognizable ethos of presumed intimacy around the illegally 'present' commodity. In the market for luxury and other expensive goods, where the price mechanism is widely viewed and commonly accepted to be rigged in favour of copyright and patent holders, resort by the economically disadvantaged to accumulate illegal counterfeits, is a perfectly acceptable part of everyday life (Rutter and Bryce 2008; Wall and Large 2010; Treadwell 2012). What is ultimately most remarkable about the trade is the tenacity with which the great majority who are separated on economic grounds from the world of luxury and high priced commodities, crave even the most questionable social attachment to the world of luxury goods sanctioned by the general price mechanism. Counterfeit consumption is a two edged sword. Outwardly it undercuts the general price mechanism, and therefore constitutes a critical departure from conventional relations. Simultaneously, and contrarily, it seeks to acquire the status of involvement with relations of luxury consumption with which the consumers concerned would otherwise be debarred by reason of property disqualification, i.e. it is a form of hyper-consumerism (Hayward 2004). For the most part, exchange relations are thoroughly parasitic.

The counterfeit trade may damage the margins of multi-national producers of luxury goods. But it does not seek to replace or transcend the luxury gap set by the general price mechanism. Counterfeit commerce seizes the cultural capital attached to luxury and expensive commodities which are legally protected by copyright and patent and transfers them to duplicates or knock-offs which are sold at prices that are within the price range of ordinary consumers.

Despite the common location in irregular retail settings, it is a mistake to see the trade solely in terms of improvised exchange points and opportunistic transactions. The normalization of counterfeit commerce in everyday life is linked to the growing audacity and sophistication of retail exchange relationships. For example, Yang (2014) reports that in 2011, an entire 'fake' Apple store stocked with counterfeit Apple goods was discovered in the southern Chinese city of Kuming. The store featured the trademark Apple glass spiral staircase and was manned by employees dressed in blue T shirts with Apple nametags. Counterfeit commerce has always been unapologetic in pursuing effective pricing policies and credible brand design values to bring luxury goods into the pockets of ordinary consumers. The fake Apple store in China and the development of branded kiosk trading suggests that some suppliers are stepping up the retail process by imitating the retail arrangements of legitimate brand suppliers in order to enhance the authority of the counterfeit. Consecutively, supply chains to wholesale purchasers of pharmaceutical, computer and spare parts industries, especially in the developing world, are expanding. Supply gateways built around wholesale, clandestine deals and furtive exchange points evolve their own rituals of *omerta*. At every level, from production, through to exchange and consumption, intimate presumptions of social inclusion and social exclusion accrete around these economic transactions. *Omerta* and gestural economies of group belonging may make the difference between smooth trading or criminal liability.

Parallel changes in the organization of retail exchange relationships have boosted counterfeit commerce. The internet provides multiple new opportunities for identity theft, credit card fraud, hacking and, because servers can change sites at will, the non-delivery of goods and services (Newman and Clarke 2003). E-commerce sites like *eBay*, *Craiglist* and half.com, have not developed effective regulatory mechanisms to guarantee the same standards of probity in exchange relationships that consumers expect from exchange relationships in regular trade settings. The faith and trust in the orthodox price mechanism and the validity of transactions attached to it therefore comes with a complete counter-world of phony prices, affixed to fake commodities and illegal transactions. It is a mistake to think that counterfeit commerce is an abnormal feature of consumer culture. In short, it is a routine feature which extends over all age groups, ethnicities and is gender neutral (Rutter and Bryce 2008: 1158).

Counterfeit goods may be divided into two categories. *Deceptive counterfeits* are knock offs carrying a legitimate brand name which hoodwink consumers into believing that they are buying the real thing. *Non-deceptive counterfeits* are fake, branded commodities that are designed and recognized as inauthentic by specific consumer information points, such as quality, purchase location, price or materials used to make the product (Juggessur and Cohen 2009). In both cases, the imprimatur of the brand conveys authority with retailers and consumers. The consumption of counterfeits is indissoluble from questions of surplus and scarcity under capitalism. Price advantage and value for money are the chief motivating factors for consumers to engage in the purchase of knock-offs (Kim and Karpova 2010: 80; Hendriana, Mayasari and Gunadi 2103: 63). Deceptive counterfeits are a means for the economically disadvantaged to symbolically participate in cultures of social exclusivity, despite the non-deceptive counterfeit commodity being recognized by all and sundry as an inferior fake. Kitsch culture possesses its own repertoire and hierarchy of social distinction. The deceptive counterfeit is the material foundation for much of these relations. As Brunner (1994) argues, the authenticity of a product is based not only in copyright law, but in interpretation. However, while politicized readings of the consumption of non-deceptive counterfeits may apply to some sections of the consumer market it begs the question of why this has not precipitated a truly destabilizing social movement of anti-consumption capable of challenging the *status quo*. To be sure, in the *Occupy* protests of 2011–12 that colonized public space in many of the world's biggest cities anti-consumerism was a signature theme.

Occupy was not successful in toppling the general price mechanism or the vested interests behind it. More mundanely, while counterfeit commerce challenges many of the central principles of capitalism, notably copyright and fair trade, it is in no real sense genuinely oppositional. It does not seek to overturn or replace the price mechanism. Rather it aims to dismantle the operation of the general price mechanism so as to enable wider participation in social exclusivity. The emphasis is upon gaining competitive price advantage and accumulating status. This interpretation is strengthened by the observation that the exchange of counterfeits is associated with elements of carnivalesque culture. Buying a fake luxury good is celebrated as a small way of beating price inflation in the pharmaceutical, spare parts and luxury goods sector. Culturally speaking, the consumption of fake commodities bearing luxury brands which are known to be knock-offs is inherently gestural. The consumption of fake *Rolex* watches or *Louis Vuitton* handbags allows consumers who are excluded or marginalized from the luxury goods market to symbolically join it, while, at one and the same time, providing the means to comment upon the vanity and price inflation of this market.

The most obvious victims of counterfeit commerce are holders of copyright and patent. Trade loss to European companies in the clothing and footwear market is put at E1,266 million; E55 million in the perfumes and cosmetics sector; E627 million in toys and sports commodities; and E292 million in pharmaceuticals (Blakeney 2009: 7). US Border control reports that the top 5 brands counterfeited are *Louis Vitton, Gucci, Microsoft, Nike* and *Prada* (Kim and Karpova 2010). All of these figures offer nothing more than a rough and ready guide to the extent of counterfeit commerce since, in the nature of things, non-deceptive fakes are never recorded. Viewed from the standpoint that equates counterfeit commerce with a blow against the system, this damage to corporate margins is rightful retribution. Anti-capitalist sentiment is a powerful force. It exploits and develops presumed intimacy. For social groups that regard themselves to be subject to social exclusion or marginalization tend to develop concentrated emotions around the principle of social inclusion and antagonism against the mechanisms of property disqualification. However, in flaunting the morality of the general price mechanism producers of counterfeit commodities plays fast and loose with separate moral codes. The World Health Organization estimates that ten per cent of global medication consists of counterfeit products, with an increase of 80 per cent between 2000 and 2006. In 2001, Chinese authorities investigated 480,000 incidents involving counterfeit drugs and attributed 192,000 deaths to counterfeit drug use (Chang 2009:

1516). The absence of independent regulators means that fake pharmaceutical commodities carry significant risks of toxicity, morbidity and mortality. While all consumers are equally at risk, the danger is concentrated in the lowest quartile of Western consumers and in the developing world (Newton et al. 2006: 602; Healey 2012). Aldhous (2005) reports that research by the Ministry of Health in Cambodia into a sample of antibiotics and pain killers available on the market discovered that 3.5 per cent consisted of below 60 per cent of the labelled active ingredient. In Haiti (1990), eighty-nine children died after taking fake cough medicine containing anti-freeze; in 1996 more than 2,500 Nigerians reportedly died after receiving a fake meningitis vaccine (Kontink 2003: 46). Counterfeiting is also well established in the spare parts trade of the motor and aeroplane industries, with obvious implications for public health and safety. In the USA the Federal Trade Commission (FTC) estimates that counterfeiting in the auto industry accounts for $3 billion turnover and, globally, $12 billion (Mele 2004: 16). The US Federal Aviation Administration (FAA) submit that two per cent, or 520,000 of the 26 million aeroplane parts installed each year are fake (Wotherspoon and Cheng 2009: 32). The hazard posed to consumers arising from the unregulated, counterfeit trade need hardly be stressed. There are also implications for employment and public finance. In the USA the counterfeit trade is thought to be responsible for the loss of 750,00 jobs a year; in New York alone, counterfeit sales are estimated to account for £23 billion in turnover, i.e. a loss to Taxation authorities of $1 billion. The counterfeit trade avoids generating tax revenues and therefore deprives the Exchequer of income to invest in public projects.

Despite the risks of morbidity, counterfeit commerce is an entrenched and growing component of the capitalist world economy. Price advantage is obviously a motive behind its prolific growth and rude health. However, the popularity of non-deceptive counterfeits suggests that the exchange process carries a chic quality. That is, it communicates social differentiation around presumed intimacy with getting something for nothing, and achieving competitive price advantage which compliant consumers can never attain. As to exposing the inflation and vanity of the luxury goods trade, the popularity of non-deceptive knock-offs suggests that there may be an element in some sectors of the trade in unmasking the pretensions of capitalist exchange and the injustices of the general price mechanism. However, there is little evidence to support the view that counterfeit consumption constitutes a radical collective push against capitalism. When all is said and done the trade in non-deceptive counterfeits remains steadfast to the essential principles of consumer culture. The trade is informally institutionalized wherever there are urban population concentrations. Moreover, the rise of the internet is clearly expanding and drawing more people to dabble in circumventing the general price mechanism. Strong relations of righteous indignation derive from beating the system. These are not attached to labels of deviant conduct let alone criminal behaviour. Counterfeit consumption affords consumers who break (unjust) laws of supply and demand with positive social status and presumed intimacy. It implies that consumers who observe copyright and patent law across the board are mugs. However, while it is tacitly critical of the system that supports the genuine price mechanism, it is entirely parasitic and produces no coherent set of practices and aims to transcend the status quo.

11

Nuda Veritas

What may we conclude from the three case studies of gestural economies and the associated phalanx of speech illustrators and emblems?
There is no way of absenting gestural economies and presumed intimacy from social life. All claims to do so are groundless. In both
formal and informal institutions presumed intimacy is a basic con-
stituent of most social relationships. To some degree it is a necessary
part of civic culture. What the Romans called *nuda veritas* (the naked
truth) is above what managed democracy can endure. There is too
much call for double-entry bookkeeping, not to mention an indefati-
gable delight in playing games. Hence, the practice of presumed
intimacy is something with which we have all learned to live. It is
hard to envisage how one can get along with others without exhibiting the public face of general empathy, solicitude and some form of
identity for statistical men and women with whom we otherwise
maintain standards of principled non-communication. But these qualities of healthy democracy have been degraded by programmed
institutional accelerated intimacy designed to attain acceptance,
approval and in countless other ways, to curry favour on tap. This
has created the conditions for votive behaviour and principled non-
communication to grow like bindweed. It does not follow that real
intimacy has vanished from daily life. Notwithstanding this, the
ubiquity of salaried accelerated intimacy through the labour of the
caring, professions, education and other sectors of the service
economy, makes questions of trust and reliability permanently fraught
and insistent. From relationships with over-worked general practi-
tioners working in community Health Centres to the prime time

celebrity para-confessional, consumers have half a mind on what calibre of truth, sincerity and accountability is really being set before them. Many social categories make the business of exhibiting presumed intimacy *de rigueur* not merely to soothe anxieties about medical or work conditions, but also to forestall searching questions about the legal basis of the exchange relationship (Gamson 2011: 1062). Medical, educational and other forms of salaried service work are beset with the need to be vigilant about the threats of entrapment and litigation. Consecutively, para-social relationships with statistical men and women further chronically confuse the emotional boundaries between emotional nearness and remoteness. We have access to wider forms of data than ever before and superficially, have emotionally satisfying relations with familiar strangers via the global media. But the illusion of cybernetic togetherness, through the media and the para-social union of watchers that it supports, plus the event diet concocted by the media, cannot overcome the inner reality of cybernetic solitude. The latter is at the emotional heart of market-based forms of organization. In the end, under the market form, we live and die, alone together. The conscious and subconscious realization of this dogs all attempts to foster and harness presumed intimacy as an affirmative force.

Is there any way out? Bryan Turner (2006) holds that biological vulnerability is something that humans share regardless of cultural diversity. He posits vulnerability as the foundation for a new theory of human rights. Since all of us are locked into a precarious, finite existence, the localized challenges and responsibilities that we recognize may conceivably, be elevated into a socially inclusive, superior settlement of rights that might make ordinary social relations become more mutually considerate and genuinely intimate. At the core of this is reinvigorated civic engagement. Under managed democracy it suits vested interests to permit dis-involvement, bystander mentality and a fixation with consumerism, to rule the day (Cohen 2001; Wolin 2008). Turner's (2006) emphasis on the universal predicament of vulnerability points a way forward to actively develop secular forms of brotherhood (and sisterhood). This train of thought is of the utmost importance for anyone interested in the question of making presumed intimacy a lively, positive, affirmative force in moral life. For one cannot acknowledge common vulnerability without showing and expressing intimacy. To acknowledge that we are all vulnerable is to concede that we all share the same species predicament. The acceptance of intimacy is therefore theoretically, the other side of the coin of species vulnerability. The devil is in the detail. In managed democracies the scale and volume of relationships utilizing presumed intimacy in public and professional life as a technique to acquire acceptance, approval and manage consent has metastasized (Wolin 2008). Routinely, speech illustrators and emblems of emotional famil-iarity are employed as the prelude to new relationships, not their divi-dend. Barbara Ehrenreich (2009) is right to object to the auto-pilot response of medical and para-medical staff in response to the diagno-sis of her breast cancer. The 'positive thinking' that she was subjected to is a grotesque form of intimacy It reflects an amalgam of adminis-tratively dictated emotional presumption and professional didacti-cism that comes close to social impertinence. Plainly speaking, it is managerial bait to set the trap of compliance and lure acquiescence to the standards and objectives of professional authority. Scripted diagnosis and counselling for patients suffering life threatening disease is part of the same audit culture employed to pre-empt complaint in other sectors of society, such as employment relations, schools or the assessment of research output in higher education. It has half an eye on minimizing the involvement of an ombudsman and ensuring that there is no legal basis for clients to remonstrate on matters of due process. It scarcely lifts its gaze above the level of standard deviation from the median. Its fear of entrapment and litigation means that it lacks vision and aspiration. Of course, salaried service workers involved in sensitive areas of emotional labour have real feelings. They are capable of transferring genuine emotion to those whose vulnerability is laid bare. However, they operate with case-load struc-tures and optimal commercial targets of service delivery that have the effect of automating and homogenizing services. Therapy culture has evolved a well shielded, cosy, but really, somewhat toxic climate in which the insistence upon the impertinence of unearned complicity is deplored as a personality defect (Furedi 2003).[1] For want of mean-ingful, empowered general commonality with others the ass is con-fused with the lion. We assent to the prepared entreaties of political leaders, health workers, educators, psychoanalysts, human relations personnel and other workers in the sector of emotional labour because most of us mainline on acceptance and approval. Free speech is a sacrosanct value in managed democracies. It is the first characteristic which is said to differentiate them from authoritarian regimes. Yet typically, free speech in managed democracies encourages a politics that is high wired to personality instead of character. It inflates and dramatizes the value of 'the occasion' in mobilizing attention and attaining social and political impact (Schmitt 1919). The result is the absurdity of minatory democracy, i.e. a multi-fronted, interstitial, interchange of politics that is, for the most part, unable to break out of gridlock. For it is incapable of generating the necessary level of solidarity to achieve viable momentum for change. By extension, a type of politics that is incapable of rising above the immediate dilemmas of the occasion, the event or the incident thrives. Moreover, it is lionized by *dramatis personae* in public life, for it presents countless opportunities to achieve social impact and court acclaim. These are at the nucleus of Schmitt's (1919) account of personality politics. It would certainly be wrong to maintain that this politics is 'without opposition'.[2] On the contrary, dissatisfaction with spin and political posturing is commonplace. The reinvigoration of democracy is a *cause célèbre*. But achieving a hale and solid popular front in this respect is ruefully elusive.

Consider the well publicized recent *Occupy* protests of 2011–12. The protesters portrayed the mass occupations of public metropolitan space throughout many urban centres in the world as a reclamation of civic rights and, *ipso facto*, a challenge to the corporate-state axis. That is, public spaces were popularly re-inhabited. In the bargain, the authority of the police and the state to regulate public space, and corporate advertizers to commodify was said to be dealt a hammer blow. Even critics of the tactics used by *Occupy* and the inconvenience that it visited upon ordinary public life, celebrated the undertaking to give power to the people as a worthwhile cause. Additionally, *Occupy* was effective in recasting public awareness of the causes and magnitude of inequality. 'We are the 99 per cent' quickly became a mantra for understanding the dynamics and scale of market inequality. In some quarters it is submitted to have transformed the terms of debate (Castells 2012; Gitlin 2012a). Against this, there is reason to believe that the proposition muddles the incident of transitory temporal derailment with system change. The staged, personality-based aspects of the event must not be minimized. Although *Occupy* pilloried many aspects of personality politics and the organization of everyday life around 'the occasion', it unwittingly found itself enmeshed in the same machinery. For example, the driving forces behind the movement were well versed in using modes of drama in reporting events, pioneered by the media, to coax preferred readings out of public opinion. The same para-social technologies that enable watchers to conduct emotional identification and votive behaviour with celebrities and statistical men and women for the purposes of system compliance were utilized to strive for critical mass support for system transformation. Similar, untested categories of emotional convergence with statistical men and women who are geographically remote and culturally distant were invoked. *Occupy* was a highly public, relatively prolonged and – by courtesy of the media – richly documented protest. Unlike organized, party-based politics, it advocated a political structure based upon 'horizontalism' and 'the people's mic' as a society-wide lever of social transformation.[3] Indeed, it explicitly eschewed leaders, party discipline and the formulation of a coherent strategy of objectives, on the grounds that these characteristics are what produced the technical contradictions of managed democracy in the first place.[4] This is like trying to solve entrenched, entangled, intricate social, economic and political problems by waving a wand. True, *Occupy* went beyond arm-chair theorizing and micro-politics to disrupt key metropolitan nodal points in market society. In passing, it should be noted again, the crucial importance of densely populated urban space as a site of challenge and resistance in contemporary culture and society. In the age of casualized, disaggregated labour, 'seize the city' has become a more pertinent cry for challenge and opposition than 'seize the factory'. No-one should under-estimate the transformative power of mass public protests. They have the capacity to dislocate social order and intensify moral density (Thompson 1991b: 185–351). Even if we confine ourselves to the last few years, Tiananmen, Tahir, Syntagma and Gezi Park, achieved durable, demonstrable political and economic changes[5] Yet if one looks at *Occupy* in aggregate, and with hindsight, three things stand out. Firstly, it was recognized by the media to be a vivid contrast in what might be called the ontology of resistance. In an age where the politics of challenge and resistance have been dominated with micro-politics, it was a case of civil disturbance that went well beyond the conventions and *lex loci of* community opposition to pinpoint general antagonisms in the system. It sought to revitalize the conventions of the Ancient Greek *agora* and apply them on an industrial, global scale.[6] Sociologists with an historical bent (and professional historians) refer to major derailments of temporal order as World Historical Events (WHEs) (Wallerstein 1989; White 2008). Conceptually speaking, they involve the escalation of moral density and are transparently, anti-systemic. They are expressed, by agents who pursue them, and watchers who experience and interpret them, as the fulfilment of widely felt system contradictions. At one extreme, WHEs refer to incidents like the French Revolution (1789), the Bolshevik Revolution (1917), the Nazi invasion of Poland (1939), Pearl Harbour (1942) and 9/11 (2001). However, in an age in which the media is a key moral force organizing popular agendas and influencing opinion, it is appropriate to speak of 'event hyperinflation', i.e. the attribution of significant derailment of temporal order to a much more varied, spasmodic, less historically momentous, number of incidents and episodes. While *Occupy* stressed the value of community and locality, the cadence of the event was for global, anti-systemic derailment. Consecutively, it was portrayed as the end of a particular kind of (debased) politics geared to the compulsion of making the contradictions of managed democracy palatable to the people. *Occupy* spokesmen and proselytizers seized upon the propaganda of WHEs by presenting the occupations as a 'signpost' in history (Hobsbawm 1978: 130). This was faithfully represented and, to some degree dramatically conveyed, in media representations of the day. But by invoking the standard of a unified *polis* ('the 99 per cent') it created a rod for its own back. As the protests evolved, the media seized upon obvious disagreements and schisms between activists, supporters and bystanders. This plunged the notion of a unified *polis* into hot water. The public profile of *Occupy* atrophied because it was unable to construct a robust, incisive popular front. In part, this reflected the doctrinal rejection of elected leaders, party forms of political discipline and a binding programme of goals.

Secondly, *Occupy* was extremely mediagenic. As with the *Arab Spring* it made extensive use of modern communication technologies (especially the internet and hand held devices) to convey action. Simultaneously, it enlisted the commercial and state media to register and publicize the drama of temporal derailment at local, national and global levels. Typically, TV film crews came fast on the heels of police vans and squad cars. Indeed, in many cases, they were already waiting for the police to arrive, having been tipped-off by media-savvy *Occupy* insiders. The televised nature of the protest lends itself to the festive and the 'playing out' of antagonisms through various forms of street theatre. *Occupy* contributed to this by foregrounding the celebratory and educational qualities of derailment (musical performance, the people's 'University', on-site libraries, debates). In doing so the actions of televised statistical men and women were used to make bold, vivid, but unproven, links with conditions in the altogether greater mass of statistical men and women (the 99 per cent). The majority desisted from enlisting in direct action. Nonetheless, the protesters affected a relationship of presumed intimacy with them. Doctrinally, they were presented as the reserve support of frontline protesters.

Thirdly, to date, the balance of evidence supports the conclusion that it is self-deception or outright deceit to attribute to *Occupy* fundamental, durable system change. Rather, it was a spasmodic, derailment of social order that momentarily dramatized deep system contradictions. 2011–12 was not 1917 or even 9/11. The protests succeeded in venting pressure and publicizing the core antagonisms at the heart of the system. They did not bring the system to its knees and they failed to produce a new, higher democratic settlement.

The question posed by these three observations about *Occupy* is, what type of politics is being claimed and ostensibly pre-figured here? Of course, real frustrations and hopes were at the heart of the movement, but their expression was unable to cut free from the gravitational pull of the gestural economy. Gestural economies organized around intensely commodified markets propagate votive behaviour on an industrial scale because the opportunities of displaying indignation are literally numberless. The minatory element in managed democracies thrives on the anxieties of not being heard or recognized. While some groups speak in muffled voices which are semi-noticed or not heard, the minatory form of managed democracy encourages a cacophony of sound and fury in order to dispel the formation of cohesive themes to produce meaningful system change. *Occupy* is a form of politics born out of a blister (the economic recession and its origins and effects), that grabbed the mediagenic capacity of the occasion (the occupation), but proved to be fettered by a reliance upon 'the occasion' and media networks as a means to spring into action and grab public attention, i.e. it is primarily incident-based, bound by the wheel of drama and reactive. The grievances that *Occupy* articulated reflect communal disquiet with the way things have gone, and are going, in managed democracy. Community is advocated as the oxygen for reinvigorating democracy (Wolin 2008: 288–92). However, the idea that community vitalities and grievances can be elevated into a hale and enduring popular front by social media must be handled with caution. The digital crowd operates mostly through relations of presumed intimacy with statistical men and women. What is missing is the lived, cumulative, face-to-face experience of common injustice and exploitation of labourers in the workplace and the ghetto. The grinding, face-to-face engagement with direct, common material conditions of injustice and the accompanying assault on the emotions, is most propitious for the creation of affirmative intimacy over presumed intimacy. It might even be said that the internet and hand-held devices in general are a bad measure to achieve affirmative intimacy because they produce accelerated intimacy, i.e. a form of connection that foregrounds only certain elements of speech illustrators and emblems (what the screen and audio system show you) and leaves the rest to presumption.

Occupy's lofty disdain with organized political parties, elected leaders and party forms of discipline condemns it to the margins. Some commentators submit that, despite this, it is perfectly plausible to propose that *Occupy can* play a useful role in generating a popular front against the elite management of democracy. For example, David Harvey (2013: 162–3) ventures that the movement has in it the

capacity to build alliances and coalitions with students, the unemployed and the other victims of 'the Party of Wall Street'. He goes
further, *Occupy* has a duty to publicize exploitation in the workplace,
especially the form suffered by immigrant workers on minimum wage
and forge links with creative workers, whose labour power is routinely commodified by the corporate-state axis. Similar submissions
are made by other respected commentators on the Left (Castells
2012; Gitlin 2012a).

What are we to make of this? While the heart supports the argument, the head must decree that it represents an expression of hope
rather than a tenable case. Making the injustices of the workplace
and the ghetto a global *cause célèbre*, is a rabbit that successive social
movements that challenge the rule of capital, over many years, have
failed to pull from the hat. The absence of meaningful solidarity in
the *polis* has been precisely the pitfall for anti-systemic national and
global organizations that aspire to combat and transcend capitalism.
Whither the popular front is a legitimate question of all pro-
democratic movements seeking a global shift in the balance of power.
If temporal derailments like the *Occupy* protests have fallen short in
precipitating system change must we confine ourselves to political
quiescence, i.e. the acceptance that market logic is insurmountable?
Might it perhaps, be more honourable and realistic to remain
nonplussed in the face of strident appeals to change the system? For
might apathy be said to be a fair measure of the powerlessness of
individuals before the leviathan of the corporate-state axis? I am
reminded of what the poet Yeats wrote in 1919 in *The Second
Coming*:

> The best lack all conviction, while the worst
> Are full of passionate intensity

One resounding refusal to all of this way of thinking was supplied
in France in 2007 by the self-styled group of anarchists known as
'The Invisible Committee'. They herald a swarm of apparently disconnected incidents of global derailment as evidence of general,
evolving, spontaneous community hostility to the contradictions of
the system e.g. Argentine *piqueteros*, the emergence of free street
kitchens in New Orleans after the Hurricane (2005), the riots in 2005
in *Clicy-sous-Bois* (an Eastern suburb of Paris comprising mainly an
immigrant, low paid population), the occupations of public buildings
in Oaxaca, Mexico (2006), the Black Bloc protests against the *cara-
binieri* at the G8 summit in Genoa (2007). In the view of The Invisible
Committee it is folly to suppose that the contradictions of the system
can ever be synthesized. If one reads the tea leaves aright, the whole

show is in an imminent state of collapse. This anticipates many of the claims made by the *Occupy* movement. Is it a tenable jeremiad?

The Invisible Committee

'The Coming Insurrection' (The Invisible Committee 2009) is a political tract originally published in 2007 by an anonymous group, since alleged by French police to be an anarchic cell, the *Tarnac Nine*.[7] Drawing upon the traditions of Revolutionary Marxism, The Situationists and Ecological Radicals, the book contends that capitalism generates insoluble crises in the self, social relations, work, the commercialization for profit of emotional labour, the economy, the city, the environment and civilization, *in toto*. The unregulated market is condemned for destroying a language of common experience and fuelling the inexhaustible corporate urge to maximize profits. Satisfying the needs of shareholders imposes high barriers on the capacity for organizations to reform themselves (The Invisible Committee 2009: 15, 26). The traditional Durkheimian notion of modern society as a system of mutual obligations and reciprocities has depleted into 'the metaphor of a *network* to describe the connection of cybernetic solitude' (The Invisible Committee 2009: 40, emphasis in original).

Published on the eve of the global financial collapse in 2008, the book predicts the inability of capitalism to utilize idle resources and fall back on inflated asset values rather than production to achieve the illusion of economic growth. Ineffective demand and rising indebtedness fuse to intensify the crisis in the investment class. Low wages and prolonged unemployment oblige propertyless labourers to forestall on mortgage repayments. In addition, the inexorable depletion of oil reserves together with the degradation produced by exploiting fossil fuels portends imminent economic and environmental catastrophe. Insurrection – the spontaneous attack on organized power – is inevitable. To be sure, it is actively demanded by The Invisible Committee.

A generation earlier the Situationists also devised and proselytized a disapproving vocabulary conveying system exhaustion, personal disintegration, urban distemper and fictive capital (Debord 1987, 1990; McDonough 2009). They wrote against the backdrop of the affluent society and apparent ecological stability. Despite this, their critique achieved wide, enduring circulation. Manifestly, the high-wired, staccato-style pages of 'The Coming Insurrection' are willing heirs to this type of reasoning. If the content is not exactly new, it is given additional charge by the economic collapse of 2008 – the most serious since the Great Depression of the inter-war years – and, crucially, rising fears about the capacity of the global economy to recover. The Invisible Committee (2009) deplore the coporate-state attrition of the environment, not least because it unequivocally exposes the self-destructive logic of capitalist accumulation. While this unfolds most apocalyptically at the structural level, it virally infects emotional relations at the personal level. Nowhere more so than in the field of intimacy. *Prima facie*, in ordinary public life presumed intimacy soothes and calms. At least that is its outward intent. The Invisible Committee will have none of this. Presumed intimacy is nothing but a shibboleth for an economically and emotionally exhausted system that cannot regenerate itself and is determined to linger on in a moribund state for as long as possible:

> Under the auspices of "intimacy", we come to it looking for everything that has so obviously deserted contemporary social relations: warmth, simplicity, truth, a life without theatre or spectator. But once the romantic enchantment has passed, "intimacy" strips itself bare: it is itself a social invention, it speaks the language of glamour magazines and psychology. (The Invisible Committee 2009: 41)

Celebrity culture, life coaching and salaried positive thinking have sprayed everyday life so deep with their treacherous hue that ordinary emotions and vocabulary that convey intimacy are shot through with artfulness, contrivance and unsafe assumptions. According to The Invisible Committee (2009: 42) this is actually a disguised 'blessing'. For it creates 'the ideal conditions for a wild, massive experimentation with new arrangements, new fidelities' (The Invisible Committee 2009: 42).

The central thrust of The Invisible Committee jeremiad is that dominant values in the West are soaked through in ultimately self-denying values of emotional duplicity and cultural relativism. A conditional perspective is no way to confront and handle the ultimate problems facing the West and (because of Western domination), the globe). Cultural Relativism is repudiated as substituting representation for integrity, i.e. in the terminology used in this study it succours presumed intimacy and reinforces the gridlock of minatory democracy. Allied with concerns about the nature of civic prudence, centring upon ineffective demand and tumorous indebtedness then, is racing scepticism about the probity and validity of the entire system.

The Situationists knew that a house built upon sand must fall. They regarded spectacular capital as fictive capital, i.e. based in asset values rather than productive values.[8] The catalysts of exposure were seen as 'situations'. 'Our central purpose is the construction of situations', explained Debord (2009: 94), 'i.e. the concrete construction of temporary settings of life and their transformations into a higher passionate nature.' They elected to work within the system in order to change it by covertly and determinedly undermining it. Similarly, The Invisible Committee (2009: 125, 99) urges adherents to 'jam everything' and to 'expect nothing from organizations'. A digitally connected, commune structure is advocated as the antidote to the estranging effect of corporate-state domination. What comes after jamming is less clear. The Invisible Committee envisages jamming to exploit and develop a commune structure. However, the content of this structure and its part in post-jamming social reconstruction is a matter of conjecture. In *The Coming Insurrection* the accent is upon forcing system contradiction to a terminal spasm. As with the *Occupy* protests that came after it, the document respects the value of a micro-politics of resistance waged through networks of communes. However, the scope of political ambition is plainly directed at world change.

The Road Ahead

The Invisible Committee and *Occupy* belong to a long, mostly honourable, tradition of agitprop and *refusenik* politics. This reflects the antinomy between Modernity 1 and Modernity 2 alluded to earlier.[9] Both The Invisible Committee and *Occupy* draw on immense reserves of popular indignation with the smug impertinence of the system, i.e. capitalism purports to produce profit for all and to annihilate barriers of social exclusion in favour of free market independence, while simultaneously, and covertly, bolstering and extending elite power with the compulsive object of intensifying organized social and economic inequality. Both *Occupy* and The Invisible Committee proffer *stateless solutions* to civil disorder and moral decay. The compact between the state and the corporation is rejected as a busted flush. Instead, the re-birth of the *agora* is envisaged. Nothing less than a 24-carat form of communal populism is at stake. It discards the legislative and executive arms of the corporate-state axis. The gridlock of the minatory form of managed democracy is not fundamentally the result of the orchestrated repression of interests. Rather, it results from the automative, instinct of legislators, chief executives and service personnel in the corporate-state axis to cling on to power by attending to, and protecting, the sectional interests of majority voters and stockholders (Stockman 1986). These narrow, sectional ends are respected above and beyond considerations that apply to the general interests of the lives of others, i.e. the statistical men and women who make up 'society', 'the global population', or what have you. Against this, a devil's advocate might say that stateless solutions discount the validity of corporate-state arrangements and expertise at their peril. The industrial or, as some would have it, the post-industrial, scale of human relations is now in fundamental respects global, rather than merely regional and national. It cannot do without salaried, trained service labourers who operate beyond the boundaries of community. Wolin (2008: 290–2) is correct to insist that the revitalization of democracy requires committed public servants with the capacity to combine knowledge and accomplishment with respect for defending and promoting democratic values, diminishing inequalities and protecting the environment. Given the present dispensation in the minatory form of managed democracy this is a tall order. To make matters worse, it is not sufficient. What is also needed is even more daunting. Namely, to persuade Chief Executives of corporations, their service staff and their shareholders, that they have ethical responsibilities for the lives of others. Now, of course, today Social Responsibility is a standard feature of the public face of multi-nationals. Yet conversely, the profit margins of corporations depend upon driving down costs (wages, supplies and production), and defending, and wherever opportunity allows, increasing prices. In some cases, notably, for example, in the armaments, tobacco, alcohol and gambling sectors, multi-national corporations profess social responsibility while producing commodities that result in addiction, illness, higher rates of mortality and environmental degradation. Stateless solutions are right to ask, what price Social Responsibility here? But they are wrong to write off the cultural capital accumulated by these agents and the wider corporate-state axis in unqualified, deficit terms. Stateless solutions will fail, because ultimately, some form of state organization, acting at the behest of the people but involving trained, skilled salaried staff to ensure optimal efficiency in the social and economic infrastructure, is unavoidable. On the whole the dismissal of 'the system' by The Invisible Committee and *Occupy* is too airy and apocalyptic. More modest and pragmatic forms of resistance, designed to unpick the facade of the corporate-state axis and make connections between community, regional, national and global levels, are required.

Political forms interested in getting beyond presumed intimacy and the gestural economy might start with what is, in many ways, the Achilles heel of the system, i.e. the pecuniary basis for judging the value of moral relationships. This gets to the heart of the question of trust which is the essence of organic solidarity. For it is an attempt to quantify trust relations by monetary discipline. Both Left and Right portray the mantra of value for money as the essence of virtuous politics. This contributes to the monetization of public and private relations. In societies that have moved beyond discredited regimes of clan-based domination and slave labour, presumed intimacy is part of the portfolio of profit maximization. There is an obvious tension when what is done in the name of the people is subject to the discipline of financial bean-counting.

Perhaps above any other issue in collective life, citizens are entitled to assume that governments recognize that their primary duty is to protect the citizenry from physical danger. Chimerical risk management is a parody of the real anxieties and fears that citizens face, because it exaggerates the horizon of hazard. Yet the privatization of military services means that few Western governments wholly control the forces that they profess to command. Deborah Avant (2006) points out that strictly speaking, there is nothing new about defence out-sourcing in America. From the beginning of the Republic, civilians were used to provide logistics and weapons support. Until the Second World War resources were concentrated in basic ration supply, the provision of uniforms, transport support and weapons inventory. However, the involvement of private contractors escalated significantly during the Vietnam War. This entailed the deployment of civilian contractors to direct involvement in military zones of operation. The Pentagon funded civilian contractors to provide policing and military training to the South Vietnamese Army. At the height of hostilities in Vietnam, the *Vinnell* Corporation employed 5000 people in Vietnam building military bases, repairing equipment and running military warehouses.

Since the end of the Vietnam war, escalation has proceeded a-pace. Civilian contractors have been directly involved in large numbers, often under no-open-bid protection agreements, to provide and service military hardware, communications networks, barrack construction and facilities, food and hospitality to troops stationed in the Gulf, Bosnia, Afghanistan and Iraq. Avant (2006) reports that the estimated ratio of contractors to military deployed to Theatres of Conflict is steadily moving towards near parity – 1: 58 in the Gulf War; 1: 15 in Bosnia and 1:6 in Iraq. Contract operations have extended to include the employment of mercenaries namely in East Timor and the Middle East (employed by *Global Risk Strategies*) and Chile and El Salvador (employed by *Blackwater* and *Triple Canopy*). American security companies such as *Halliburton, DynCorp, Kroll,*

Triple Canopy and *Custer Battles* have enjoyed dramatic growth in turnover. They have been joined by British companies such as *Aegis*, *Olive Security* and *Global Risk Strategies* and other corporations from dominant national civilian security providers such as France, Israel, South Africa and Saudi Arabia. Serious outsourcing of national security provision to the private sector began in the early 1980s. The late Chalmers Johnson (2010: 101–3) recounts that it was then that, Ronald Reagan created the 'Private Sector Survey on Cost Control' (1982). Eventually, this became known as the Grace Commission, because the survey was headed by the conservative business mogul J. Peter Grace, chairman of the *W. R. Grace Corporation*, one of the largest chemical corporations in the world. The Grace Commission set a marker that in modern democracies national security systems could be privatized in the interests of 'value for money' and budgetary prudence. This took full control of the military out of the hands of elected governments and introduced new shared arrangements between government and often, foreign multi-nationals. The pre-sumed intimacy that Washington or Whitehall purport to possess with national citizens is now subject to ratification with the Executive Boards of military service suppliers who are not solely accountable to Presidents or Prime Ministers. As Johnson (2010) goes on to show, the biggest boost to this process of farming out the security functions of the state to private contractors occurred in the Clinton years. At the culmination of Clinton's first term over 100,000 Pentagon jobs had been taken over by private security providers. At the end of his second term in 2001, 360,000 federal jobs had been redeployed and government spending on private contractors was 44 percent higher than in 1993. Troops in Iraq and Afghanistan were supplied with food, laundry and other personal services by the *KBR Corporation*, while *Blackwater Worldwide* ran security and analytical services in the regions for the CIA. Where the USA led, much of the rest of the Western world followed. Currently, in the UK the largest employer on the London Stock Exchange, with operations in more than 120 countries and over 618,000 employees, is the 'security solutions' provider, *G4S*. In 2013, the company reported underlying revenue of £7.54 billion.

Nor has the privatization and out-sourcing of domestic security services stopped with the military sector. The privatization of prisons has made significant inroads in the ownership and control of penal institutions in the USA, the UK, Canada and Australia (Lundahl et al. 2009; Azzi 2010; Scott 2013; Younhee and Price 2014). In the USA the range of involvement stretches from partial out-sourcing of operations (e.g. of food and recreational provision to complete corporate ownership of prison facilities and services (Yim and Price 2014: 259). The move was motivated by cost efficiency consider-ations following the rise of prison populations that commenced in the early 1970s. In 1973 the US prison population stood at 220,000 inmates. By 2003, it had soared to approximately 1,470,045 (Livanou et al. 2006: 189). Underfunding and overcrowding were the catalysts to redistributing some, or all, prison operations from state control (Ethridge and Marquart 1993; Shichor 1995). Some commentators point to strong ideological overtones in the drive to privatize (Wright 2010; Yim and Price 2014). Thus, the conviction that 'the market knows best' has often been the starting point of the reallocation of services and ownership to private corporations rather than the *con-sequence* of prudent investigation. Currently, in England and Wales, 84,000 people are in prison (Meek, Gojkovic, Mills 2013). In the UK at large, eight per cent of the prison population are in privately con-trolled penal institutions, compared with three per cent of the prison population in the USA (Cooper and Taylor 2005: 497–8). In the light of aforementioned remarks about the incursion of private corpora-tions into military service provision, it is notable that in 2011 Brit-ain's leading private military service provider, the *G4S* corporation, successfully took over ownership of Her Majesty's Prison, Birming-ham from the public sector (Ludlow 2014: 70). This is an example of *bespoke aggregation*, i.e. the development of services in different sectors of a sector of the economy by a provider intent upon achiev-ing quasi-monopoly control. Competitive tendering has been cham-pioned by enthusiasts as a means to inject capital into the penal infrastructure, improve industrial relations by rolling back the power of Prison Officers' Association (the Trade Union for Prison, Correctional and Secure Psychiatric Workers) and remedy poor performance. In practice, successful private tendering may provide a sop to ideologically driven opinion, but it has not exactly resulted in real autonomy for privately run penal institutions (Ludlow 2014:71). Private providers remain bound by legal provision which remains entrenched in elected government.[10] Additionally, allocating ownership and out-sourcing to companies responsible for different operations of penal service (education, medical care, sanitation, reha-bilitation etc.) creates challenges of delivering fully integrated man-agement. In short, the academic jury is out on the costs and benefits of the private provision of penal operations over public sector delivery.

Nonetheless, parallel movements of privatization are evident in the provision of health services, policing, transport, waste disposal, care for the elderly, child care and, of course, education. For example, most University students in Britain reading this book are paying substantial fees for a span of education that my generation, and postwar generations before me, were given for free, and urged to be celebrated as a civic virtue. In England fees for higher education were introduced in 1998 and set at £1,000 per year; they climbed to £3,000 a year in 2004; and in 2012 a fee of £9,000 per year was introduced. Private debt has replaced a hard won, prized and notable civic right. When a society switches to use profit-driven corporations to assist in delivering basic services formally delivered as a right of citizenship, government statements of presumed intimacy do not leave much in the way of after-glow.

We have come to a treacherous and dangerous pass. Encouraging the sort of moral density that Durkheim believed to be the *sine qua non* of the good (organic) society is hobbled by the widespread perception that public life is profoundly insincere and ultimately at the behest of corporate plunder. The connections between statistical men and women and the corporate-state axis are not mediated by inclusive occupational groupings or any sort of meaningful, alternative collective entity. This is obscured by the connections and apparent transparency delivered by the internet. The latter certainly multiplies connections. Simultaneously it violates the equilibrium between emotional nearness and remoteness that Simmel (1950) submits makes the distinction between solidarity and strangeness viable. Contact with spatially remote and culturally distinct people is magically made to appear emotionally near, while pressures of work and the routines of domestic life make relations with the physically close household, street or village often emotionally remote. World events communicated by the media, in little more than attention-grabbing headlines, haul us into emotionally aroused identification with statistical men and women, while in domestic and community settings, sleeping dogs are left to slumber. An emotional world composed of the fast and loose exhibition of emotion with people that we have never physically met and about whom our knowledge is mostly confined to media soundbites, is stagnant because it has no robust standard of personal involvement. In contrast, a world of domestic somnambulism, where the real emotions of those with whom we share our days are not even noticed, contributes to emotional bottlenecks and chasms of estrangement that cease to make life navigable. The question is, how 'moral' is the density produced by the internet? Typically, the emotional bind that is its main currency, reinforces the dynamic of the gestural economy, since it encourages votive behaviour as a substitute for really getting to grips with the lives of others, whether they be kith and kin or statistical men and women separated from us by the magnitude of physical and cultural distance. The commonplace reciprocity and mutuality between people that Durkheim (2013) envisaged under organic solidarity only exists in uneven, spasmodic distributions. In 'free', market society the name of the game is the maximization of personal property. Of course, there are notional restraints upon action and provisional responsibilities for others with inferior fixed or variable capital assets. These are catered to by the speech illustrators and emblems in the gestural economy. Presumed intimacy draws its lifeblood from the automative, heat-seeking, energy rush of the feel-good factor in the gestural economy. It is eminently reasonable to maintain that this may reflect genuine feelings of reciprocity and mutuality. Indeed, it is calumny to profess that real emotional feelings and connections with strangers do not exist. However, in a society where the race for acceptance and approval masks a *realpolitik* of personality politics spurred by the headlong compulsion to jockey for competitive, acquisitive advantage, to seize the occasion, to make a mark and get ahead, they are constantly left champing in the stalls. It bears repeating that it is groundless to propose that gestural economies and presumed intimacies can be absented from social life. However, that is no reason to be brain-blind about them. The reflecting pool of managed democracy holds up an image of the world that is fit for purpose. That purpose, doggedly sought by the corporate-state axis, is to maximize the veneer of order and predictability and, by these means, to minimize dissent and derailment. This omits a contrary, savoury detail: dissent and nonconformity are integral to what democracy means. It is unrealistic to dream of re-staging the *agora* on the global arena. We will never achieve solid emotional connections with global apparitions of statistical men and women. The world population is too vast, intricately differentiated and its growth rate too hyper-prolific. Notwithstanding this, it *is* realistic to aim for a transfusion of energy in democracy to make it more alert to, and sceptical of, the omnipresence of presumed intimacy and the gestural economy in everyday life. Public concern needs to be heightened about the nature of the command lines that deliver indispensable public services. The balance between private profit and public interest needs to be re-interrogated. Real accountability in public services depends upon knowing exactly who owns operations, how ownership fits in with wider business portfolios and what bid arrangements have been sanctioned by state officials. Today, when matters of this sort percolate into public consciousness, they are seldom permitted to bulk one whit more than small print. In 2003 the award of a 'no-bid' contract to *Halliburton* to re-build the infrastructure of Iraq's oil industry stirred up so much mud in the public sphere that it eventually led to the contract being rescinded. What is ultimately telling about this episode is the smug assumption of central command in managed democracy that they can slip it through under cover of the chimerical risk management argument, i.e. the details of the contract are so sensitive to public interest that they should on no account be subject to competitive tender. In other words, the public must be protected from themselves for their own best interests. For from the flight deck of the corporate-state axis, is it not the case that the public is a mystery even unto themselves? The privatization of essentials has positioned multi-nationals to take unilateral decisions, nominally in the public interest, without voluntarily disclosing them in the public sphere. In June 2014 an open letter, posted on the *War On Want* website, that included Noam Chomsky, Archbishop Desmond Tutu, Alice Walker and Angela Davis among signatories, joined other Human Rights activists in alleging a history of torture and systematic ill treatment of Palestinian prisoners, including children kept in solitary confinement, at the Ofer prison, located in Israel's occupied West Bank, and the Kishon and Moskobiyyeh detention/interrogation Units (www.waronwant.org). All of these security facilities are operated by *G4S*.

The subtle configuration of structural relationships between power and culture are obscured by mainstream media. The melancholy addiction to media weekly news rounds of global events that portray the world as a collection of isolated, disconnected calamities, dominates, and is actively encouraged, by media networks and programme schedulers. Votive behaviour, presumed intimacy and the reinforcement of the gestural economy go hand in hand with event-based para-social relationships. When a WHE (World Historical Event) is covered by the media the reassuring image of 'team world' mobilizing and intervening to take care of things is activated. The configurations of structural power that cause WHEs to give the appearance of de-railing social order rarely make prime time and are accessible to the public mainly through personal research and study.

In such circumstances it is tempting to call for nothing less than urgent and wholesale moral renewal. We cannot stomach any more spin and lies. We want our leaders and professionals to tell us the truth and keep their promises. It is abominable that others should take it upon themselves to pull the wool over our eyes and purport to act in our best interests. Without further ado, presumed intimacy, votive behaviour and the entire gestural economy must be consigned to the dustbin of history. This line of thinking does not get very far. In fact, it falls at the first hurdle. All pleas for 'post-hypocrisy' cannot overcome the fact that hypocrisy and anti-hypocrisy are bound together in a Gordian knot (Shklar 1984; Runciman 2008: 197). It may even be the case that there is a genetic disposition towards duplicity in the species. In other words, it is in our nature to pretend, dissemble and lie (Jay 2010: 22–4). If this is so, it explains why presumed intimacy is integral in the human condition. Life is made-up of inescapable fictions and half-truths. To think otherwise is to be naive. Yet duplicity and presumed intimacy would mean nothing without veracity and emotional integrity. We only recognize a compulsive liar because we know what trust and truth-telling mean. The war between lies and truth, presumed intimacy and emotional integrity, may be permanent, but battles can be won. Lost ground can be regained and fortified. The capstone of robust democracy is intimacy with respect for truth. A minatory, managed form of democracy wherein this does not abide must fall. Presumed intimacy may sparkle and delight, but in relation to vigorous moral density, it is as thin and insubstantial as quicksilver. It seldom transcends 'the occasion'. For the spray-on solutions and demi-measures that it proffers, bristle with hidden contradictions that will, in the sureness of time, bring the whole edifice down. Since time immemorial we have lived among familiar strangers. But never in such numbers, or with so many emotional triggers, primed by vested interests, to produce preferred readings. In robustly contemplating the world of para-social relations, composed of apparitions, consisting of remote, one dimensional celebrities and statistical men and women, we may hope to actually grasp how our sense of being alone, together is sustained. Through these means, the face and character of the vested interests that support the stupendous masquerade of managed democracy will become less furtive and evasive.

Notes

1 Living with Statistical Men and Women

1. The note of qualification reflects the appreciation that the media oper-
    ates as a gatekeeper of world news. The 'framing' function raises
    obvious and difficult questions about the nature of journalistic inde-
    pendence and the relationship between media frames and vested inter-
    ests (Castells 2009). To believe what we see on-screen is not necessarily
    empowering at all. Empowerment requires developing critical distance
    from media information and a methodology and theoretical perspective
    that enables us to weigh data and make judgements in the balance.
2. Rachel was an American political peace activist who belonged to the
    pro-Palestinian group, 'International Solidarity Movement' (ISM). She
    was crushed to death by an Israel Defence Forces (IDF) armoured
    bulldozer in Rafah during the second Palestinian intifada.
3. To confine ourselves to only recent examples of Western political vol-
    unteers for the ISM and the IDF, Thomas Hurndell, a British photog-
    raphy student was shot by an IDF sniper in January 2004, and later
    died in hospital; Brian Avery was shot in the face, suffering permanent
    disfigurement in April 2004 by IDF forces in the West Bank town of
    Jenin; and 18-year-old Furkan Dogan, a Turkish-American citizen, was
    allegedly shot by the IDF while participating in the Gaza Freedom
    flotilla raid (organized by the Free Gaza Movement and the Turkish
    Foundation for Human Rights and Freedoms and Humanitarian Relief)
    to bring humanitarian and construction materials of relief by sea to
    breach the Israeli blockade of the Gaza Strip.
4. A platitude in what used to be called 'Development Studies' and is now
    more commonly expressed in 'Globalization Studies' is that individuals
    throughout the world are inter-connected. In Globalization Studies the
    burden of this idea has become more political. In addition to a focus
    on the 'development gap' between the economically affluent and poor

countries of the world, is the realization that modern technology allows ordinary people on the wrong side of the development gap to engage in terrorist activity as an expedient of political protest.

5. Milgram was ahead of his time in being interested in the depth of moral commitments in modern civic culture. In a number of path-breaking experiments he studied how far people would go to remove intimacy in particular social settings. The 'Lost Letter Experiment' is one example. He dispersed 400 sealed self-addressed envelopes in public places to see what would happen to them. The addresses were deliberately composed to test moral judgements. Among letters to supposedly fellow citizens, such as 'Walter Carnap', were letters to morally positive institutions, such as medical research institutes, and controversial political organizations, like the Communist Party and the Nazi Party. The letters were 'left' under car windscreen wipers, telephone booths, on streets and in shops. The aim of the research was to discover how many letters reached their destinations via the intervention of the strangers that found them. Milgram found that more people mailed letters to socially desirable groups, such as the personal address and the Medical Research institute. These achieved, respectively, a 72 per cent and 71 per cent rate of return. In contrast, only 25 per cent of the letters addressed to the Communist Party or Nazi Party reached their destinations. One interesting additional finding was that 50 per cent of the letters to the Communist Party, 32 per cent to the Nazi Party, 25 per cent to the Medical Research Institute and 10 per cent to 'Walter Carnap', had been opened. Presumably, people were checking if the envelopes contained donations. Milgram's study revealed how hidden prejudice and stereotypes operate in civic culture. Civic obligations are often skin deep. Beneath the veneer of presumed intimacy, deeper forces of group differentiation and personal advantage are at work.

6. The term 'background expectancies' is associated with the work of Harold Garfinkel (1967). Social outcomes are the result of tacit, complex judgements in which an underlying pattern is deciphered out of a temporally qualified succession of appearances. Background expectancies are 'seen' but not codified (Garfinkel 1967: 118). Garfinkels' emphasis on the arbitrary, mutable nature of taken for granted social consensus is not without interest for students of moral behaviour.

7. By the term 'event consciousness' I mean a perspective on life which sees the world as a succession of disconnected episodes, incidents and emergencies. This is the staple fare in prime time news bulletins. It is a media induced and supported form of consciousness. But of course, it suits vested business and government interests to privilege episodes, incidents and emergencies over processes and structures. In the work of Sheldon Wolin (2008) this is recognized as a central plank of 'managed democracy'.

8. The regional inflection of para-social relationship requires us to revise the concept of *habitus*. Para-social interaction influences our sense of

self and mental maps of the world. Horton and Wohl (1956) treated it as producing convergent responses in culture. It is more accurate to think of it as multi-polar, i.e. providing multiple modes of interpretation and meaning in variance to group membership and setting.

9. Accelerated intimacy has become a widespread feature of modern organizational settings. The humanization of the work place through the management style of Human Relations encourages managers to open up emotionally to the private concerns and wellbeing of workers. Ehrenreich's (2009) squib against 'positive thinking' rightly exposes the absurdity and impertinence that this development can produce in ordinary social relations, i.e. when salaried staff claim to really know the pain you are going through when you suffer a major illness or bereavement. Where 'reaching out' is programmatic and goal-driven it carries an air of insincerity. In the extremity of our pain we may neglect or refuse to accept this. However, like Furedi's (2003) deymstifying book on counselling, Ehrenreich (2009) encourages us to make the link between salaried caring and social control.

10. By the term 'casualization of labour' is meant the rise of part-time and fixed term employment contracts. De-industrialization (especially the contraction of steel, coal, printing, the docks and car manufacture), unemployment and legislation curbing union powers (banning tactics such as secondary picketing) are the main reasons for the decline in union power.

11. Bonding through the celebration and defence of space is, of course, not confined to the city. Alliances and struggles formed in defence of the country can also produce a potent sense of group belonging and collective narrative. However, the capital accumulation concentrated in cities means that the struggles and challenges over them create bigger waves and greater long-term threats to the system (Harvey 2013).

12. Authoritarian populism means the political engineering of popular identification with economic and political policies designed to limit popular power. The concept is most closely associated with the work of Stuart Hall (Hall and Jacques 1983; Hall 1988).

2 Chimerical Risk Management

1. Pascal reasoned that it is better for humans to believe that God does exist since to do so will be recognized and rewarded in the Afterlife. If they turn out to be wrong, they will have lost little in the way of pleasure or bounty. Certainly, set against the prospect of everlasting life in heaven, Pascal maintained, the risk of being wrong is trifling.

2. How the popular notion of freedom suffers from John Locke's fateful equation between individual freedom and property! By tying 'the natural right' of property to individual labour Locke exposes the proper limits of government, but fails to grasp the exultant mettle of reform.

3. This was also the kernel of Durkheim's objection to rule by the state under organic solidarity. When the mechanics of *imperium* are too remote from the people, the *polis* feel disenfranchised. For Durkheim, the solution is to create 'occupational; groupings' with tangible, real powers at a midway point between the state and the people. The contraction of trade union power since the early 80s in most Western democracies seems to invalidate the potential of occupational groupings. At the same time, new opportunities for hatching and exerting civic power are provided by the city, volunteering and the web.

4. In the *Republic* Plato's (2007) 'noble lie' is, he believes, reasonable to achieve political stability. The noble lie is the means by which rulers persuade the gullible to follow their best interests. The proviso, is that the noble lie is uttered by leaders who are themselves noble. They possess superior mental and spiritual powers or, to borrow Machiavelli's (1898) term *virtu*. The link between Machiavelli and Plato should not be pushed too far, since most commentators agree that Machiavelli's thinking was far more indebted to Xenophon (Jay 2010: 150). Plato's notion of the noble lie was allowed to rest almost forgotten, until the twentieth century, when earth shaking events in Germany, Russia, China and the responses to them in Britain, France, Italy and the USA, revived interest. Above all, in the controversial philosophy of Leo Strauss (2013), obscurantism, mendacity and misdirection are identified as key parts of the tool box of state craft.

5. 'We Make Us' is a phrase, I stumbled across in November of 2011 on a visit to Melbourne, Australia. It was written in chalk on a paving stone in Spring Street, near the *Occupy* encampment in the Treasury Gardens. Who knows if the author ever did a course in Sociology? But the phrase would not be a bad starting point for Sociology:1

6. Votive behaviour is related to the psychological needs for acceptance and approval. Rationally, the problems of the world exceed the capacity of any individual to solve them. Bystander mentality is the natural bedfellow of this cognitive judgement. But its frank articulation is likely to invite stigma. Votive behaviour is a strategy of risk incubation, i.e. to make a pledge to help is a promissory note delivered in the knowledge that it will never be delivered in order to achieve circumstantial acceptance and approval.

7. Another of Cohen's (2011) concepts is germane here: moral panic. The media is instrumental in inflating popular anxieties about social, political and economic issues. Anxiety inflation is a mechanism for achieving conformity and compliance.

3   The Shockwaves of Trauma

1. The bombing of the Alfred P. Murrah Building (1995) killed 168 people and injured more than 680. The motivation behind the attack was

allegedly, anger at the federal government's handling of civil disturbances at Ruby Ridge (1992) and the Waco siege (1993).

2. This finding appears to confirm the argument made by Hume, Smith
    and Simmel that intensity of emotional identification has a propensity
    to be higher in cases where there is direct or close physical propinquity.
    This in turn raises questions about the emotional intensity of para-
    social relationships with celebrities and statistical men and women. In
    particular, it implies that the degree of isolation among members of
    audiences involved in para-social relationships and the role of the
    media in framing data is decisive.

3. The Santa Monica massacre (2013) which resulted in the deaths of six
    people, was committed by a lone shooter, John Aawahri. The
    Washington Navy Yard (2013) shooting involved 12 fatalities. It was
    carried out by Aaron Alexis, who was alleged by the media to suffer
    from mental delusions.

4. Identification in this respect, may be confined to mere votive behaviour.
    The effect is to achieve group acceptance and approval. But the mecha-
    nism is not primarily identifying with the plight of those at risk. Rather,
    it takes the form of identifying with the representation of the personal
    reaction of the celebrity involved to this plight.

5. It also connects up with Guy Debord's (1987) important argument that,
    in 'the society of the spectacle', screen and print contemplation of
    images has replaced direct action. Interestingly, Debord also argues that
    celebrities represent a combination of human qualities or 'joie de vivre'
    that is absent from the routine lives of the *polis* (Jappe 1999: 6).

6. Speculation that the increase in the rate was the *result* of Monroe's
    suicide is hazardous. Her own death may be interpreted as related to
    wider issues of *anomie* arising from general features of the social, politi-
    cal and economic context, especially the cold war.

7. It may be a fallacy to assume that the responses by celebrities on social
    networking sites are made *by celebrities themselves*. It is entirely con-
    sistent with what is known of the role of cultural intermediaries in
    celebrity promotion to posit third party involvement in the apparent
    conduct of texts between celebrities and fans.

4   The Lost Neighbour Proposition and the Collateral Damage Problem

1. For a stranger to claim to 'feel your pain' or 'know what you are going
    through' was once dismissed as an impertinence. The opening up of
    emotions that has accompanied the postwar ascent of therapy culture
    has widened emotional access, but arguably, weakened the depth of
    emotional commitment (Furedi 2003). Emotional identification is a
    tool of accelerated intimacy. Feeling (or appearing to feel), caring (or
    affecting to care) for strangers establishes common ground. Ehrenreich's

(2009) argument is that salaried, emotional labour may be sincere, but it is also often built on pillars of sand. That is, it is a discursive manoeuvre that, for a culturally literate person, is likely to fragment with familiarity. In Hochschild's (1983) work it is referred to as 'spray on' sincerity. Aptly so.

2. Furedi's (2003) penetrating critique of therapy culture extends much further than professional boundaries e.g. in counselling, social work and psycho-therapy. At least the level of votive behaviour, civic culture demands recognition of the plight of the victims and those in wretched conditions as a condition of civic acceptance and approval. We are urged to care and emote, even before we know the substance of what we are being asked to care about and why emotional identification is appropriate. Not to openly declare care or to withhold emotion is linked to personal inadequacy and civic default.

3. The ethical objections to the lost neighbour experiment need hardly be laboured. To exclude a neighbour from a community arbitrarily risks mobilizing deep emotions. If my next door neighbour apparently disappears overnight and the police and ancillary social workers fail to find her, I may experience deep anxiety and distress. But there is the rub. In the spirit of Milgram's work the aim is to reveal the moral density of affective relations with others. The depth of the moral responsibilities that we feel in respect of neighbours is the point at issue. Once ethical forms are introduced into the process, there is an argument that responses are de-naturalized. That is, respondents are aware that they are involved in an institutional, somewhat artificial process, and cease to behave naturally. This raises important and controversial issues about the legitimacy of research methodologies. To go into them fully here would be to deflect attention from the main purpose at hand. This is not however, to imply that they are insubstantial. On the contrary, in the task of building a relevant, public Sociology they are among the most urgent issues of the day.

4. The West should be under no illusions about the moral effect that these deaths have on radicalizing opinion among Muslims. The total comfortably eclipses the number of victims who died at the World Center attacks on 11 September 2001, i.e. 2,996 (including 19 hijackers). For those militant Muslims who advocate terrorism, collateral damage in Pakistan, Yemen and Somalia provides a moral justification to vindicate armed attacks on the West.

5. It is easy to propose that all salaried carers practise the sort of 'spray on sincerity' in caring for strangers that Hochschild's (1983) work identified in modern salaried life. However, to do so goes too far. Care workers are often sincere in the emotions they invest in strangers under their charge. Professional training teaches individuals how to harness and distribute emotional investment, but it would be wrong to say that it always results in 'spray on' forms of empathy.

6. Celebrity may be defined as the accumulation of attention capital via self-promotion and exposure management. Van Kriekan's (2012) useful

concept of 'attention capital' draws necessary attention to the role of investment and asset management in the conduct of social impact. By connecting it with self-promotion and exposure management the crucial influence of cultural intermediaries is incorporated into the perspective. The task of cultural intermediaries is to manage self-promotion of celebrities and exposure management to realize optimum asset management of attention capital.

7.   Bauman's (1987) influential discussion of legislators and interpreters continues to be a helpful resource in understanding modernity. Legislators seek to elucidate or produce rules of conduct. These rules do not always follow the Enlightenment precedent of cleaving to a rational metric. The sort of legislative apparatus in the conduct of life devised by Hitler, Stalin, Mao, Pol Pot, Muammar al-Gaddafi or Saddam Hussein can hardly be said to be 'rational'. What they shared in common is that each, in their own way, regarded themselves to be enforceable over all aspects of social life. Interpreters are constitutionally drawn to the ambivalence and irregularities of rules. They reject the notion that the conduct of social life is a process of unfolding, binding collective legislated order. For them, the conduct of life is mostly circumstantial and social life itself is irrepressibly dynamic, and hence cannot be confined by a legislative order. There is pathos in the Janus face of modernity. The tragedy of modernity 1 is to unintentionally create the conditions whereby Modernity 2 becomes inevitable. Just as the fate of Modernity 2 is to inevitably produce a backlash that will see the mind-set of Modernity 1 straining to correct error and redeem order.

5   Horizontal Frontierism: The Juggernaut of Character

1.   The term 'Old Corruption' refers to 'the widespread use of pensions, sinecures and gratuitous emoluments granted to persons whom the British government, between the earlier eighteenth century and the Age of Reform, wished to buy, reward or bribe' (Rubinstein 1983: 55). The term was coined by William Cobbett. It fell out of use for nigh on a century, before being revived by radical neo-Marxist historians and used as a shibboleth in the language of class based movements dedicated to resistance (Thompson 1978: 258–60; Stedman Jones 1984).

2.   This genre of popular fiction provided a non-annotated, emotionally absorbing vehicle to inculcate the central principles of American character to readers. Cowboy fiction and, later, cowboy films provided escapist entertainment for mass audiences who were none too critical of the versions of history and reality being presented to them.

3.   American neo-liberal ideology has great difficulty in acknowledging any valid role for the state in supporting and developing enterprise culture. After the recession of 2008 Federal support for the bankrupt components of the banking system and 'quantitative easing' (i.e.

increasing the circulation of money by printing currency) was depicted as incidental in the recovery. Support for the banks and central planning of finance was effectively the nationalization of the economy. But it was never spoken of as such. In addition neo-liberal ideology proved extremely effective in portraying the recession as a cyclical downturn. Whereas in fact, it was the result of profiteering and unregulated risk management by the banks and other economic institutions. The managed economy is the accessory of 'managed democracy', but such is the tenacious hold of American neo-liberal ideology that the terms can never be used in critical discussion without being subject to censure that they are 'exaggerations' or gross 'distortions' (Wolin 2008).

4. Inequalities in the USA today are higher than at any time since 1927. The top one per cent of US earners accounted for 19.3 per cent of household income. In 2012 pre-tax income for the top one per cent rose 19.6 per cent compared to an increase of one per cent for the rest of Americans (Saez 2013).

6 The Accentuation of Personality

1. The figurational sociologist, Robert van Kriekan (2012) is right to point to Court society as providing precedents of personality performance and presumed intimacy that were imitated in the age of achieved celebrity. Attention capital is a form of risk capital that can produce windfall gains or catastrophic losses (Van Kriekan 2012: 56).
2. Carl Schmitt (1888–1985) is a controversial figure owing to his membership of the Nazi party (1933), participation in the burning books by Jewish authors and statements of support for Hitler's notorious 'Night of the Long Knives'. His constitutional and political theory remains influential. *Political Romanticism* contains penetrating insights about the dynamics of personality. Their implications are not confined to political figures but rather, extend to achieved celebrity *in toto*. His work remains one of the best critiques of personality, since underlying it is a staunch preference for character.
3. The distinction is between the hedgehog (who views the world through a single defining idea) and the fox (who rejects the idea of singularity and privilege plurality). It has become a famous and popular distinction in philosophy and social science. It does not require much of a leap to identify the hedgehog with character and the fox with personality.
4. Informal life coaching in this sense, is the accessory of para-social forms of interaction. The celebrity personality is not remote from the urban crowd. Technology makes them 'close'. Technology is the means of emotional intimacy, but the spur behind it is the inadequacy of kith and kin relations. The celebrity informal life coach offers the urban crowd life insights and lifestyle tips that are valued as more glamorous and relevant in the business of gaining acceptance and approval in wider social circles.

5.   In the UK in 2011 the median full-time salary was £26,200 per year, while the top ten per cent earned £52,600 (Cribb 2013). The 'Office for National Statistics' (2014) reports that Britain's richest one per cent hold as much wealth as the poorest 55 per cent of the population.

6.   To treat character as a 'front' (or 'public face') to be switched in and out of, is, of course, symptomatic of the cast of mind associated with personality. Principle and consistency are defined as resources to be applied in given settings to achieve personal advantage and impact. The obligations and responsibilities that follow principle and consistency are not necessarily acknowledged in subsequent encounters. 'Fronting', fit for 'the occasion', is the name of the game.

7   Vertical Frontierism: Four Case Studies

1.   Joseph Roach (2007) has devoted an entire book to an analysis of 'it'. Drawing on a variety of sources, he argues that 'it' is a combination of sexual magnetism (to both sexes), unselfconsciousness, presence, personality entitlement and confidence. To use his (2007: 8) own term, this account is a trifle 'polymorphous'. For it not only associates 'it' with a multitude of traits, but the traits are themselves contradictory. Elsewhere in his book he makes contradiction the essence of 'it': ' "It" is the power of apparently effortless embodiment of contradictory qualities simultaneously: strength *and* vulnerability, innocence *and* experience, and singularity *and* typicality . . . the possessor of It keeps a precarious balance between such mutually exclusive alternatives, suspended at the tipping point like a tightrope dancer on one foot; and the empathetic tension of waiting for the apparently inevitable fall makes for breathless spectatorship' (Roach 2007: 8). This combination of personality traits rather suggests a rather disagreeable individual. To be sure, many people who encounter those who purport to possess 'it' indeed, find them disagreeable and irritating. Perhaps, Roach ought to have added 'daring' to his list of personality traits. For clearly, while one might find those who purport to possess 'it' disagreeable and irritating, the jeopardy posed to boundaries is attractive. Roach's (2007) discussion recalls many aspects of Schmitt's (1919) analysis of personality dynamics and the importance of 'the occasion'. Not least, the equation of social impact with challenging and breaking boundaries.

2.   Celebrity is a social construction. It always consists of two elements: the *public face*, which is for the consumption of the public; and the *private face*, which is the sense of self that celebrities have of themselves. Reflexivity in human affairs is always challenging, since it requires individuals to confront the question of how *habitus* contributes to issues of embodiment and emplacement. The challenge is heightened in the case of celebrity since acclaim is based upon the accumulation

of attention capital for the public face. The private face of the celebrity is in danger of suffering atrophy, so that stars may complain that they do not know who they are any more.

9 The Gestural Economy

1. Since personal conduct is always *situated behaviour* it follows that it bears the imprimatur of the balance of power relationships in which willed (and unwilled) gestural acts occur.
2. The term 'ratio dynamics' is designed to convey that the ratio of the balance of power relations between an individual and the patterns of power in which agency and cognitive intentions unfold move up and down. Gesture is an important communicative mechanism in registering movements in the ratio of power between individuals and groups.
3. Weber's (1968) classical model of bureaucracy identifies written, codified rules and circumscribed commitment to normatively prescribed, formal authority as the basis of legitimate rule. He contrasted the bureaucratic form, which he associated with industrialization and democratization, with traditional and charismatic forms of rule, both of which demanded ultimate commitment to the rulers and the system of command surrounding them.
4. This about face in protocol and convention of course, established rising economic and maritime power of the industrializing Western nations. Asia, Africa and Latin America could not ignore the increasingly favourable ratio dynamics in favour of Western interests. The loss of Courtly and Tribal presage in these areas of the world, and the degradation and humiliation associated with it, proved decisive in the twentieth century e.g. in the pan-Asian discomfort with the attempt to create a new world power order that guaranteed Western supremacy established, after the Treaty of Versailles (1919). In particular, it was an important factor in the militarization of Japan and its recognition of the USA as an oppressor.
5. Supporters of Edward Said's (1991) absorbing and highly influential critique of 'Orientalism' need no reminder of the condescending views that many so-called 'civilized' Englightenment *savants* applied to the East. Orientalism was undoubtedly racist. Conversely, it should not be assumed that racial condescension was singular to the Occident. The system of power in traditional Han Chinese Court society privileged the Emperor as the centre of the civilized world. Obeisance to the Emperor was integral to the Chinese model of suzeranity. This model identified the Emperor and his Court as the apex of the world order and, so 'naturally', positioned the rulers of other lands and their people as subjects, with all of the unspoken, binding obligations that this implied.

6. The polarization between 'the one per cent and the 99 per cent was of course, the slogan of the *Occupy* movement in the protests and occupations of public space in 2011–12. Some respected commentators on the Left regarded this as a game changing intervention, i.e. it dramatically popularized consciousness of the inequality and injustice that is endemic to capitalism (Castells 2012; Gitlin 2012b). Against this, David Runciman (2012) is properly sceptical. He describes 'the 99 per cent' as 'a concept that comes apart on close scrutiny' (Runciman 2012: 7). The problem is that 99 per cent unity among people on any issue or any type of social composition is improbable. Analogously, the characterization of the one per cent as a unified composite with the same beliefs and interests is a caricature. Eligibility to belong to the one per cent starts for those with a household income of $350,000. But the 0.1 per cent with incomes in the millions or billions cannot realistically be placed on a par with the 0.99 per cent. Even within the 0.99 per cent there are blatant divisions of status, values, beliefs etc. So the caricature of 'the one per cent' and 'the 99 per cent' are not helpful analytic metaphors because they are intrinsically false constructs. Runciman (2012) tellingly goes on to note that a crucial division that the *Occupy* sloganeers ignored was between *Occupy activists* and *Occupy sympathesizers*. Activists consisted of a high proportion of unemployed, propertyless labourers who constitute a categorical minority of the so-called 99 per cent. It is surely a grossly inflated claim to suggest that this categorical division is secondary to an ontological assumption of victimhood.
7. The phrase has been one of the enduring from *The Communist Manifesto* (Marx and Engels 1968: 31–63). But it is a 'clumpish' term (Thompson 1991a: 13). That is, it abbreviates difference, variety and *lex loci* ('the law of the place) which are inevitably features of work cultures and replaces them with the false emulsion of metaphorical unity. Customs, habits and other communicated principles of difference are intrinsic to the experience of labour and other cultural categories (Thompson 1991; Winslow 2014). It is really no surprise that the phrase 'workers of the world unite' failed to live up to its billing. The symbolic weight of the billing was too great to encompass reality. Workers did in fact, have something more to lose than their 'chains', i.e. the labouring and community traditions and the *habitus* of geographical place and social position that contributed ontological meaning.
8. FCUK is the trade name of *French Connection UK*. It is a branch of the so-called 'shockvertising' pioneered by *Benetton* in the 1980s. Shockvertising is designed to generate instant attention capital. It is an aspect of the gestural economy which frequently addresses civil rights issues, climate change and corporate power, but in a way that prioritizes aesthetic identification over concrete action. Shopping at FCUK is a type of votive behaviour which conveys consciousness of the inequalities and injustices of the system while at the same time contributing to the profit margins that perpetuate the system.

10 Institutional and Counter-Institutional Gestural Economies

1. Said's (1991) *Orientalism* still provides the most arresting account of how Occidentalism socially constructed the Orient as backward and inferior.
2. Decentring and deconstruction are the enemies of progressive politics because they bestow authority upon the position that agreement and resolution are possible and more than arbitrary. The anti-Hegelian thrust in postmodernism was carried too far. The Frankfurt School did enough to question Hegelian logic by means of the principle of negative dialectics, i.e. Adorno's (1992) thesis that there is no transcendence or unity. For Adorno, Hegel's approach conjures the spell of catastrophic force because it posits grand, elemental unities beyond the respect for individual difference and anomaly. Postmodernism *contra* Hegel leads to the same impasse, but for different reasons, i.e. postmodernism holds that every grand narrative proclaiming unity is a con-trick. Progressive politics today has one foot in each swamp. We live with an urgent need to recognize unity in the midst of difference and difference in the midst of revisionist sentiments.

11 Nuda Veritas

1. Furedi's (2003) account of 'therapy culture' and its discontents is required reading for understanding the peculiar delusions of modern 'caring' culture. It is not that this culture is incapable of comprehensive care. It is that it makes automatic assumptions about the content and means of care without fully appreciating the social dimensions of personal problems. For example, mood-stabilizing medication prescriptions for children increased by 400 per cent between 2002 and 2013 (Leader 2013). Hardly any psychoanalysts have related mood stabilizing personality disorders to social conditions. Interestingly, Simmel (1903) does anticipate these connections in his discussion of the relationships between the balsa and neurasthenic personalities and modernity. The temporary, fugitive, unstable character of modern social conditions is one factor in the manic episodes associated with bipolar personality disorder.
2. The phrase 'society, without opposition' is associated with the Frankfurt School critique of mature capitalism (Marcuse 1964). Many aspects of this critique remain of interest. However, although it has tremendous metaphorical power, the 'one dimensional man' thesis misses the real state of managed democracy which is one of cacophony. The free reign given to voices, provided that they do not over-step legal, ethical boundaries, has produced a din of noise that is unable to resolve itself

into binding keynotes. This suits the multi-national executives and state civil servants situated at the tiller of the corporate-state axis very well since paralysis of effective opposition is the desired state of optimally governed managed democracy (Wolin 2008).

3. The philosophy of horizontalism derives from *horizontalidad*, the system of organization devised by protesters in Argentina in 2001. It is credited with ejecting five consecutive elected governments and created new neighbourhood assemblies. Horizontalism stands for self-management and direct democracy. It rejects conventional notions of political leaders in favour of equal, organic group power (Sitrin 2012: 74). The meaning of the term 'the people's mic' is self-explanatory.

4. To be clear, the technical provision of leaders, party discipline and defined goals are not in themselves corrupting. The problem is that in the minatory form of managed democracy they operate to fulfil the wishes of the vested interests that covertly govern the entire system. *Occupy* was right to object to corruption, but horizontalism and the people's mic simply do not translate to regional, national or global levels of political intervention. 'In an age where identities are potentially plural and changing', writes Wolin (2008: 290), 'a unified demos is no longer possible: instead of *a* demos, democratic citizens' (emphasis in the original). That is, instead of *agora*-type forms political decision making the emphasis should be upon creating educated, well informed citizens with the powers to implement their majority will in the production and reproduction of the social order.

5. Hayden White (2008: 18–20) makes a couple of important contributions to clarify WHEs. To begin with, WHEs are anti-systemic. They are literally shocks to the system. WHEs like the mass demonstration in Tiananmen Square (1989), the assembly beneath the Brandenberg Gate and the dismantling of the Berlin Wall (1989), 9/11, were major dislocations of routine in which the precarious nature of the system was unquestionably exposed and various sorts of adaptive responses were elicited. In the second place, White (2008: 18–20) observes that it is necessary to twin the idea of the WHE with the notion of a double occurence. That is, WHEs are acted out as first, dislocation, and second, the 'filling out' or 'fulfilment' of an earlier Event or Event sequence. Naturally, they are experienced and interpreted from multiple viewpoints and vantages. However, unlike purely personal incidents, their decisive quality is that they operate as a benchmark against which trajectories of inter-subjective readings of history are mapped. You know where you were when 9/11 happened and many people have the same feeling about the Arab Spring (2011) and Occupy (2011–12).

6. Tiananmen, Tahir, Syntagama and Gezi achieved some of the immediate goals that sparked the protests and filtered through the system of organized politics to elicit new conciliations and constitutional reform. Some of these were considerable. For example, post-Tahir eventually ousted President Hosni Mubarak from office and reinforced the pace of civil disobedience in the wider so-called 'Arab Spring'. Besides Egypt,

this led to political change in Tunisia, Libya, Yemen and Syria. However, nowhere have the changes exactly amounted to power to the people. In Libya the overthrow of loyalist forces in 2011, has not resulted in stable government. Schisms between the central government and rival, armed militias have produced a post-Gaddafi history of disorder and chaos. In Yemen, the protests eventually led to the downfall of President Saleh, but he was succeeded by his Vice President Hadi (the only candidate), who continues with broadly the same policies. In Syria the protests triggered civil war in the country which, at the time of writing, remains intense, bloody and unresolved. Post-Mubarak Egypt underwent the trauma of the military seizure of power, the rise of the Muslim Brotherhood, national violence and unrest and the removal of the democratically elected President (Mohamed Morsi) by a militarily led *coup d'etat* in 2013.

7. The Tarnac 9 refer to a group of nine radicals aged between twenty-two and thirty-four, alleged to be anarchist terrorists plotting the overthrow of the state. They were arrested in 2008. The ring leader, Julien Coupat is said to have authored 'The Coming Insurrection'. He and his associates were accused by the French state for inciting and planning armed struggle. The arrests produced a wave of complaint in France that the state had acted precipitately, in a misinformed way. The Tarnac 9 were eventually released. Coupat spent six months in prison.

8. Investment, using borrowed money, in over-valued property and stock markets is not currently, even remotely, matched to sustainable growth. It is estimated that GDP in 2013 amounted to $74.909 trillion. World debt as a proportion to output in 2013 was 212 per cent, compared with 180 per cent in 2008 (Buttiglione et al. 2014).

9. To remind the reader, Modernity 1 strives to impose a rational grid upon social life whereas Modernity 2 strains to demonstrate that all rational grids over-simplify social reality and present a barrier to innovation. In some respects the division mirrors the polarity between Hegel and Adorno. According to Hegel (1956, 1977) social development is a process of resolution, i.e. thesis, anti-thesis leads to synthesis. Against this, Adorno (1966) argued for negative dialectics, i.e. that there is no durable synthesis from the antimony between thesis and anti-thesis.

10. The political rhetoric of 'freedom' that animated the movement to establish Academies in the English school system falls foul of the same qualification. New Labour and the Coalition government that succeeded it, promoted Academies in the interest of producing diversity and freeing education from restrictive Local Authority controls. In actuality, the state retains tight controls over educational standards and provision. What may have been crowd pleasing to the public, inured by the popular media to tales of classroom disorder and falling standards, disguised centrist regulation and control (Curtis 2009: 114–15).

References

Adams, J. Q. (1909–10) 'J. Q. Adams on the Opium War', *Massachusetts Historical Society Proceedings*, 43: 295–325

Adams, V., Van Hattum, T. and English, D. (2009) 'Chronic disaster syndrome: Disaster capitalism and the eviction of the poor from New Orleans', *American Ethnologist*, 36 (4): 615–36

Adorno, T. (1966) *Negative Dialectics*, London, Routledge

___ (1981) *In Search of Wagner*, London, New Left Books

___ (1992) *The Culture Industry*, London, Routledge

___ (2000) *The Psychological Technique of Martin Luther Thomas' Radio Addresses*, Stanford, Stanford University Press

Adorno, T. and Horkheimer, M. (1979) *Dialectic of Enlightenment*, London, Verso

Aldhous, P. (2005) 'Counterfeit pharmaceuticals: Murder by medicine', *Nature*, 434: 132–6

Alexander, J. (2011) *Performance and Power*, Cambridge, Polity.

Allen, N. (2008) 'Council bans brainstorming', *Daily Telegraph*, 20.6.2008

Andrews, M. (2006) *Charles Dickens and His Performing Selves*, Oxford, Oxford University Press

Aronowitz, S. (2004) *How Class Works*, New Haven, Yale University Press

___ (2012) *Taking It Big: C. Wright Mills and the Making of Political Intellectuals*, New York, Columbia University Press

Azzi, N. (2010) 'Canada's prison privatization experiment: A critique', UMI Dissertation Publishing, York University, Toronto

Bailyn, B. (1976) *The Ordeal of Thomas Hutchinson*, Cambridge, Harvard University/Belknap Press.

Barber, B. (2012) 'What democracy looks like', *Contexts*, 11 (2): 14–16

Baudrillard, J. (1986) *The Evil Demon of Images*, Sydney, Power Institute

___ (2004) *The Gulf War Did Not Take Place*, Sydney, Power Institute

Bauman, Z. (1987) *Legislators and Interpreters*, Cambridge, Polity
___ (2000) *Liquid Modernity*, Cambridge, Polity
___ (2006) *Liquid Times*, Cambridge, Polity
Bauman, Z. and Tester, K. (2001) *Conversations With Bauman*, Cambridge, Polity
Barnes, V., Treiber, V., and Ludwig, D. (2005) 'African-American adolescents' stress responses after the 9/11/01 terrorist attacks', *Journal of Adolescent Health*, 36 (3): 201–7
Batson, C., Chang, J., Orr, R and Rowland, J. (2002) 'Empathy, attitudes and actions', *Journal of Personality and Social Psychology*, 72, 105–18
Beck, U. and Cronin, C. (2006) *Cosmopolitan Vision*, Cambridge, Polity
Beniger, J. (1987) 'Personalization of mass media and the growth of pseudo-community', *Communication Research*, 14 (3): 352–71
Benoit, W. and Henson, J. (2009) 'President Bush's image repair discourse on Hurricane Katrina', *Public Relations Review*, 35 (1): 40–6
Bergen, P. and Tiedemann, K. (2010) *The Year of the Drone: An Analysis of US Drone Strikes in Pakistan*, New America Foundation (http://counterterrorism.newamerica.net)
Berger, A. (2008) 'Tourism in Society', *Society*, 45 (4): 327–9
Bernays, E. (1928) *Propaganda*, New York, Ig Books
Best, J. (2001) *Damned Lies and Statistics*, Berkley, University of California Press
Bevis, M. (2001) 'Dickens in public', *Essays in Criticism*, 51 (3): 330–52
Bhatt, C. (2012) 'Human rights and the transformations of war', *Sociology*, 46 (5): 219–23
Billington, R. (1958) 'How the frontier shaped American character', *American Heritage*, 9 (3): 4–12
___ (1966) *America's Frontier Heritage*, San Francisco, Holt, Rinehart and Winston.
Bird, R. (2008) 'Counterfeit drugs: A global consumer perspective', *Wake Forest Intellectual Property Journal*, 8 (3): 287–404
Blakeney, M. (2009) 'International proposals for the criminal enforcement of intellectual property rights', Queen Mary School of Law, Legal Studies Research Paper, No. 29.2009 (http://papers.ssrn.com/sol3/papers.cfm?abstract_id=1476964)
Blyton, P. and Jenkins, J. (2007) *Key Concepts in Work*, London, Sage
Boholm, A. (1998) 'Visual images and risk messages: Commemorating Chernobyl', *Risk, Decision and Policy*, 3 (2): 125–43
Bourdieu, P. (1977) *Outline of a Theory of Practice*, Cambridge, Cambridge University Press
___ (1984) *Distinction*, London, Routledge
___ (1993) *The Field of Cultural Production*, Cambridge, Polity
___ (1996) *The Rules of Art*, Cambridge, Polity
___ (1999) *The Weight of the World*, Cambridge, Polity
Bowen, P., Van Heerikhuizen, B., Emirbayer, M. (2012) 'Elias and Bourdieu', *Journal of Classical Sociology*, 12 (1): 69–93

Boys, J. (2011) 'What's so extraordinary about rendition?' *The International Journal of Human Rights*, 15 (4): 589–604

Bull, P. (1987) *Posture and Gesture*, Oxford, Pergamon

Bubnys, E. (1982) 'Nativity and the distribution of wealth: Chicago 1870', *Explorations in Economic History*, 19 (2): 101–9

Bush, G. W. (2001) 'Freedom at war with fear' (http://www.whitehouse.gov/news/releases/2001/09/20010920-8.html)

Butsch, R. (2008) *Citizen Audience*, New York, Routledge

Buttiglione, L., Lane, P., Reichin, L. and Reinhart, V. (2014) 'Deleveraging? What Deleveraging?', 16th Geneva Report on the World Economy, International Center for Monetary and Banking Studies, Geneva

Brinkley, D. (2006) *The Great Deluge*, New York, William Murrow

Brunner, E. (1994) 'Abraham Lincoln as authentic reproduction', *American Anthropologist*, 96 (2): 397–412

Brown, W. (1926) 'The psychology of Character II', *Journal of Neurology and Psychopathology*, 7 (26): 125–31

Calhoun, C. (2012a) *The Roots of Radicalism*, Chicago, Chicago University Press

___ (2012b) 'Response', (given to) Gitlin, T. 'Occupy's predicament: The moment and prospects of the movement', Public Lecture, Sheik Zayed Theatre, London School of Economics, 18.10.2012

Calloway, C. (1951) 'Is dope killing our musicians?', *Ebony*, February 1951

Carey, J. (1988) *Communication as Culture*, New York, Routledge

Carlyle, T. (2012) *On Heroes, Hero Worship, and the Heroic in History*, CreateSpace Independent Publishing Platform

Castells, M. (2009) *Communication Power*, Oxford, Oxford University Press

___ (2012) *Networks of Outrage and Hope*, Cambridge, Polity

Caughey, J. (1984) *Imaginary Social Worlds*, Lincoln, University of Nebraska Press

CensusScope (2006) University of Michigan Social Science Data Analysis Network (2006: Segregation: Dissimilarity Indices (http://www.censuscope.org.us)

Chabot, C. B. (1976) 'Melville's the confidence man: A "poisonous" reading', *Psychoanalytic Review*, 63 (4): 571–85

Chae-Mi, L. and Youn-Kyoung, K. (2011) 'Older consumers' TV home shopping: Loneliness, parasocial interaction, and perceived convenience', *Psychology and Marketing*, 28 (8): 763–80

Chang, M. (2009) 'Is the drugstore safe? Counterfeit diabetes products on the shelves', *Journal of Diabetes Science and Technology*, 3 (6): 1516–20

Chaudry, P. and Stumpf, S. (2011) 'Consumer complicity with counterfeit products', *Journal of Consumer Marketing*, 28 (2): 139–51

Chia, S. and Poo, Y.-L. (2009) 'Media, celebrities and fans', *Journalism and Mass Communications Quarterly*, 86 (1): 23–44

Chomsky, N. (2012) *Occupy*, London, Penguin

Chory-Asad, R. and Yanen, A. (2005) 'Hopelessness and loneliness as predictors of older adults' involvement with favourite television performers', *Journal of Broadcasting and Electronic Media*, 49 (2): 182–201

Christopher, J., Richardson, F. and Slife, B. (2008) 'Thinking through positive psychology', *Theory and Psychology*, 18 (5): 555–61

Cigler, B. (2006/7) 'Hurricane Katrina: Two intergovernmental challenges', *Public Manager*, 35 (4): 3–7

Clarkson, P. (1996) *The Bystander (An End to Innocence in Human Relationships?)*, London, Whurr Publications

Cohen, J. (1999) 'Favourite characters of teenage viewers of Israeli serials', *Journal of Broadcasting and Electronic Media*, 43: 327–45

___ 2001) 'Defining identification: A theoretical look at identification of audiences with media characters', *Mass Communication and Society*, 4: 245–64

___ (2004) 'Parasocial break-up from favourite television characters', *Journal of Social and Personal Relationships*, 21 (2): 187–202

Cohen, S. (2001) *States of Denial*, Cambridge, Polity

___ (2011) *Folk Devils and Moral Panics*, London, Routledge

Cole, T. and Leets, L. (1999) 'Attachment styles and intimate television viewing', *Journal of Personal and Social Relationships*, 16: 495–511

Coleman, F. M. (2003) 'The encoded frontier: from open space to ad space', *Capitalism Nature Socialism*, 14 (2): 135–62

Collini, S. (2012) *What Are Universities For?*, London, Penguin

Collins, P. (1975) 'Introduction', pp: xxv–xxvii, in Collins, P. (ed.) *Charles Dickens: The Public Readings*, Oxford, Clarendon Press

Comfort, L., Birkland, T., Cigler, B. and Nance, E. (2010) 'Retrospectives and Prospectives on Hurricane Katrina: Five Years and Counting', *Public Administration Review*, 70 (5): 669–78

Compton, W. (2005) *Introduction to Positive Psychology*, Belmont, CA., Thomson Wadsworth

Cooper, C. and Taylor, P. (2005) 'Independently verified reductionism: prison privatization in Scotland, *Human Relations*, 58 (4): 497–522

Cooper, R. (1997) 'The visibility of social systems', in Hetherington, K. and Munro, R. (eds) *Ideas of Difference*, Oxford, Blackwell

Couldry, N. (2008) 'Mediatization or mediation?' *New Media and Society*, 10 (3): 373–91

___ (2012) *Media, Society, World*, Cambridge, Polity

Corner, J. and Kendall, S. D. (2007) 'Terrorism: The psychological impact on youth', *Clinical Psychology: Science and Practice'*, 14 (3): 179–212

Curran, J. (2010) 'Entertaining Democracy', in Curran, J. (ed.) *Media and Society*, London, Bloomsbury 38–62

Curry, R. (1996) *Too Much of a Good Thing: Mae West as a Cultural Icon*, Minneapolis, University of Minnesota Press

Curtis, A. (2009) 'Academies and school diversity', *Management in Education*, 23 (3): 113–17

Cribb, J. (2013) 'Income inequality in the UK' *Institute of Fiscal Studies*, http://www.ifs.org.uk/docs/ER_JC_2013.pdf

Davis, L. and Siegel, L. (2000) 'Posttraumatic stress disorder in children and adolescents', *Clinical Child and Family Psychology Review*, 3 (3): 135–54

Debord, G. (1987) *Society of the Spectacle*, London, Rebel Press

___ (1990) *Comments on the Society of the Spectacle*, London, Verso

___ (2009) 'Toward a situationist international', in McDonough, T.(ed.) *The Situationists and The City*, London, Verso: 94–9

Delaporte, Y. and Shaw, E. (2009) 'Gesture and signs through history', *Gesture*, 9 (1): 35–60

Department for Business Innovation London, and Skills (2013a) *Trade Union Membership 2012*

Department for Business, Innovation and Skills (2013b) *Participation Rates in Higher Education, Years 2006/7–2011–12*, London, info@bis.gsi .gov.uk

Der Derian, J. (2009) *Virtuous War: Mapping the Military-industrial-media-entertainment Network*, 2nd edn, New York, Routledge

Dohnt, H. and Tiggemann, M. (2006) 'The contribution of peer and media influences to the development of body satisfaction and self-esteem in young girls', *Developmental Psychology*, 42 (6): 929–36

Douglas, M. (2002) *Purity and Danger*, London, Routledge

Downer, A. (1966) *The Eminent Tragedian: William Charles Macready*, Cambridge, Harvard University Press

Dumont, M., Yzerbyt, V., Wigboldus, D. and Gordjin, E. (2003) 'Social categorization and fear reactions to the September 11th terrorist attacks', *Personality and Social Psychology Bulletin*, 29 (12): 1509–20

Durkheim, E. (2013) *The Division of Labour in Society*, Basingstoke, Palgrave (2nd edn)

Drake, S. C. and Clayton, Jr, H. R. (1945/1993) *Black Metropolis*, Chicago, Chicago University Press

Dreyfus, L. (2010) *Wagner and the Erotic Impulse*, Cambridge, Cambridge University Press

Dworkin, R. (2011) *Justice for Hedgehogs*, Cambridge, Belknap, Harvard University Press

Dundes, L. and Rajapaksa, S. (2004) 'Just deserts? An examination of Sri Lankans's reactions to 9/11', *Studies in Conflict and Terrorism*, 27 (1): 31–45

Dunning, E. and Elias, N. (2013) *Norbert Elias and Modern Sociology*, London, Bloomsbury Academic

Dynes, R. and Rodriguez, H. (2007) 'Finding and framing Katrina: The social construction of disaster', in Brunsma, D., Overfelt, D., and Picou, J. (eds) *The Sociology of Katrina*, Lanham, Rowman and Littlefield, pp. 23–33

Easterly, W. (2007) *The White Man's Burden*, Oxford, Oxford University Press

___ (2014) *The Tyranny of Experts*, New York, Basic Civitas

Eaton, R. (1921) 'Social Fatalism', *The Philosophical Review*, 30 (4): 380–92

Ehrenreich, B. (2009) *Smile Or Die*, London, Granta

Eichenweld, W. (2001) 'The "I don't care girl" ', *American History*, 36 (5): 26

Elias, N. and Dunning, G. (1986) *The Quest For Excitement*, Oxford, Blackwell

Elliott, A. (2010) ' "I want to look like that!": Cosmetic surgery and celebrity culture', *Cultural Sociology*, 5 (4): 463–77

Eisenberg, N. and Silver, R. (2011) 'Growing up in the shadow of terrorism: Youth in America after 9/11', *American Psychologist*, 66 (6): 468–81

Eurostat (2013) *Tertiary Education Statistics* (epp.eurostat.ec.europa.ed/statistics)

Erdman, A. (2012) *Queen of Vaudeville: The Story of Eva Tanguay*, Ithaca, Cornell University Press

Erkman, P. and Friesen, W. (1969) 'The repertoire of non-verbal behaviour', *Semiotica*, 1: 49–98

Ethridge, P. and Marquart, J. (1993) 'Private prisons in Texas: The new penology for profit', *Justice Quarterly*, 10: 29–48

Ewen, S. (1998) *PR! A Social History of Spin*, New York, Basic

Fairbank, J. (1942) 'Tributary's trade and China's relations with the West', *The Far Eastern Quarterly*, 1 (2): 129–49

Farrel, N. (2012) 'Celebrity Politics: Bono, Product (RED) and the Legitimising of Philanthrocapitalism', *British Journal of Politics and International Relations*, 14 (3): 392–406

Ferguson, S. (2001) 'Dickens's public readings and the Victorian author', *Studies in English Literature*, 41 (4): 729–49

Ferrell, J., Hayward, K., Morrison, W. and Presdee, M. (eds) (2004) *Unleashing Cultural Criminology*, London, Glasshouse Press

Figley, C. (1995) 'Compassion fatigue as secondary traumatic stress disorder: an overview', in Figley, C. (ed.) *Compassion Fatigue*, New York, Brunner-Mazel pp: 1–20

Fioramonti, L. (2014) *How Numbers Rule The World: The Use and Abuse of Statistics in Global Politics*, London, Zed Books

Fox, A. (1974) *Beyond Contract: Work, Power and Trust Relations*, London, Faber and Faber

Foucault, M. (1981) *The History of Sexuality*, London, Penguin

——— (2013) *Emile Durkheim*, Cambridge, Polity

Fournier, M. (2003) *Emile Durkheim: A Biography*, Cambridge, Polity.

Forgette, R., Dettrey, B., Van Boeing, M. and Swanson, D. (2009) 'Before, Now, and after: Assessing Hurricane Katrina relief', *Population Research and Policy Review*, 28 (1): 31–44

Fu, K.-W. and Chan, C. H. (2013) 'A study of the impact of thirteen celebrity suicides on subsequent suicide rates in South Korea from 2005 to 2009', *PLoS ONE* *(1): e53870

Furedi, F. (2003) *Therapy Culture*, London, Routledge

Fullerton, C. S. and Ursano, R. J. et al. (eds) (2005) 'Psychological and pscyhopathological consequences of disasters', in Lopez-Ibor, J. *Disasters and Mental Health*, Chichester, Wiley

Fremont, W. (2004) 'Childhood reactions to terrorism-induced trauma', *Journal of the American Academy of Child and Adolescent Psychiatry*, 43 (4): 381–92

Gabler, N. (2000) *Life: The Movie*, New York, Vintage Books

Galea, S., Vlahov, D., Resnick, H., Ahren, J., Susser, E., Gold, J., Bucculvalas, M. and Kilpatrick, D. (2003) 'Trends of probable post-traumatic stress disorder in New York City after the September 11 terrorist attacks', *American Journal of Epidemiology*, 158 (6): 514–24

Gallman, R. (1994) 'Professor Pessen on the "egalitarian myth"', *Social Science History*, 2 (2): 194–207

Gamson, J. (2001) 'Normal sins: Sex scandal narratives and institutional morality tales', *Social Problems*, 48 (2): 185–205

___ (2011) 'The unwatched life is not worth living: The elevation of the ordinary in celebrity culture', *Publications of the Modern Language Association of America*, 126 (4): 1061–9

Ganzel, B., Casey, B., Glover, G., Voss, H., Temple, E. (2007) 'The aftermath of 9/11: Effect of intensity and recency of trauma on outcome', *Emotion*, 7 (2): 227–38

Gaventa, J., Tandon, R. (eds) (2010) *Globalizing Citizens*, London, Zed

Gardner, H. (1983) *Frames of Mind*, New York, Basic Books

Garfinkel, H. (1967) *Studies in Ethnomethodology*, Cambridge, Polity (revd edn 1984)

Gellner, E. (1988) *Plough, Sword and Book*, Chicago, Chicago University Press

Giddens, A. (1990) *The Consequences of Modernity*, Cambridge, Polity

Giles, D. (2002) 'Parasocial interaction: A review of the literature and a model for future research', *Media Psychology*, 4 (3): 279–305

Gitlin, J. (2010) *The Bourgeois Frontier: French Towns, French Traders and American Expansion*, New Haven, Yale University Press

Gitlin, T. (2012a) *Occupy Nation*, New York, IT Books

___ (2012b) 'Occupy's predicament: The moment and prospects of the movement', Public Lecture in the Sheikh Zayed Theatre, London School of Economics, 18/10/2001

Gleser, G., Green, B. and Winget, C. (1983) *Prolonged Psychosocial Effects of Disaster: A Study of Buffalo Creek*, New York, Academic Press

Godelier, M. (1999) *The Enigma of the Gift*, Chicago, Chicago University Press

Goffman, E. (1961) *Asylums*, London, Penguin

___ (1963) *Behaviour in Public Places*, New York, Free Press

Golem, D. (1996) *Emotional Intelligence*, New York, Bantam

Gomery, D. (1986) *The Hollywood Studio System*, St Martin's, New York

Gumperz, J., Kaltmann, H. and O'Connor, M. (1984) 'Cohesion in spoken and written discourse', in Tannen, D. (ed.) *Coherence in Spoken and Written Discourse*, Norwood, Ablex, 3–19

O'Connor, H. (2006) 'Project', *Journal of Youth Studies*, 9 (2): 159–73

Gosh, P. (2003) 'The Muslims, South Asia and the United States: A Post T-9/11 Analysis', *South Asian Survey*, 10 (1): 101–23

Graham, S. (2010) *Cities Under Siege*, London, Verso

Gramsci, A. (1971) *Prison Notebooks*, London, Lawrence and Wishart

Greenblatt, S. (1991) *Marvellous Possessions*, Chicago, Chicago University Press

Greenwood, D. (2009) 'Idealized TV friends and young women's body concerns', *Body Image*, 6 (2): 97–104

Greenwood, D., Pietromonaco, P. and Long, C. (2008) 'Young womens' attachment style and interpersonal engagement with female TV stars', *Journal of Social and Personal Relationships*, 25 (3): 387–407

Gregory, D. (2011) 'From a Viet to a kill: Drones and late modern warfare', *Theory, Culture and Society*, 28 (7–8): 188–215

Guin, U., Di Mase, D. and Tehranipoor, M. (2014) 'Counterfeit integrated circuits', *Journal of Electronic Testing*, 30 (1): 9–23

Gullberg, M. (2006) 'Some reasons for studying gesture and second language acquisition', *International Review of Applied Linguistics*, 44 (2): 103–24

Gundle, S. (2008) *Glamour*, Oxford, OUP

Habermas, J. (1997) *Between Facts and Norms*, Cambridge, Polity

___ (2002) *The Inclusion of the Other*, Cambridge, Polity

___ (2008) *Between Naturalism and Religion*, Cambridge, Polity

Haidt, J. (2001) 'The emotional dog and its rational tail' *Psychological Review*, 108: 814–34

Hagan, J. (1954) 'The poor labyrinth: The theme of social injustice in Dickens's *Great Expectations*', *Nineteenth-Century Fiction*, 9 (3): 169–78

___ (2005) 'Psychosocial implications of disaster or terrorism on children', *Pediatrics*, 116 (3): 787–95

Hall, E. (1968) 'Proxemics', *Current Anthropology*, 9: 83–108

___ (2007) 'Living with difference' (in conversation with Schwarz, B.), *Soundings*, 37 (1): 148–58

___ (1988) *The Hard Road To Renewal*, London, Verso

Hall, S. and Jacques, M. (eds) (1983) *The Politics of Thatcherism*, London, Lawrence and Wishart

Hamilton, M. (1990) 'Mae West', *Cambridge Quarterly*, 15 (4): 383–8

___ (1997) *When I'm Bad, I'm Better: Mae West, Sex and American Entertainment*, Berkley, University of California Press

Harper-Scott, J. (2011) 'Wagner, sex and capitalism', *The Wagner Journal*, 5 (2): 46–62

Harvey, D. (1985) *Consciousness and the Urban Experience*, Oxford, Blackwell

___ (2007) *A Brief History of Neo-Liberalism*, Oxford, Oxford University Press

___ (2013) *Rebel Cities*, London, Verso

Hayward, K. (2004) *City Limits: Crime, Consumer Culture and Urban Experience*, London: Glass House Press

Head, S. (2011) 'The grim threat to British universities', *New York Review of Books*, January, 13 2011

Healey, D. (2012) *Pharmageddon*, Berkley, University of California Press

Hedges, C. (2009) *Empire of Illusion*, New York, Nation Books
___ (2010) *Death of the Liberal Class*, New York, Nation Books
___ (2012) 'The Cancer in Occupy', *Truthdig*, 6.02.2012
Hegel, G. W. F. (1956) *The Philosophy of History*, New York, Dover
___ (1977) *Phenomenology of Spirit*, Oxford, Oxford University Press
Heidegger, M. (1978) *Being and Time*, Oxford, Blackwell
Hendriana, E., Mayasari, A. and Gunadi, W. (2013) 'Why do college students buy counterfeit movies?', *International Journal of e-Education, e-Business, e-Management and e-Learning*, 22 (4): 353–71
Henkel, K., Dovidio, J. and Gaertner, S. (2006) 'institutional discrimination, indiviudal racism, and Hurricane Katrina', *Analyses of Social Issues and Public Policy*, 6 (1): 99–124
Hesmondhalgh, D. (2006) 'Bourdieu, the media and cultural production', *Media, Culture and Society*, 28 (2): 211–31
Hevia, J. (2009) ' "The ultimate gesture of deference and debasement": Kowtowing in China', *Past and Present*, 203 (4): 212–34
Hjarvard, S. (2004) 'From bricks to bytes: The mediatization of a global toy industry', in Bondjeberg, I. and Golding, P. (eds) *European Culture and Intellect*, Bristol, Intellect, 43–63
___ (2009) 'Soft individualism: Media and the changing social character', in Lundby, K. (ed.) *Mediatization*, New York, Peter Laing: 159–77
Hobsbawm, E. (1978) '1968: A retrospective', *Marxism Today*, May, 130–8
Hochschild, A. (1983) *The Managed Heart*, Berkley, University of California Press
___ (2003) *The Commercialization of Intimate Life*, Berkley, University of California Press
Holmes, E., Cresswell, C. and O'Connor, T. (2007) 'Posttraumatic stress syndromes in London school children following September 11, 2001', *Journal of Behavior Therapy and Experimental Psychiatry*, 38 (4): 474–90
Hodkinson, P. (2011) *Media, Culture and Society*, London, Sage
Horney, K. (1939) *New Ways in Psychoanalysis*, Norton, New York
Horton, D. and Wohl, R. (1956) 'Mass communication and para-social interaction: Observations and intimacy at a distance', *Psychiatry*, 19: 215–29
Hudson, L., Owens, C. and Callen, D. (2012) 'Drone Warfare in Yemen: Fostering Emirates Through Counterterrorism?' *Middle East Policy*, 19 (3): 142–56
Hume, D. (1742) *A Treatise on Human Nature*, London, Penguin
___ (1751) *An Enquiry Concerning the Principles Of Morals*, Oxford, Oxford University Press
Huntington, S. (2002) *The Clash of Civilizations*, New York, Free Press
Huizinga, J. (1950) *The Waning of the Middle Ages*, London, Arnold
Illouz, E. (2007) *Cold Intimacies*, Cambridge, Polity
Inglis, D. (2009) 'Cosmopolitan sociology and the classical canon: Ferdinand Tonnies and the emergence of global Gesellschaft', *British Journal of Sociology*, 60 (4): 813–32

Inglis, F. (2010) *A Short History of Celebrity*, Princeton, Princeton University Press

Invisible Committee (2009) *The Coming Insurrection*, Los Angeles, Semiotext(e)

Iyer, A. and Oldmeadow, J. (2006) 'Picture this: Emotional and political responses to photographs of the Kenneth Bigley kidnapping', *European Journal of Social Psychology*, 36 (5): 635–47

Jacoby, I. and Chestnut, R. (1978) *Brand Loyalty: Measurement and Management* New York, Wiley

Jappe, A. (1999) *Guy Debord*, Berkley, University of California Press

Jay, M. (2010) *The Virtues of Mendacity*, Charlottesville, University of Virginia Press

Jenkins, H. (2006) *Textual Poachers: Television Fans and Participatory Culture*, New York, Routledge

Jiuping, X. and Xiaocui, S. (2011) 'Post-traumatic stress disorder among survivors of the Wenchaun earthquake one year after', *Comprehensive Psychiatry*, 52 (4): 431–7

Joffre, H. (2008) 'The power of visual material: persuasion, emotion and identification', *Diogenes*, 217: 84–93

Johnson, C. (2000) *Blowback*, New York, Little Brown

___ (2010) *Dismantling the Empire*, New York, Metropolitan Books

Katz, B. (2006) 'Concentrated poverty in New Orleans and other American cities', *The Chronicle of Higher Education*, 21.10.2006

Katz, J. (1999) *How Emotions Work*, Chicago, Chicago University Press

Keane, J. (2009) *The Life and Death of Democracy*, New York, Norton

Kelly, J. (2012) 'The decline of British trade unionism', *Industrial Relations Journal*, 43 (4): 348–58

Kendon, A. (1997) 'Gesture', *Annual Review of Anthropology*, 26 (1): 109–28

___ (2007) *Gesture: Visible Action as Utterance*, Cambridge, Cambridge University Press

___ (2012) 'Language and kinesic complexity' *Gesture*, 12 (3): 308–26

Kernberg, O. (1967) 'Borderline personality organization', *Journal of American Psychoanalytic Association*, 15: 641–85

___ (1989) 'Narcissistic personality disorder in childhood', *Psychiatric Clinics of North America*, 12: 671–94

Kim, K. (2013) 'Which country has the highest reported incidents of rape?' *Global Post*, 18.03.2013

Kim, H. and Karpova, E. (2010) 'Consumer attitudes toward fashion counterfeits', *Clothing and Textiles Research Journal*, 28 (2): 79–94

Kim, Y. and Price, B. (2014) 'Revisiting prison privatization: An examination of the magnitude of prison privatization', *Administration and Society*, 63 (3): 255–75

King, B. (2008) 'Stardom, celebrity and the para-confession', *Social Semiotics*, 18 (2): 115–32

King, T., and Dennis, C.(2006) 'Unethical consumers', *Qualitative Market Research*, 9 (3): 282–96

Kirsch, M. (ed.) (2006) *Inclusion and Exclusion in the Global Arena*, London, Routledge

Kleinfeld, J. and Kleinfeld, A. (2004) 'Cowboy nation and American character', *Society*, 4 (3): 43–50

Kontink, L. (2003) 'Counterfeits: The cost of combat', *Pharmaceutical Executive*, November 2003: 46–58

Kracauer, S. (1960) *Theory of Film*, Oxford, Oxford University Press

___ (2012) *Siegfried Kracauer's American Writings* (eds) Von Moltke, J. and Rawson, K. Berkley, University of California Press

Kroplin, E. (1989) *Richard Wagner*, Leipzin, Deutscher Verlag fur Musik

Kunreuther, H. and Pauly, M. (2006) 'Rules rather than discretion: Lessons from Hurricane Katrina', *Journal of Risk Uncertainty*, 33 (1): 101–16

Lambert, A. (2013) *Intimacy and Friendship on Facebook*, Basingstoke, Palgrave

Lasch, C. (1979) *The Culture of Narcissism*, London, Abacus

Lavalle, K.and Feagin, J. (2006) 'Hurricane Katrina: The race and class debate', *Monthly Review*, 58 (2): 52–66

Leader, D. (2013) *Strictly Bipolar*, London, Penguin

Leary, W. and Allen, A. (2011) 'Personality and persona: Personality processes in self presentation', *Journal of Personality*, 79 (6): 1191–218

Lee, S.-H. and Workman, J. (2011) 'Attitudes toward counterfeit purchase and ethical beliefs among Korean and American university students', *Family and Consumer Sciences Research Journal*, 39 (3): 289–305

Levin, A. (2005) 'New Orleans police chief quits', *USA Today*, p. 5A

Levinas, E. (2005) *Humanism of the Other*, Chicago, University of Illinois Press, Champaign

Levitt, J. and Whitaker, M. (eds) (2009) *Hurricane Katrina: America's Unnatural Disaster*, Lincoln, University Of Nebraska Press

Lewis, S. and Reese, S. (2009) 'What is the war on terror? Framing through the eyes of journalists', *Journalism and Mass Communications Quarterly*, 86 (1): 85–102

Linklater, A. (1997) *The Transformation of Political Community*, Cambridge, Polity

Lippman, W. (2007) *Public Opinion*, Sioux Falls, NuVision

Livanou, M., Basgoglu, M., Lukemeyer, A. and McCorkle, R. (2006) 'Traumatic stress responses in treatment-seeking earthquake survivors in Turkey'; 'Privatization of prisons: Impact on prison conditions', *American Review of Public Administration*, 36 (2): 189–2006

Lockwood, D. (1958) *The Blackcoated Worker*, Oxford, Clarenden Press

Lopez-Ibor, G., Christodoulou, G., Maj, M., Sartorius, N., and Okasha, A. (eds) (2005) *Disasters and Mental Health*, Chichester, John Wiley

Lo-Shu, F. (1967) *A Documentary Chronicle of Sino-Western Relations, 1644–1820* (2 vols.), Tucson, University of Arizona Press

Lowenthal, L. (1961) *Literature, Culture and Society*, New York, Prentice Hall

Ludlow, A. (2014) 'Transforming Rehabilitation: What lessons might be learned from prison privatisation?' *European Journal of Probation*, 6: 67–81

Lundahl, B., Kunz, C., Brownwell, C., Harris, N. and Van Fleet, R. (2009) 'Prison privatization: A meta-analysis of cost and quality of confinement', *Research on Social Work Practice*, 19 (4): 383–94

Lukes, S. (1973) *Emile Durkheim*, Harmondsworth, Penguin

MacCannell, D. (2011) *The Ethics of Sightseeing*, Berkley, University of California Press

McCorkle, S. (2001) 'The immortality of Mae West', *Heritage*, 52 (6): 48–58

McCutcheon, L., Lange, R. and Huron, J. (2002) 'Conceptualization and measurement of celebrity worship', *British Journal of Psychology*, 93: 67–87

McCutcheon, L. Maltby, J., Houran, J. and Ashe, D. (2004) *Celebrity Worshippers: Inside the Mind of the Stargazers*, Baltimore, PublishAmerica

McDonough, T. (ed.) (2009) *The Situationists and the City*, London, Verso

Machiavelli, N. (1898) *History of Florence (Together With The Prince)*, London, George Bell and Sons

McIntosh II, A. P. (2002) 'Property rights on Western ranches: Federal rangeland policy and a model for valuation', PhD thesis, New Mexico State University

McLuhan, M. (2001) *Understanding Media*, London, Routledge

McNeill, D. (1992) *Hand and Mind: What Gestures Reveal About Thought*, Chicago, University of Chicago Press

McQuail, D., Blumler, D. and Brown, J. (1972) 'The television audience: A revised perspective', in McQuail, D. (ed.) *Sociology of Mass Communications*, Harmondsworth, Penguin

Madley, B. (2008) 'California's Yuki Indians: Defining genocide in native American history', *Western Historical Quarterly*, 39: 303–32

Maltby, J., Day, L., McCutcheon, L., Houran, J. and Ashe, D. (2006) 'Extreme celebrity worship, fan proneness and dissociation' *Personality and Individual Differences*, 40: 273–83

Mann, M. (1973) *Consciousness and Action Among the Western Working Class*, London, Macmillan

Manning, A. (2005) 'Accidents, infections new worry, clinics say', *USA Today*, p. 3A

Marcuse, H. (1964) *One Dimensional Man*, London, Abacus

Marsh, D., Hart, P. and Tindall, K. (2010) 'Celebrity politics: The politics of late modernity?' *Political Studies*, 8 (3): 322–40

Marshall, P. (1997) *Celebrity and Power*, Minneapolis, University of Minnesota Press

Martinko, M., Breaux, D., Martinez, A., Summers, J. and Harvey, P. (2009) 'Hurricane Katrina and attributions of responsibility', *Organizational Dynamics*, 38 (1): 52–63

Marx, K. (1854) 'The English middle class', *New York Tribune*, 1 August 1854, p. 4

___ (1964) *The Economic and Philosophic Manuscripts of 1844*, New York, International Publishers

Marx, K. and Engels, F. (1968) *Selected Works in One Volume*, London, Lawrence and Wishart

Masten, A. and Chatsworth, J. (1998) 'The development of competence in favourable and unfavourable environments', *American Psychologist*, 53(2): 205–20.

Masten, M., Petrie, C. Braga, A. and McLaughlin, B. (2002) *Deadly Lessons: Understanding Lethal School Violence*, National Research Council, Washington DC

Mauss, M. (1990) *The Gift*, New York, Norton Books

Matsumoto, D., Hwang, H. (2013) 'Cultural similarities and differences in emblematic gestures', *Journal of Nonverbal Behavior*, 37: 1–27

Meehan, E. (2006) 'Hurricane Katrina and Bush's vacation: Contexts for decoding', *Critical Studies in Media Communication*, 23 (1): 85–90

Meek,R., Gojkovic, D. and Mills, A. (2013) 'The involvement of nonprofit organizations In prisoner reentry in the UK', *Journal of Offender Rehabilitation*, 52 (5): 338–57

Mele, J. (2004) 'Counterfeit parts: buyers beware', *Fleet Owner*, 99 (3): 16–20

Mellen, J. (1974) 'The Mae West nobody knows', in Braudy, L. and Cohen, M. (eds) (1974) *Film Theory and Criticism*, Oxford, Oxford University Press, pp. 576–83

Mendle, M. (1985) *Dangerous Positions: Mixed Government, the Estates of the Realm, and the answer to the xix propositions'*, University Al, University of Alabama Press

Merton, R.(1946) *Mass Persuasion*, New York, Harper and Bros

Milgram, S. (1971) 'The frozen world of the familiar stranger', an interview with Carol Tavris, *Psychology Today*, 8 (1): 70–80

___ (1992) *The Individual in a Social World*, New York, McGraw Hill

Miller, D. and Sinanan, J. (2014) *Webcam*, Cambridge, Polity

Millington, B. (2012) *Richard Wagner: The Sorcerer of Bayreuth*, London, Thames and Hudson

Ministry of Justice, Home Office and the Office for National Statistics (2013) *An Overview of Sexual Offending in England and Wales*, www.justice.gov.uk

Miron, A., Branscombe, N. Schmitt, M. (2006) 'Collective guilt as distress over illegitimate intergroup inequality', *Group Processes and Intergroup Relations*, 9, 163–80

Mitzman, A. (1973) *Sociology and Estrangement*, New York, Knopf

Morgan, G., Wisenski, D. and Skifka, L. (2011) 'The expulsion from Disneyland: The social psychological impact of 9/11', *American Psychologist*, 66 (6): 447–54

Moyo, D. (2009) *Dead Aid*, New York, Farrar, Strauss and Giroux

Moxon, D. (2011) 'Consumer culture and the 2011 riots', *Sociological Research Online*, 16 (4): 19

Mullan, B. and Taylor, L. (1986) *Uninvited Guests*, London, Chatto and Windus

Mullan, J. (1988) *Sentiment and Sociability: The Language of Feeling in the Eighteenth Century*, Oxford, Clarendon Press

Nasaw, D. (1993) *Going Out: The Rise and Fall of Public Entertainment*, New York, Basic Books

Newton, P. N. et al. (2006) 'Counterfeit anti-infective drugs', *The Lancet Infectious Diseases*, 6 (9): 602–13

9/11 Commission Report (2004) *Final report of the National Commission on Terrorist Attacks upon the United States*, New York, Norton

Nordgren, F., McConnell, M. Loewenstein, G. (2011) 'What constitutes torture?' *Psychological Science*, doi: 10.1177/09567961 Online First Article

Norris, F. and Rosen, C. (2009) 'Innovations in disaster mental health services and evaluation' *Administration and Policy in Mental health and Mental Health Services Research*, 36: 159–64

North, C., King, R., Folwer, R., Polatin, P., LaGrone, A. and Pepe, P. (2008) 'Psychiatric disorders among transported hurricane evacuees', *Psychiatric Annals*, 38, 104–13

North, C. (2010) 'A tale of two studies of two disasters: Comparing psychosocial responses to disaster among Oklahoma City bombing survivors and Hurricane Katrina evacuees', *Rehabilitation Psychology*, 55 (3): 241–6

Norum, P. S. and Cuno, A. (2011) 'Analysis of the demand for counterfeit goods', *Journal of Fashion Marketing and Management*, 15 (1): 27–40

Office of National Statistics (2014) 'Personal Wealth and Income' www .ons.gov.uk

Olshansky, R. (2006) 'Planning after Hurricane Katrina', *Journal of American Planning Association*, 72 (2): 147–53

Otto, M., Hennin, A., HIrshfield-Becker, D., Pollack, M., Biederman, J. and Rosenbaum, J. (2007) 'Posttraumatic stress disorder symptoms following media exposure to tragic events: Impact of 9/11 on children at risk for anxiety disorders', *Journal of Anxiety Disorders*, 21 (7): 888–902

Papachirssi, Z. and Rubin, A. (2000) 'Predictors of internet use', *Journal of Broadcasting and Electronic Media*, 44, 175–96

Parker, C., Stern, E., Paglia, E. and Brown, C. (2009) 'Preventable catastrophe? The Hurricane Katrina disaster revisited', *Journal of Contingencies and Crisis Management*, 17 (4): 206–20

Parker, L. and Frank, T. (2005) 'Federal official, mayor disagree', *USA Today*, p. 1A

Paulos, E. and Goodman, E. (2004) 'The familiar stranger: Anxiety, comfort and play in public places', ACM SIGCHI 223–30

Peck, J. (2008) *The Age of Oprah*, New York, Paradigm

Peek, L. (2003) 'Reactions and response: Muslim students' experiences on New York city campuses post 9/11', *Journal of Muslim Minority Affairs*, 23 (2): 271–83

Pessen, E. (1976) 'The egalitarian myth and the American social reality', *American Historical Review*, 76, October: 989–1034.

Phillips, D. (1974) 'The influence of suggestion on suicide: Substantive and theoretical implications of the Werther effect', *American Sociological Review*, 39: 340–54

Pine, D. and Charney, D. (2002) 'Children, stress and sensitization', *Biological Psychicatry*, 52 (8): 773–5

Pine, D. and Cohen, J. (2002) 'Trauma in children and adolescents', *Biological Psychiatry*, 51(7): 519–31.

Pinsky, D. and Young, M. (2009) *The Mirror Effect*, New York, Harper

Plato (2007) *The Republic*, London, Penguin

Power, M. (1994) *The Audit Explosion*, London, Demos

Publishing Association (2014) *Publishing Association Statistics Yearbook 2014*, London, Publishing Association

Randle, J. (2013) 'Low-Flying Drones', *London Review of Books*, 20 March 2013

Ray, M and Malhi, P. (2005) 'Reactions of Indian adolescents to the 9/11 terrorist attacks', *Indian Journal of Pediatrics*, 72 (3): 217–21

Rhodes, L. (1998) 'Panoptical intimacies', *Public Culture*, 10 (2): 285–311

Rieff, P. (1965) *The Triumph of the Therapeutic*, New York, Harper and Row

Riesman, D., Glazer, N. and Denney, R. (1950) *The Lonely Crowd*, New Haven, University Press

Roach, J. (2007) *it*, Ann Arbor, University of Michigan Press

Robertson, P. (1996) *Guilty Pleasures: Feminist Camp from Mae West to Madonna*, Durham, Duke University Press

Robertson, R. (1992) *Globalization*, London, Sage

Rojek, C. (1995) *Decentring Leisure*, London, Sage

___ (2000) *Leisure and Culture*, Basingstoke, Macmillan

Roosevelt, T. (1889) *The Winning of the West*, Fairford, Echo Library.

Rosen, C. (2005) 'The overpraised American', *Policy Review*, 133 (Oct/Nov): 27–43

Rosen, C. and Cohen, M. (2010) 'Subgroups of New York City children at high risk of PTSD after the September 11 attacks', *Psychiatric Services*, 61 (1): 64–9

Rosen, J. (2009) 'Vanishing act: In search of Eva Tanguay, the first rock star', *Slate*, 1.12.2009

Rosenberg, B. (1985) ' "Resurrection" and "Little Dorrit": Tolstoy and Dickens reconsidered', *Studies in the Novel*, 17 (1): 27–38

Rubinstein, W. (1983) 'The end of "old corruption" in Britain', *Past and Present*, 101 (1): 55–86

Runciman, D. (2008) *Political Hypocrisy*, Princeton, Princeton University Press

___ (2012) 'Stiffed', *London Review of Books*, 34 (20): 7–9

Rust, R. and Oliver, R. (eds) (1994) *Service Quality*. Thousand Oaks, Sage

Rutter, J. and Bryce, J. (2008) 'The consumption of counterfeit goods: 2Here be pirates2?', *Sociological Review*, 42 (6): 1146–64

Saez, E. (2013) 'Striking it richer: The evolution of top incomes in the United States', http://eml.berkeley.edu/~saez/saez-UStopincomes-2012.pdf

Said, E. (1991) *Orientalism*, London, Penguin

Salcioglu, D. and Kalender, D. (2002) *Journal of Nervous and Mental Disease*, 190 (12): 816–23

Sandler, W. (2012) 'Dedicated gestures and the emergence of sign language', *Gesture*, 12 (3): 265–307

Sauer, F. and Schornig, N. (2012) 'Killer drones: The "silver bullet" of democratic warfare?' *Security Dialogue*, 43 (4): 363–80

Sayer, D. (2015) *Rank Hypocrisies: The Insult of the REF*, London, Sage

Scannell, P. (1996) *Radio, Television and Modern Life*, Oxford, Blackwell

Scharf, M. (2010) 'The T-Team (torture team) (Is there a war on terror? Torture, rendition, Guantanamo, and Obama's preventative detention', *Journal of International Law*, 19 (1): 129–43

Schickel, R. (1985) *Intimate Strangers*, New York, Doubleday

Schmitt, C. (1919) *Political Romanticism*, Cambridge, MIT Press

Schulz, W. (2004) 'Reconsidering mediatization as an analytical concept', *European Journal of Communication*, 19 (1): 87–101

Scott, D. (ed.) (2013) *Why Prison?*, Cambridge, Cambridge University Press

Scott, M. and Lyman, S. (1968) 'Accounts', *American Sociological Review*, 33, 46–62

Seligman, M. and Csikszentmihalyi, M. (2000) 'Positive psychology: An introduction', *American Psychologist*, 55: 5–14

Seeger, M., Sellnow, T. and Ulmer, R. (2003) *Communication and Organizational Crisis*, Westport, Praeger

Sennett, R. (2003) *The Fall of Public Man* (2nd edn), London, Penguin

Shichor, D. (1995) *Punishment For Profit*, Thousand Oaks, Sage

Shklar, J. (1984) *Ordinary Vices*, Cambirdge MA, Bellknap Press

Silverstone, R. (2002) 'Complicity and collusion in the mediation of everyday life', *New Literary History*, 33 (4): 761–80

Simmel, G. (1903) 'The metropolis and mental life', in Simmel, G. (1971) *On Individuality and Social Forms*, Chicago, Chicago University Press

___ (1904) 'Fashion', in Simmel, G. (1971)

___ (1907, 1990) *The Philosophy of Money*, London, Routledge

___ (1911) 'The adventurer', in Simmel, G. (1971)

___ (1950) 'The stranger', in Wolf, K. (1950) (ed.) *The Sociology of Georg Simmel*, New York, Free Press

Simonson, P. (2006) 'Celebrity, public image, and American political life', *Political Communication*, 23 (3): 271–84

Sitrin, M. (2012) 'Horizontalism and the Occupy movements', *Dissent*, 59 (2): 74–5

Smith, A. (1790) *The Theory of Moral Sentiments*, London, Penguin

Snyder, C. and Lopez, S. (2002) *Handbook of Positive Psychology*, Oxford, Oxford University Press

Shalev, A. (2004) 'Further lessons from 9/11: Does stress equal trauma?', *Psychiatry*, 67 (2): 174–7

Slater, M. (2012) *The Great Charles Dickens Scandal*, Princeton, Princeton University Press

Slatta, R. (1990) *Cowboys of the Americas*, New Haven, Yale University Press

___ (2001) *Comparing Cowboys and Frontiers: New Perspectives on the History of the Americas*, Norman, Oklahoma University Press

Slotkin, R. (1973) *Regeneration Through Violence*, Norman, University of Oklahoma Press.

___ (1985) *The Fatal Environment*, Norman, University of Oklahoma Press.

___ (1992) *Gunfighter Nation*, Norman, University of Oklahoma Press.

Smith, E. R. (1993) 'Social identity and social emotions', in McKie, D. and Hamilton, D. (eds) *Affect, Cognition and Stereotyping*, San Diego, CA: Academic Press, pp. 297–315

___ (1999) 'Affective and cognitive implications of a group becoming part of the self', in Abrams, D. and Hogg, A. (eds) *Social Identity and Social Cognition*, Oxford, Blackwell pp 183–96

Sommer, J. (2012) 'The war against too much of everything', *New York Times*, 22.12.2012

Stack, S. (1987) 'Celebrities and suicide: A taxonomy and analysis, 1948–83', *American Sociological Review*, 52 (3): 401–12

Staake, T. (2012) 'Business strategies in the counterfeit market' *Journal of Business Research*, 65: 658–65

Stedman Jones, G. (1984) *Languages of Class*, Cambridge, Cambridge University Press

___ (2008) 'The redemptive power of violence? Carlyle, Marx and Dickens', *History Workshop Journal*, 65 (1): 1–22

Steiner, C. with Perry, P. (1999) *Achieving Emotional Literacy*, London, Bloomsbury Academic

Stearns, A. and Burns, J. (2011) 'About the human condition in the Works of Dickens and Marx', *CLC Web: Comparative Literature and Culture*, 13 (4): 2–11

Steuter, E. and Wills, D. (2010) 'The vermin have struck again': Dehumanizing the enemy in post 9/11 media representations' *Media, War and Conflict*, 3 (2): 152–67

Stever, G. (2011) 'Celebrity worship: Critiquing a construct', *Journal of Applied Social Psychology*, 41 (6): 1356–70

Sternheimer, K. (2011) *Celebrity Culture and the American Dream*, London, Routledge

Stockman, D. (1986) *The Triumph of Politics*, London, Coronet

Stone, W. (2011) 'The decline of trade unions in the US and Canada', *Global Research* (www.globalresearch.ca)

Studlar, G. (1996) *This Mad Masquerade*, New York, Columbia University Press

Strauss, L. (2013) *On Tyranny*, Chicago, Chicago University Press

Street, J. (2012) 'Do celebrity politics matter?' *British Journal of Politics and International Relations*, 14 (3): 346–56

Strathern, M. (2000) 'The tyranny of transparency', *British Educational Research Journal*, 26 (3): 309–21

Sue Carter, C., Pournajafi-Nazarloo, H., Ziegler, T., White-Traut, R., Bello, D. and Schwertz, D. (2007) 'Behaviorial associations and potential as a salivary biomarker', *Annals of The New York Academy of Sciences*, 1098: 312–22

Sylves, R. and Waugh, W. (eds) (1996) *Disaster Management in the US and Canada*, Springfield, Charles C. Thomas

Taithe, B. (2007) 'Horror, abjection and compassion: From Dunant to compassion fatigue', *New Formations*, 62 (1): 123–36

Tarrant, M., Branscombe, N. Warner, R. and Weston, D. (2012) 'Social Identity and perceptions of torture', *Journal of Experimental Social Psychology*, 48 (2): 513–18

Taylor, A., Gessen, K. and editors from n + 1 (2011) *Occupy: Scenes from Occupied America*, London, Verso

Thompson, E. P. (1978) 'The peculiarities of the English' pp. 245–302, in Thompson, E. P. *The Poverty of Theory*, London, Merlin

___ (1991a) *Customs in Common*, London, Penguin

___ (1991b) 'The moral economy of the English crowd in the eighteenth century' and 'The moral economy reviewed', pp. 185–351 in Thompson, E. P. (1991)

Tian, Q. and Hofner, C. (2010) 'Parasocial interaction with liked, neutral, and disliked characters on a Popular TV Series', *Mass Communication and Society*, 13 (3): 250–69

Tonnies, F. (2003) *Community and Society*, New York, Dover

Tucker, W. (1965) 'Max Weber's *Verstehen*', *The Sociological Quarterly*, 6 (2): 157–65T

Turner, B. S. (2009) *Can We Live Forever?*, London, Anthem Press

___ (2006) *Vulnerability and Human Rights*, University Park, Penn State University Press

Turner, B. S. and Khondker, H. H. (2010) *Globalization East and West*, London, Sage

Turner, B. S. and Rojek, C. (2001) *Society and Culture: Principles of Scarcity and Solidarity*, London, Sage

Turner, G. (2004) *Understanding Celebrity*, London, Sage

___ (2009) *Ordinary People and the Media*. London, Sage

Turner, F. J. (1893) 'The significance of the frontier in American History', *Proceedings of the State Historical Society Wisconsin*, 14, December 1893

Turner, J. (2007) *Human Emotions*, New York, Routledge

Turner, J. and Stets, J. (2006) 'Sociological theories of human emotions', *Annual Review of Sociology*, 32: 25–52

Traugott, M. et al. (2002) 'How Americans responded: A study of public reactions to 9/11', *Political Science and Politics*, 35 (3): 511–16

Treadwell, J. (2012) 'From the car boot to booting up? e-Bay, online counterfeit crime and the transformation of the criminal market place', *Criminology and Criminal Justice*, 12 (2): 175–91

Trippett, D. (2010) 'Wagner studies and the "paralactic drift"', *Cambridge Opera Journal*, 22 (2): 235–55

US Department of Homeland Security (2004) *Final Draft: National Response Plan*, June 30 (http://www.dhs.gov)

Valentine, G. (2008) 'Living With Difference: Reflections on geographies of encounter', *Progress in Human Geography*, 32 (3): 323–37

Van Kriekan, R. (2012) *Celebrity Society*, London, Routledge

Vandervort, B. (2006) *Indian Wars of Canada, Mexico and the United States 1812–1900*, London, Routledge

Vazsonyi, N. (2008) 'Beethoven instrumentalized: Richard Wagner's self-marketing and media Image', *Music and Letters*, 89 (2): 195–211

___ (2012) *Richard Wagner: Self-Promotion and the Making of a Brand*, Cambridge, Cambridge University Press

Verma, G., Bagley, C., and Jha, M. (eds) (2007) *International Perspectives on Educational Diversity and Inclusion*, London, Routledge

Wacquant, L.(1989) 'Toward a reflexive sociology: A workshop with Pierre Bourdieu', *Sociological Theory*, 7 (1): 26–63

Wagner, R. (1975) *Daus Braune Buch: Tagebuchaufzeich-nungen 1865* (ed.) Bergeld, J., Munich, Piper

Wall, D. and Large, J. (2010) 'Jailhouse frocks: Locating the public interest in policing counterfeit luxury fashion goods', *British Journal of Criminology*, 50: 1094–116

Wall, T. and Monahan, T. (2011) 'Surveillance and violence from afar: The politics of drones and liminal security-scapes', *Theoretical Criminology*, 15 (3): 239–54

Wallace, M. and Junisbai, A. (2003) 'finding class consciousness in the new economy', *Research in Social Stratification and Mobility*, 20 : 385–421

Wallerstein, I. (1989) 'The French Revolution as a world historical event', *Social Research*, 56 (1): 33–52

Waugh, W. (2006) *Shelter From The Storm: Repairing the National Emergency Management System After Hurricane Katrina*, Thousand Oaks, Sage

Ware, B. and Linkugel, W. (1973) 'They spoke in defense of themselves: On the general criticism of *apologia*', *Quarterly Journal Speech*, 59: 273–83

Watts, J. (2001) *Mae West: An icon in Black and White*, New York, Oxford University Press

Weber, M. (1947) *The Theory of Social and Economic Organization*, New York, Oxford University Press

___ (1946) (edited by Gerth, H. and Mills, C. W.) *From Max Weber*, London, RKP

___ (1968) *Economy And Society*, Vols. 1 and 2, Berkley, University of California Press

White, H. (2008) 'The Historical Event', *Differences*, 19 (2): 9–34

Whyte, W. F. (1943/1993) *Street Corner Society*, Chicago, Chicago University Press

Wiedmann, K. P., Hennigs, N. and Klarmann C. (2012) 'Luxury consumption in the trade-off between genuine and counterfeit goods', *Journal of Brand Management*, 19: 544–66

Wilshire, H., Neilsen, J. and Hazlett, R. (2008) *The American West at Risk: Science, Myths, and Politics of Land Abuse and Recovery*, New York, Oxford University Press

Wilmeth, D. B. and Miller, T.(1996) *Cambridge Guide to American Theatre*, Cambridge, Cambridge University Press

Williams, L. (1975) 'What does Mae West have that all the men want', *Frontiers*, 1 (1): 118–21

Wills, G. (1993) *Lincoln At Gettysburg*, New York, Simon and Schuster

Winslow, C. (ed.) (2014) *E. P. Thompson and the Making of the New Left*, London, Lawrence and Wishart

Wolin, S. (2008) *Democracy Inc*, Princeton University Press, Princeton

Woods, J. (2011) 'The 9/11 effect: Towards a social science of the terrorist threat', *Social Science Journal*, 48 (1): 213–33

Wortis-Leider, E. (1997) *Becoming Mae West*, New York, Farrar, Stauss and Giroux

Wright, E. O. (1997) *Class Counts*, Cambridge, Cambridge University Press

Wright, K. (2010) 'Strange bedfellows? Reaffirming rehabilitation and prison privatization', *Journal of Offender Rehabilitation*, 49: 74–90

Wouters, C. (2007) *Informalization: Manners and Emotions Since 1890*, London, Sage

Wotherspoon, D. and Cheng, M. (2009) 'Web of deceit', *Risk Management*, 56 (8): 32–6

Yang, Y., Yeh, C., Chen, C., Lee, I. H. and Lee, C. K. (2003) 'Psychiatric morbidity and posttraumatic symptoms among earthquake victims in primary care clinics', *General Hospital Psychiatry*, 25 (4): 253–61

Young, J. (1999) *The Exclusive Society*, London, Sage

Younhee, K. and Price, B. (2014) 'Revisiting prison privatization', *Administration and Society*, 46 (3): 255–75

Yzerbyt, V., Dumont, M., Wigbolud, D. and Gordjiin, E. (2003) 'I feel for us: The impact of categorization and identification on emotions and action tendencies', *British Journal of Social Psychology*, 42: 533–49

Zerzan, J. (2005) *Against Civilization*, Port Townsend, Feral House

___ (2012) *Future Primitive Revisited*, Port Townsend, Feral House

Author Index

Subject Index